GROW!

Meditations and prayers for new Christians

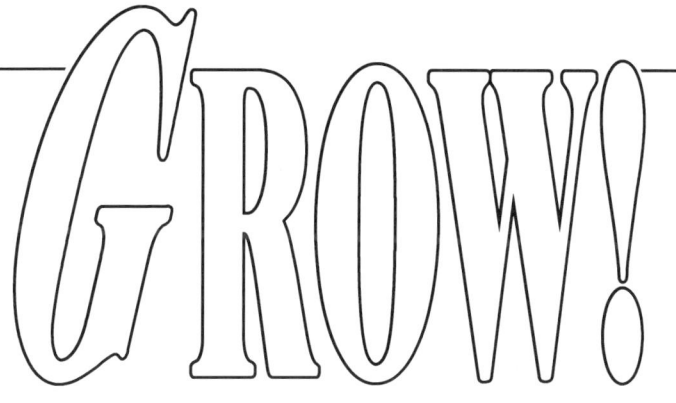

GROW!

Meditations and prayers for new Christians

ROWLAND CROUCHER

The Joint Board of Christian Education
Melbourne

Published by
THE JOINT BOARD OF CHRISTIAN EDUCATION
Second Floor, 10 Queen Street, Melbourne 3000, Australia

GROW! Meditations and prayers for new Christians

National Library of Australia
   Cataloguing-in-Publication entry.

Croucher, Rowland.
   Grow!

   ISBN: 0 85819 822 3.

   1. Meditations. 2. Prayers. I. Joint Board of Christian
      Education. II. Title.

242

First printed 1992.

Cover photograph: Joy Merritt
Additional photographs: Jennifer Wait (page 9),
   Coo-ee Picture Library (page 55), Joy Merritt (pages 111, 155)

Cover design by Kelvin Young
Text design by Kelvin Young, Jennifer Wait
Typeset by MacKenzies in Caslon
Printed by Australian Print Group   JB92/3061

Contents

Foreword

This is a book for new Christians, or those who want to know more about the Christian faith. Clergy and Christian leaders have constantly told me they needed it — they couldn't think of one book that answered most of the questions a thoughtful enquirer is likely to ask.

Was it G. B. Shaw who talked about those who are dead at thirty and buried at sixty? The assumption in *Grow!* is just that: you want to learn, to grow, to become mature in your faith and thinking.

We major here on issues of theology and spirituality. Subsequent volumes tackle ethical and other issues. We have used the proven format of the gratifyingly popular series of devotional books (published by Albatross/Lion).

The idea for this book was conceived in a car trip from Sydney to Melbourne, two days before Christmas 1989, with the help of Jan, Amanda and her friend Judith, and Lindy. Thanks also to David and Christine Silvana, Grace, Sue, Elaine and Jane for research and editing help. And to Hugh McGinlay of JBCE for his patient advice and encouragement.

My prayer is that you will 'grow in grace and knowledge' (2 Peter 3:18) and discover the purpose for which God your creator and redeemer gave you life and new life!

Shalom!

Rowland Croucher

John Mark Ministries
7 Bangor Court
Heathmont
Victoria 3135
Australia

Beginning the Christian life

1

Welcome to the family

For it was you who formed my inward parts; you knit me together in my mother's womb.

But now thus says the Lord, he who created you... I have called you by name, you are mine.

The counsel of the Lord stands forever, the thoughts of his heart to all generations. Happy is the nation whose God is the Lord, the people whom he has chosen as his heritage.

I will be their God, and they shall be my people... they shall all know me, from the least of them to the greatest.

As Jesus passed along the Sea of Galilee, he saw Simon and his brother Andrew casting a net into the sea — for they were fishermen. And Jesus said to them, 'Follow me and I will make you fish for people'.

This is the work of God, that you believe in him whom he has sent.

But you are a chosen race, a royal priesthood, a holy nation, God's own people, in order that you may proclaim the mighty acts of him who called you out of darkness into his marvellous light.

He chose us in Christ before the foundation of the world to be holy and blameless before him in love. He destined us for adoption as his children through Jesus Christ.

For we are what he has made us, created in Christ Jesus for good works, which God prepared beforehand to be our way of life.

So if anyone is in Christ, there is a new creation: everything old has passed away; see, everything has become new!

Now if you are unwilling to serve the Lord, choose this day whom you will serve... but as for me and my household, we will serve the Lord.

But to all who received him, who believed in his name, he gave power to become children of God.

Psalm 139:13; Isaiah 43:1; Psalm 33:11, 12; Jeremiah 31:33, 34; Mark 1:16, 17; John 6:29; 1 Peter 2:9; Ephesians 1:4-6; Ephesians 2:10; 2 Corinthians 5:17; Joshua 24:15; John 1:12.

At the graveside of Willie Loman in Arthur Miller's *Death of a Salesman*, one of the characters standing by says, 'He never really knew who he was'.

Who am I? Does anyone care about me? Where can I find meaning for my life? And after death, what then? Or, to paraphrase the philosopher Kant, why is there anything at all? Why not nothing? The search for identity, love, meaning and immortality is as relevant and urgent for you and me as it has been for people down the ages.

Christianity begins by teaching that we humans are like God, made in his image. Although that image is marred by evil we have done, and evil done to us, God loves you and has a significant purpose for your life. You were planned, not an accident; God wants you to become a whole person in this life, and share heaven with him in the next.

So, as the Negro spiritual says, 'Get on board!' How? Start being nicer to people? Believe in Christianity? Go to church? Agree with certain dogmas? They're good, but if that's all you do, you could be seduced into believing 'I'm just as much a Christian as anybody else!' No, being a true Christian starts somewhere else.

In essence, a Christian is 'called' by Christ and then chooses to follow him.

There are four ideas here: I am chosen, by Jesus Christ, but I also choose to obey him, my Master and Lord.

The early Christians often told the story of Peter, a fiery, quick-tempered fisherman. Jesus, whom he knew, said to him, 'I have chosen you to follow me: with a few others we're going to change the world!' Later he asked Peter and his friends, 'Who do you think I am?' Peter said, 'You are the Christ, Son of the living God!' Peter often failed as a Christian, but Jesus kept after him: 'Do you love me, Peter? You've let me — and yourself — down. But come on, you're forgiven, let's start again. I've got a strategic job for you. Trust me, follow me, obey me; I will never leave you or forsake you — even to the end of time!' For 'Peter', substitute your own name...

1. You are chosen! Any friendship, or love affair, involves two people choosing each other. Christianity is a relationship, too, between you and Someone who has always loved you.

2. You are chosen by Jesus. Friendships or love affairs begin with the question: Who is this person? What's he or she like? Can I trust him or her?

So who is Jesus? He was a Jew from Galilee, a frontier province of the Roman Empire, and he claimed to have a very special relationship with God. He was truly human, but also, uniquely, the Son of God. Indeed, Christians assert he was and is God. If you want to know what God is like, look at Jesus; as the 'Jesus freaks' used to say, if God is like Jesus, nothing is too good to be true!

Now if Jesus is God, he created the whole universe (and you), he died for you, he cares for you, and he will be your judge! Problem is, when you've done wrong, you have not only sinned against yourself and others, but, supremely, against him too. So you must face up to that, by repenting. That is, you change your mind, and instead of rebelling against Jesus, you turn your life around and do what he wants you to do.

3. So you have to make a choice. Jesus invites you to 'come, follow me'. Your response can be dramatic (particularly if you've been running from him!) as with one of the early Christians, Saul, on the Damascus Road. Or it can be a gradual awareness that the Christian values you learned from childhood are true for you personally, and you make a quiet but serious decision to give your life over to Jesus.

4. Being a Christian is a sincere commitment to obey Jesus, whatever the cost. And there is a cost. How much? Everything! G. K. Chesterton once said it's not that Christianity has been tried and found wanting but that it has been found hard and not tried.

But let's get one thing straight: it's not Christianity as such you're committed to. Christianity has brought great good to our world (the notion of charity, the concept of inalienable human rights, the limitations of the power of the State — all derive from our Christian heritage). But Christianity as a religious system, said theologian Karl Barth, stands as much under the judgment of the gospel as other religions. Sometimes, for example, Christians have backed an unjust ideology — like Nazism.

Nor is your primary commitment to a church or denomination, although you should belong to a Christian community.

No, you commit yourself to Jesus Christ, and follow other people and systems only as they authentically follow him. Study

13

his life in the gospels; ask 'what does he want me to do?'; do in your world what he did in his.

But you say, 'I don't have much faith'. No problem: most of the best Christians started with little faith. Faith grows as you exercise it. As you get to know Jesus better, and do his will for you, faith will grow.

Jesus said we come into his kingdom — or under his rule — as a child. We come to God as Father. Childlike trust is unafraid: perfect love drives out fear (1 John 4:18). Children are impressionable — they believe anything someone in authority tells them — so we, too, trust God in everything.

Children are willing to accept correction (Hebrews 12:7), so if times get tough, we tell ourselves again that God knows what he's doing: it's all, only, for our good.

Children are expressive: they are spontaneous and uninhibited in the way they express their joy and their trust.

You're set for an exciting, hard adventure: hang in there!

Some Bible passages to study: Mark 1:16-18, Luke 5:1-11, 9:18-27, John 3:1-17. Then go back to Mark and read it through.

Pascal once said there is a God-shaped vacuum within every person. How does a person become a Christian? The process is not difficult to understand. It can be explained as easily as ABC:

A represents the truth that all have sinned. It calls me to admit my sins. To be a Christian, I must acknowledge my sins.

B stands for belief in the Lord Jesus Christ. I must call on him, receive him, trust him, and worship him, recognising who he is and what he has done for me.

C stands for something Paul requires in Romans 10:9 — I must confess that the risen Christ is my Lord and Saviour. That seals the transaction.

When I have admitted my sins, believed in Jesus, and confessed Christ as my Saviour, I am a Christian, ready to 'grow in the grace and knowledge of our Lord and Saviour Jesus Christ' (2 Peter 3:18).

J. I. Packer,
'Becoming a Christian', in LaVonne Neff et al. (eds), *Practical Christianity*, Wheaton, Illinois: Tyndale House Publishers Inc., 1988, pp. 26-27.

Hi! You have made or are about to make, the most important decision of your life: to commit your life to Jesus Christ.

You are saved by God's grace (which has come to us in Jesus), through faith. Faith is trust. It's reaching out to receive Christ.

So to become a Christian it doesn't matter how much faith you've got. It's the object of your faith that's important. God asks for your faith and then provides it. The faith he gives is not a blind leap into the dark. It rests on the one thing you can be sure of — God's loving faithfulness, his promise to do what he's said he would do.

Becoming a Christian won't solve all your problems: it may increase them! God's not going to give you everything you want (some things may not be good for you). You don't get a package that includes perfect health, success, popularity, prestige or financial blessing.

Faith means hanging on to a good God, knowing he has your best interests always in mind, and he'll see you through. Real faith accepts problems rather than demanding always to be freed from them. God will be with you in your trials: he may deliver you *from* them, or *through* them.

Joni Eareckson Tada became paralysed after a diving accident. She has matured remarkably since then, and having bedsores for nine months wasn't funny. Her problem has remained, but God has used it to open up a remarkable ministry to disabled people through her.

Corrie ten Boom was not rescued from the Nazi police in Holland, but had to endure the privations and tortures of a prison camp. Since then her strong faith has been an inspiration to thousands.

Rowland Croucher
(from an unpublished sermon).

A Christian is someone who responds to the call of Christ. First and always Christianity is a relationship to a Person. In that sense it differs from great world religions like... Hinduism, and it differs from Communism and the other rival secular faiths that compete for our allegiance today. All these direct our loyalty to a theological system, a code of ethics, a philosophy or an ideology, but Christianity alone directs our loyalty to a Person. Where Christ is, there is Christianity, and the Christian is a person who tries to be a follower of Jesus Christ.

A. Leonard Griffith,
What is a Christian?, London: Lutterworth, 1962, pp. 11-12.

The foundation of the Christian faith is a person — Jesus Christ. In this, Christianity is different from most other major religions. Almost all the others are based on a philosophical proposition — something to believe or adhere to. Christianity is based on the identity of its founder, Jesus Christ...

If you took Buddha out of Buddhism, you'd still basically have Buddhism; if you took Confucius out of Confucianism, you'd still have Confucianism. These are both ethical systems. If you took Muhammad out of Islam, you'd still have Islam, because it all depends upon Allah, not Muhammad. But if you took Christ out of Christianity, you would no longer have Christianity, because Christianity is Jesus Christ...

Josh McDowell,
'Jesus Christ: The Foundation of Faith' in LaVonne Neff et al. (eds), *Practical Christianity*, Wheaton, Illinois: Tyndale House Publishers Inc., 1988, pp. 180-81.

Let's say you see a lake with ice on it. It's only about a quarter of an inch thick, but if you really believe, the ice will hold you, won't it? Of course not. You can have all the faith in the world, but if the object of your faith, the ice, is unreliable, you will fall into the lake.

But suppose the ice is two feet thick. You, however, have little faith. You say, 'Boy, I don't know if I should walk out there. But by faith, I guess I'll do it'. Your faith is small, but the object is trustworthy. You go out on the ice, and even though your faith is weak, the ice holds you.

My salvation is not based on my faith; it is based on who Jesus Christ is... The important factor is not the amount of your faith. It is the fact that you put your faith in Jesus Christ. And that makes all the difference in the world.

Josh McDowell,
'A False Concept of Faith' in LaVonne Neff et al. (eds), *Practical Christianity*, Wheaton, Illinois: Tyndale House Publishers Inc., 1988, p. 183.

God, I give you my life, my future, my job, my friendships, my marriage and home, my body and soul. Augustine of Hippo wrote centuries ago that God wants to give us a great gift. He wants to give us the gift of an intimate relationship with him. He wants us to enter the fullness of his life, the love, joy, and peace within the Trinity. But he can't give it to us because our hands are full. What are they full of? They're full of ourselves. We must put ourselves down and stand before God with empty hands before we can receive his gift... It is the faith of a child that enables us to offer empty hands to God.

Kenneth Swanson,
Uncommon Prayer, New York: Ballantine, 1987, p. 197.

How can ordinary people respond to this extraordinary call? Where do we begin? We begin as Peter and Andrew did. We begin by turning our back on all that captured our time, energy and resources. We begin by turning and following Jesus. We begin by sitting at his feet and learning from him. We begin by recognising that God is and that God reaches out in love through Jesus Christ to bring us back to our Creator. Once we decide to turn to God, we must, like the prodigal, also turn away from the past. We must, in repentance, turn away from all that was destroying us, our lives, and relationships, and through the One who died in our stead find new beginnings and forgiveness of our sins.

Tom Sine,
Taking Discipleship Seriously: A Radical Biblical Approach, Valley Forge: Judson Press, 1985, p. 23.

We cannot partake deeply in the life of God unless we change profoundly. It is therefore essential that we should go to God in order that he should transform and change us, and that is why, to begin with we should ask for conversion. Conversion in Latin means a turn, a change in direction... Conversion begins but it never ends. It is an increasing process in which we gradually become more and more what we should be, until, after the day of judgment, these categories of fall, conversion and righteousness disappear and are replaced by new categories of a new life. As Christ says, 'I make all things new' (Revelation 21:5).

Metropolitan Anthony of Sourozh,
'Meditation and Worship', in John Garvey (ed.), *Modern Spirituality: An Anthology*, London: Darton, Longman and Todd, 1986, pp. 36, 37.

According to the text in St John (17:3), eternal life is in knowing God, not in knowing that we know God.

Simon Tugwell,
'The Beatitudes' in John Garvey (ed.), *Modern Spirituality: An Anthology*, London: Darton, Longman and Todd, 1985, p. 62.

Christians are not atheists; they worship God the Father, the Son and the Holy Spirit. The state has nothing to fear from them. Christ's kingdom is not of this world. The empire has no better subjects than the Christians — look at the change in their character and their lives since they left the service of demons. They pay tribute, give to the poor, avoid swearing, and love everybody.

Justin Martyr,
First Apology, quoted in James C. Hefley, 'A Defender of the Faith' in LaVonne Neff et al. (eds), *Practical Christianity*, Wheaton, Illinois: Tyndale House Publishers Inc., 1988, p. 96.

He picked up the book, and was amazed by what he read. A calm and moving meditation on the Cross began to make everything plain. Christ himself had paid the price of sin. The new birth was a gift, not a reward; George had only to accept it. But he could not surrender all his efforts. Days passed until a morning came when he threw himself on his bed and uttered his first cry of utter helplessness — all previous prayers had been conscious attempts to win God's favour.

Suddenly George Whitefield realised he was happy — and knew why: he had thrown himself, without reserve, into God's almighty hands, and someone unseen had removed his burden and replaced it with the joy of God's presence. George laughed aloud at the simplicity of it...

John Pollock,
'The Awakening That Spanned Two Continents' in LaVonne Neff et al. (eds), *Practical Christianity*, Wheaton, Illinois: Tyndale House Publishers Inc., 1988, p. 97.

Praise to the God and Father of our Lord Jesus Christ. We have been given new birth into a living hope by the raising of Jesus Christ from the dead.

We are a chosen race, a royal priesthood, a dedicated nation; we are a people claimed by God to proclaim the triumphs of Christ.

Christ has called us from darkness into his marvellous light. We who were not a people at all, are now God's people. We were outside God's mercy once, but now we are blessed and forgiven.

Kneel in prayer to the Father, from whom every family in heaven and on earth takes its name; that out of the treasures of glory God may grant us strength and power through the spirit in our inmost being; that Christ, through faith, may dwell in our hearts in love.

A New Zealand Prayer Book, Auckland: Collins, 1989, pp. 117, 121.

Thank you, Lord God, for calling me to your service, and adopting me into your family. Loving Lord, I commit my whole life to you: Holy Father, help me to become the person you destined me to be; Victorious Jesus, conquer my fears and resistance; Holy Spirit, teach me your truth; Master, I'm yours: take me as I am and make me what you want me to be.

A benediction
And now may the grace of the Lord Jesus Christ, the love of God, and the communion of the Holy Spirit be with you. Amen.

2

One more time: 'Who am I?'

God said, 'Let us make humankind in our image, according to our likeness...'

So God created humankind in his image, in the image of God he created them; male and female he created them.

God blessed them, and God said to them, 'Be fruitful and multiply, and fill the earth and subdue it; and have dominion over... every living thing that moves upon the earth'. When God created humankind, he made them in the likeness of God. Male and female he created them, and he blessed them...

When I look at your heavens, the work of your fingers, the moon and the stars that you have established; what are human beings that you are mindful of them, mortals that you care for them?

Just as we have borne the image of the man of dust, we will also bear the image of the man of heaven.

Surely I know the plans I have for you, says the Lord, plans for your welfare and not for harm, to give you a future with hope. Then when you call upon me and come and pray to me, I will hear you. When you search for me, you will find me; if you seek me with all your heart.

Jesus said, 'I am the bread of life. Whoever comes to me will never be hungry, and whoever believes in me will never be thirsty'.

God... is rich in mercy (and a) great love with which he loved us.

As you therefore have received Christ Jesus the Lord, continue to live your lives in him... We must grow up in every way into him who is the head, into Christ. I want to know Christ and the power of his resurrection and the sharing of his sufferings...

Do not lie to one another, seeing you have... clothed yourself with the new self, which is being renewed in knowledge according to the image of its Creator. With (the tongue) we bless the Lord and Father, and with it we curse those who are made in the likeness of God.

Cast all your anxiety on him, because he cares for you.

Genesis 1:26-28; Genesis 5:1; Psalm 8:3, 4; 1 Corinthians 15:49; Jeremiah 29:11-13; John 6:35; Ephesians 2:4; Colossians 2:6; Ephesians 4:13, 15; Philippians 3:9-10; Colossians 3:9, 10; James 3:9; 1 Peter 5:7.

'Going once... going twice... gone! Sold to the gentleman with the green tie!' cried the auctioneer. One by one the man's possessions were offered — the stereo, the car, the TV. Finally only the man remained. 'And what am I offered for this man?' the auctioneer continued. 'A fine specimen...!'

Trembling with horror, he woke from his dream. But the thought troubled him. What would they have paid for him? Two thousand dollars, five thousand? More? Less?

How much am I worth?

Our inorganic elements would bring about $10: our bodies have enough fat to make a few bars of soap, enough iron for a couple of nails, enough sugar to fill a small shaker, enough phosphorous to make a box of matches, and enough lime to whitewash a shed...

The biblical question is not merely 'What are human beings?' but 'What are human beings... that you care for them?' It's about how we relate to God; how God values us. Each of us is on this planet not by chance or accident, but by design. You and I are God's idea, and very special to him. We resulted from a special creative act of God. Genesis says 'God saw everything he had made, and behold, it was very good'. Man/woman comes into being 'trailing clouds of glory'.

Humans were/are the apex of creation, made 'in the image of God'. This means we are 'like God', not in physical form (God is Spirit) but as the visible representatives on earth of the Divine Being. Nor are we simply more like God than the other animals, because we weep and laugh, or because we are the only primates to walk upright (but we begin and end life horizontally rather than perpendicularly), or whose brain is larger and cleverer (so that we can use equipment outside our own bodies, or manufacture striped toothpaste. But then, as James Thurber once wrote, 'Dogs are raising families of their own before the first anniversary of their birth; but the young of humans are practically no good at all until almost a quarter of a centur*y*'). We are more than naked (or trousered) apes. Humans are creatures who sense the difference between what things are and what they ought to be.

D. H. Lawrence sees humans in terms of 'blood, soil and sex'. Camus summarises his dilemma: 'Everything which exalts life adds at the same time to its absurdity'. In Samuel Beckett's *Waiting for Godot* human life is reduced to waiting — for someone who never comes.

Some ancient philosophers regarded humans as encased souls or animated bodies; the Bible, on the other hand, emphasises the unity of our personhood. Naturalism says we are a little higher than the tadpoles; the Bible says we are a little lower than the angels. Scientism says we are an accidental arrangement of molecules; the Bible says we are crowned with glory and honour. Behaviourism says we are complex biological machines, whose behaviour is explained in terms of inherited or environmental factors; Jesus invites us to use our God-given capacity to worship the Lord in Spirit and in truth. Marxism says all human reality can be reduced to natural processes and events; the Bible affirms our God-endowed dignity and worth.

We are like God *intellectually*: having the power to reason, imagine and think about God; *socially*: capable of loving God, others and self, of celebrating and grieving; *vocationally*: as tenants of God's good earth we are commissioned to tend it with care; *aesthetically*: delighting in the natural beauty God has created; *morally*: our conscience helps us discern the will of God and freely choose goodness; and *spiritually*: we pray and worship and can 'know' God, and we experience premonitions of immortality (long before stone was used for houses, it was used for tombs). So we are invited to exhibit the nature and qualities of our Creator. The only satisfactory way we can understand who we are is in terms of our being cared for by God, and responsible to serve and obey him in return.

But these same humans have not wanted to replicate the Divine nature. They would prefer to be served than serve; to rule than to submit; to be autonomous and selfish rather than live responsibly in community; to get along without God, rather than live in dependence upon him. Fallen human nature is such that distant wars, earthquakes or cyclones trouble us a little, but a lot less than our own toothache or the scratch on our new car. As Rousseau said, we are born free, but everywhere we are in chains. If there is one theme recurring throughout this book, it is this: you are like God, and like the devil. Humans do despicable things to each other. They're sinners. (Did you know that cannibalism was practised in Scotland, Ireland and England as recently as four hundred years ago?)

The alternative to worshipping and serving God is idolatry: making gods out of our selves or some other created thing. That's why the second commandment prohibits our making images of God. William Golding's *Lord of the Flies* graphically describes the depths to which human depravity will sink when some English school boys, marooned on a tropical island, resort to a primitive sacrificial cult in which pigs are offered to appease the mysterious Lord of the Flies.

God makes all things good, humans meddle with them and they become evil. But although the image of God in us is marred, it's still there! As Irenaeus put it in an unforgettable sentence: 'The glory of God is (humans) fully alive'.

Sigmund Freud once said that human self-esteem suffered three great blows from science. First Copernicus showed that the earth is not the centre of the universe. Then Darwin suggested that humans are not organically superior to animals. And psychoanalysis asserted that we are not 'masters in our own house'.

But how can we change and grow? Libertarians say we have complete freedom to decide this way or that. Hard determinists believe we have no free will and are therefore not ultimately responsible for our destinies. Soft determinists say we may be governed by heredity, social factors, our psychology, our sin, or even God's working in our lives, but we have some responsibility for our decisions. We can freely choose to eat of a certain tree, and die, or obediently desist, and live. Adam and Eve are 'everyperson'.

The Greeks in their wisdom said 'Know thyself!' The Hebrews would have preferred 'Know thy God!' God, more than humans, is 'the proper study of humanity'. And where is God? Look around. C. S. Lewis says somewhere that if we realised who we truly were, we'd be tempted to fall down and worship one another.

We are made up of body, soul and spirit (1 Thessalonians 5:23). What does this mean? Greek philosophers like Socrates and Plato regarded the body as a useless encumbrance from which the spirit must be freed before it can achieve its destiny. But we are not simply a soul/spirit united to a body, any more than we are a body united to a soul. We are a complex unity: and Christianity regards the body and soul and spirit very highly. When God wanted to show us what he was really like, he inhabited a human body: 'Veiled in flesh the Godhead see; Hail! the Incarnate Deity'. With our bodies we have an affinity with nature, and relate to the material universe; with our souls we have self-identity and relate to others; with our spirits we relate to God. We are like a two-storied house. The lower storey is the physical part of us — the body. The upper storey has a window looking out towards the earth, and a skylight through which we view the stars. But it's all one house!

So, use some biblical self-talk and say to yourself: 'I am important. God loves even me. I am an unrepeatable miracle of God's creation. I have significance, not because I am better or smarter than anyone else, but because I was made in his image. All through life I will be bombarded with negative feedback — from family, friends, enemies, advertisers, teachers, bosses, employees, or even my own brain. But I will agree with God about myself: he doesn't make junk. When I fail, I will learn from it and will not call myself a failure. When I succeed, I will give thanks to the One who endowed me with those gifts and abilities. When I am depressed, I will say "This, too will pass". And when elated, I shall praise him, my wonderful Lord and my God. I am important to God, and therefore to myself. I was died for. I belong to him. I am his special child. He loves me and forgives me, and I will serve him on earth and celebrate with him in heaven — forever. Wow!'

(Meursault, the hero of Camus' *The Outsider*, came early in life to the conclusion that life was meaningless. As he neared the time of his execution he tried to console himself...) 'But', I reminded myself, 'it's common knowledge that life isn't worth living anyhow'. And, on a wide view, I could see that it makes little difference whether one dies at the age of thirty or three score and ten.

Albert Camus,
The Outsider, Harmondsworth, Middlesex: Penguin Books, 1965, p. 112.

Back at the end of World War I, the French Army found itself with a very sticky situation on its hands. There were upwards of a hundred soldiers who were suffering from amnesia because of shell shock, and due to a very faulty record system, not even the army knew the identity of these individuals. In every other way these men were healthy, and if they could only be returned to their families and their native surroundings, this in itself might quicken the return of their memories. But how to discover their identity and get them back into their family groupings? Someone came up with the idea of having an Identification Rally in Paris. It would be publicised throughout the whole country, and families who had relatives missing in action would be encouraged to attend. The plan was adopted, and the moment finally came when literally thousands of people gathered in one of the great plazas of the city. A platform had been erected in the centre where all could see, and one by one these men would step up to a microphone and look out anxiously over the crowd and say, 'Please, please, is there any one here who can tell me who I am?' A reporter who covered the event said it contained as much high drama as the events of war themselves.

There is something almost mythic about this scene, for in one way or another this is exactly what each of us has been doing from the moment we emerged from our mother's womb. We are creatures in search of an identity, all of us. We are forever attempting to discover who we are and why we are here and what kinds of capacities make up our uniqueness. There is no question closer to the centre of our human mystery than the question: 'Who am I?' and we are forever looking for people who can help us at this most foundational level.

John Claypool,
'Who Am I?' unpublished sermon, Northminster Baptist Church, Jackson, Mississippi, 9 September 1979.

Dear Sir,
I am.
Yours faithfully,
G. K. Chesterton.

Shortest ever letter to *The Times* of London.

Human life has always been lived on the edge of a precipice... (Humans) propound mathematical theorems in beleaguered cities, conduct metaphysical arguments in condemned cells, make jokes on scaffolds, discuss the last new poem while advancing to the walls of Quebec, and comb their hair at Thermopylae. This is not panache: it is our nature.

C. S. Lewis,
in a sermon preached at the beginning of World War I, and published in *The Weight of Glory*, Grand Rapids, Michigan: Eerdmans, 1965, pp. 44f. Reproduced by permission of Eerdmans/Collins Publishers.

(Humans are) so the universe will have something to talk through, so God will have something to talk with, and so the rest of us will have something to talk about.

The biblical view of the history of humankind and of each individual man and woman is contained in the first three chapters of Genesis. We are created to serve God by loving him and each other in freedom and joy, but we invariably choose bondage and woe instead as prices not too high to pay for independence. To say that God drove Adam and Eve out of Eden is apparently a euphemism for saying that Adam and Eve like the rest of us made a break for it as soon as God happened to look the other way. If God really wanted to get rid of us, the chances are he wouldn't have kept hounding us every step of the way ever since.

Frederick Buechner,
Wishful Thinking: A Theological ABC, London: Collins, 1973, pp. 55, 56.

This phrase, 'the image of God', is as important as anything in Scripture... I stand in the flow of history. I know my origin. My lineage is longer than that of the Queen of England. It does not start with the Battle of Hastings. It does not start with the beginnings of good families, wherever or whenever they lived. As I look at myself in the flow of space-time reality, I see my origin in... God's creating us in his own image.

Francis Schaeffer,
Genesis in Space and Time, Downers Grove, Illinois: Inter-Varsity, 1972, pp. 48, 53-54.

When God said, 'Let us make (human persons) in our image' he once and for all provided a basis for human dignity, worth and value. He sealed forever the fact that all persons who walked this earth would have the right to see themselves as creatures of worth, value and importance... No matter how deeply sin mars our image, one fact remains: we are in his image... The Bible describes sin as an intruder into human nature. It is a foreigner — uninvited by the Creator — and it will eventually be totally eliminated from our personalities. (Therefore) sin cannot serve as the basis for our identity... No matter how far we fall short, the image of God in us will triumph... We must base our principles of self-esteem on this most basic aspect of our nature. Only in the fact that we are God's creations do we have a solid basis for self-acceptance and self-love. Once we have this foundation solidly in place, we can take a look at the extent of our sinfulness and our shortcomings. We do this in order to see our need for growth and grace, however, and not as a measure of our worth or value.

Bruce Narramore,
You're Someone Special, Grand Rapids, Michigan: Zondervan, 1978, p. 39.

(Meister Eckhart's spirituality is one) of blessing and of passing on a blessing to others by way of justice and compassion... Every creature is a word of God... Salvation for Eckhart is creativity plus justice, or creativity at justice-making... The purpose of living is not to flee the earth or run from its pleasures but to return the blessings one has received by blessing other creatures and other human generations as well... We are sons and daughters of God and therefore have divine blood within us... God is the Creator and we, the images of God, follow in God's footsteps.

Matthew Fox,
Breakthrough: Meister Eckhart's Creation Spirituality in New Translation, Garden City, New York: Doubleday, 1980, excerpts from pp. 4-46.

Aligned with that long tradition that affirms God as creator of the world, we affirm that in God's provision for the beings that issue from God's creativity, grace is built into the processes of birth, of maternal or parental care and into the orders our species has evolved for the sustenance and maintenance of life. We might call the kind of grace that comes as part of creation ordinary grace.

But in insisting upon the radical freedom of God, we must also take account of what might be called extraordinary grace — the unpredictable and unexpected manifestations of God's care and of God's claims upon our loves and our passions...

We human beings seem to have a generic vocation — a universal calling — to be related to the Ground of Being in a relationship of trust and loyalty. That vocation calls us into covenantal relationship with the transcendent and with the neighbour... Human beings are genetically potentiated — are gifted at birth — with readiness to develop in faith... We can become co-responsible with God for the quality and extensiveness of faith on earth.

James Fowler,
Stages of Faith, The Psychology of Human Development and the Quest for Meaning, San Francisco: HarperCollins*Publishers*, 1981, pp. 302-3.

Some think of a Christian as one who necessarily believes certain things. That Jesus was the son of God, say. Or that Mary was a virgin. Or that the Pope is infallible. Or that all other religions are wrong.

Some think of a Christian as one who necessarily does certain things. Such as going to church. Getting baptised. Giving up liquor and tobacco. Reading the Bible. Doing a good deed a day.

Some think of a Christian as just a Nice Guy.

Jesus said, 'I am the way, and the truth, and the life; no one comes to the Father, but by me' (John 14:6). He didn't say that any particular ethic, doctrine, or religion was the way, the truth, and the life. He said that he was. He didn't say that it was by believing or doing anything in particular that you could 'come to the Father'. He said that it was only by him — by living, participating in, being caught up by, the way of life that he embodied, that was his way.

Thus it is possible to be on Christ's way and with his mark upon you without ever having heard of Christ, and for that reason to be on your way to God though maybe you don't even believe in God.

A Christian is one who is on the way, though not necessarily very far along it, and who has at least some dim and half-baked idea of whom to thank.

Frederick Buechner,
Wishful Thinking, London: Collins, 1973, p. 14.

One idea that has influenced me greatly is that the Jesus I love in the abstract can become concrete for me in every person I meet. If I look at the person a second time, I can see through him or her to Jesus. And Jesus says to me, 'Hey, love me in this person!'

Loving Jesus through people has affected my life dramatically. Each person becomes sacred when I sense that on the other side of that person is Jesus waiting to be loved.

I want to emphasise that the person is not Jesus, the person is not God; but I can get at God through the person, and, strangely enough, God can get at me through that person too. In reality, you cannot love God without loving people. And God loves you through people...

If someone treats me like dirt and I'm about to get angry, I look at that person again and — if I'm prayerful — I can sense the presence of God on the other side of that person. When I sense God coming at me through that person, no matter how rotten the person is, my attitude toward him or her is altered.

Anthony Campolo,
'Loving Jesus through People' in Lavonne Neff et al. (eds), *Practical Christianity*, Wheaton, Illinois: Tynedale Publishers Inc., 1988, pp. 101-2.

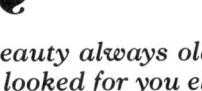

Too late have I loved you, O beauty always old and ever new. Behold you were within and I looked for you elsewhere and in my weakness I ran after the beauty in the things you had made. You were with me and I was not with you. The things you created kept me from you. You have called and have pierced my deafness. You have shone out and have lifted my blindness. You have sent out your sweetness and I have longed after you and looked for you, I have tasted you and hungered after you. And now my whole hope is in nothing else but in your great mercy O Lord, my God.

Augustine,
Praying with the Saints, Dublin: Veritas Publications, 1989, p. 19-20.

Lord, what incredible human creatures you have created. We are fearfully and wonderfully made.

Once we trudged from place to place, now we can fly faster than sound. Once we scratched the earth with crude wooden tools, now robots serve us. Once we chiselled inscriptions laboriously on parchment or stone; now we multiply words and ideas in milliseconds. Once we looked at the moon and marvelled; now we can walk on it. Someone somewhere first blew through a ram's horn; now we create mighty symphonies.

But remind us, Lord, that we have some fearful limitations. We humans possess real goodness but not sufficient goodness, real wisdom but not sufficient wisdom, real power but not sufficient power. So we need your goodness, wisdom and power. Help us, Lord, to use our intelligence to take account of the dangers that come from trusting solely in human intelligence.

You have made us for yourself, and we do not rest until we rest in you. O God, deny us peace, so that you may some day give us glory. Conquer our hearts through your sovereign power and in your mercy and love might we become the men and women you intended us to be. And if events seem to conspire against our desires, and we haven't the strength to impose our terms on life, give us the grace to accept the terms life offers us, because of our conviction that all of life is under your divine control.

As we study the majesty and glory of Jesus Christ, we see our destiny: what we could become if we too are truly in tune with your good will for us. May we become less and less enslaved by the desires of the moment, and freed by your ennobling love and forgiving grace to love you with all our heart.

We pray for your glory. Through Christ our Lord, Amen.

A benediction
Now to God who is able to strengthen you... to the only wise God, through Jesus Christ, be the glory forever! Amen.

Romans 16:25, 26

3

How much are you saved?

The Lord is my light and my salvation; whom shall I fear? The Lord is the stronghold of my life; of whom shall I be afraid?

Surely God is my salvation; I will trust, and will not be afraid, for the Lord God is my strength and my might; he has become my salvation.

For God so loved the world that he gave his only Son, so that everyone who believes in him may not perish but may have eternal life.

Believe on the Lord Jesus, and you will be saved, you and your household.

There is therefore now no condemnation for those who are in Christ Jesus. For the law of the Spirit of life in Christ Jesus has set you free from the law of sin and of death.

The goodness and loving kindness of God our Saviour appeared..., so that, having been justified by his grace, we might become heirs according to the hope of eternal life.

For by grace you have been saved through faith, and this is not your own doing; it is the gift of God — not the result of works, so that no one may boast.

For there is one God; there is also one mediator between God and humankind, Christ Jesus, himself human, who gave himself a ransom for all.

I would remind you, brothers and sisters, of the good news that I proclaimed to you... through which you are being saved, if you hold firmly to the message that I proclaimed to you... Christ died for our sins in accordance with the scriptures, he was buried, and was raised on the third day.

While we were still weak, at the right time Christ died for the ungodly. But God proves his love for us in that while we still were sinners Christ died for us. Much more surely then, now that we have been justified by his blood, will we be saved through him from the wrath of God. For if while we were enemies, we were reconciled to God through the death of his Son, much more surely, having been reconciled, will we be saved by his life.

Then Jesus told his disciples, 'If any want to become my followers, let them deny themselves and take up their cross and follow me. For those who want to save their life will lose it, and those who lose their life for my sake will find it'.

Psalm 27:1; Isaiah 12:2; John 3:16; Acts 16:31; Romans 8:1, 2; Titus 3:4, 7; Ephesians 2:8-9; 1 Timothy 2:5, 6; 1 Corinthians 15:1-4; Romans 5:1, 2, 6, 8-10; Matthew 16:24-26.

'Save the rain forests!' 'Save the whales!' But if it has not happened to you already, it will: someone will ask you in a public place 'Are you saved?' (To which a theologian retorted, 'I'll be damned if I'm not!')

'Jesus saves' can still be seen on some old church buildings or bulletin boards. (To which a Jewish student responded, 'Jesus saves, but Moses invests!')

What does it mean to be 'saved'?

On a memorable night in the Trinity Term of 1929, the great scholar C. S. Lewis, alone in his room at Magdalen College, Oxford, 'admitted that God was God, and knelt and prayed: perhaps, that night, the most dejected and reluctant convert in all England'.[1] In that moment he began to be 'saved', a term he (and the New Testament) often used.

In *The Voyage of the Dawn Treader*, C. S. Lewis has a vivid picture of what it means to be saved. Eustace, a dragon, is transformed back into a person. Eustace remembered that dragons can cast off their skin like a snake, so he began to work on himself. At first just the scales came off, but with more effort the whole skin started to peel off, and he stepped out of it altogether. He began to wash but noticed his foot was still hard and scaly. So he scratched away and finally peeled off another layer of dragon skin. But under it was still more. Then Aslan, the lion, offered to help. Though Eustace was afraid of Aslan's claws, he lay down before him. His fears were justified: the first tear was so deep it went down to his heart. When the skin was at last off him, Eustace found it 'ever so much thicker, and darker, and more knobbly looking than the others had been'. Then Aslan bathed him and dressed him in new clean clothes... You will guess who Eustace and Aslan are.

'Salvation' is a key concept in the Bible. The name Jesus (or Joshua) means 'God saves'. The Old Testament Hebrew word *yasha*, 'to save', really means to be wide open, to be free. Salvation is freedom. Not freedom to do what you like, but the opposite: freedom from whatever is binding, controlling and destroying you, and freedom to serve God and others. Jesus is our Saviour: that is, he wants to make us whole persons. 'Salvation' in the New Testament has therefore a wide range of meanings, including healing (Matthew 9:22) and rescue from danger (Matthew 8:25, Acts 17:20).

The key to being 'saved', however, means doing something about our sins. Zaccheus, a swindler, decided to return more than he'd stolen, and Jesus said 'Today, salvation has come to this house'. But you are not saved merely because you do good; you do good because you are saved. You are saved by faith in Jesus Christ, and faith is a gift — you can't 'earn' it. In an article 'I Was Decided Upon' C. S. Lewis wrote, 'It is not enough to want to get rid of one's sins. We also need to believe in the One who saves us from our sins... Because we know that we are sinners, it does not follow that we are saved'.[2] A man said to his Irish friend, 'It's great to be saved!' 'Aye', said the Irishman, 'it is. But I know something better than that'. 'Better than being saved? What can possibly be better than that?' 'The companionship of the One who has saved me', his friend responded.

So salvation is personal: Paul said 'He loved me and gave himself for me' (Galatians 2:20). Christianity is a rescue mission: rescuing sinners from death and giving them eternal life, life in all its fullness; rescuing us from selfishness, to friendship with God. It is life and health and peace and joy and fulfilment. It is a crisis (I was saved), a process (I am being saved), and a destiny (I will be saved).

It is also social. Salvation is for the whole of a person, not just for the soul of a person. Jeremiah preached against the attitude which says 'I'm safe because my religion's the right one' but is not concerned enough about ethics and justice (Jeremiah 7:1-15). A religion divorced from justice, love, mercy and honesty was also attacked by Jesus (Matthew 23:23, Luke 11:42).

Salvation is also ecological: God is concerned for all his creation. The whole universe is to be transformed (Romans 8:19-25).

And (all this and heaven too!) salvation is eternal. As the old preachers put it, we're saved for time and for eternity! Frederick Buechner says somewhere, 'To love God is to be saved... (but) you do not love God and live for him so you will go to heaven. Whichever side of the grave you happen to be talking about, to love God and live for him is heaven'.

A final word from W. E. Sangster: 'To know "full salvation" is

31

not only to be forgiven and sure of the way home; it is to be so indwelt by Christ, and so loving towards others, that we are ready (with Moses) to be blotted out of the Book of Life if these cannot be saved also. Only Christ can give us love like that. It is his love, loving in us... It can make us unafraid to face the question: "How much are you saved?"'.[3]

Different people at different stages of life need to be saved from different things. Some people have to be saved from a nagging sense of guilt that never leaves them. Other people have to be saved from a sense of meaninglessness. Other people need to be saved from terror at the brevity of life.

To be saved by faith means that if I place my trust in God, if I let my attention be focused on God, God will grasp me and will give me *yasha,* (salvation). He will give me space, room, and wholeness.

Martin Marty,
'Saved by Faith' in LaVonne Neff et al, *Practical Christianity*, Wheaton, Illinois: Tyndale House Publishers Inc., 1988, p. 185.

Nice people don't need to be saved... We never put it to ourselves quite like that, but something very like it is often at the back of our minds when we give thought (if ever we do!) to the subject of salvation... And yet the Bible knows of only two final classes, the saved and the lost. There is no in-between niche for nice people. In the last resort we must be found in one or other of these two classes, and the second doesn't sound inviting...

Leon Morris,
Salvation, Beecroft, NSW: Evangelical Tracts and Publications, n.d., p. 2.

While we may have some clear criteria whereby a person may decide whether he or she is a Christian, it may be a much more difficult thing sometimes to decide whether one is Christian!

W. Cantwell Smith,
'Christian: Noun or Adjective?' in *Questions of Religious Truth*, New York: Scribner's, 1967, pp. 99-123; quoted by Paul Trudinger, 'On Being Saved', Canberra: *St Mark's Review*, Autumn 1989, p. 22.

...It is both curious and sad that this note of salvation by grace is often muffled in much modern churchmanship. In a message to the Church of Scotland, that profound scholar, Professor Tom Torrance, deplores its absence. He claims that we have become so mesmerised by the world's material needs that we have shifted our message away from salvation by grace to salvation by social righteousness and political action. In our obsession with making the church relevant, we have made it the servant of public opinion. To be sure, the Christian is desperately concerned with social righteousness and justice. The black people of South Africa need salvation from the atrocious indignities of apartheid. The starving millions of our world need salvation from poverty and hunger and hopelessness. The victims of oppressive regimes need salvation from cruel injustices. These are all authentic Christian concerns, and must be addressed by the church. But how great and pressing is the need of all for the personal salvation graciously offered by God in Christ crucified and risen again! To withhold this gift of grace is to offer stones instead of bread, the bread of life...

John N. Gladstone,
'Magnificently Charismatic', a sermon preached in Yorkminster Park Baptist Church, Toronto, date unknown, p. 3.

The term 'full salvation' has long been loved in some evangelical circles. It is used to indicate the depth of the change Christ can work in a human life and his ability to work the change now. 'Full salvation' is not only pardon from sin but increasing deliverance from it, power to have victory over the inward as well as the outward sins, and victory not only in eternity, but in this life as well. The term grows in meaning... it now has range as well as depth. To have 'full salvation' is to be saved in our relationships as well as in our deep solitariness...

W. E. Sangster,
How Much Are You Saved? (Westminster pamphlet no. 11), London: Epworth, 1959, p. 15.

Not what these hands have done
Can save this guilty soul;
Not what this toiling flesh has borne
Can make my spirit whole.
Thy love to me,
O God, not mine,
O Lord, to thee,
Can rid me of this dark unrest
And set my spirit free.

Horatius Bonar
(in one of his hymns)

Literally, 'adding insult to injury', while Jesus hung on the cross, they said 'He saved others, himself he could not save' (Matthew 27:34)... Yet back of the voices of ridicule is a truth as deep as reality itself... They were right! Precisely because he was saving others, he could not save himself. This is the 'law of redemption' that is rooted in the very way our universe is put together. No matter what area of life you are talking about, it has always been true that 'saving others' and 'saving self' are mutually exclusive...

For many years I was troubled by all the theories of atonement that talked about 'blood sacrifice' and 'penal substitution', and it never made sense to me until I realised that not even a God can solve personal problems by the exercise of power alone. If human beings were robots or puppets or objects that could be moved around by force, then salvation could be a simple 'power transaction'. As any parent of a rebellious child knows full well, there are no easy answers to setting right a spirit that has gone wrong. Solutions relying on power wind up destroying the person you want to save. Only by getting involved with the sickness and appealing directly to the heart can resolution come. This is what the Old Testament principle 'Without the shedding of blood, there is no remission or sins' is all about.

John Claypool,
'The Paradox of Salvation', sermon preached at Broadway Baptist Church, Fort Worth, Texas. (Weekly sermons published by the church, Vol. XIV, No. 2, Nov. 3, 1974.)

I believe everyone has another self imprisoned within him or her. It may require soul surgery to bring it out, it will require repentance, a change of heart, conversion, new birth... But the real self is the person Christ loves. He sees within us hidden possibilities, he sees what we might become. Salvation is Christ's gift of 'becoming', enabling us to realise what God intended for us. In the preface to his book *The Tragic Sense of Life*, the Spanish writer Unamuno writes '...A new friend enriches our spirit... by what he causes to discover in our own selves, something which, if we had not known him, would have lain in us undeveloped'.

Ivor Bailey,
in a sermon preached from Maughan Church, Adelaide, 7 October 1973.

According to Kittel's great *Theological Dictionary of the New Testament*, the Greek word for salvation was used in the ancient world from Homer onwards of 'an acutely dynamic act in which gods or people snatch others by force from serious peril' whether the danger was a battle, a storm at sea, condemnation in a law court, illness or death... We use the same terminology today, when a surgeon saves a patient's life by an operation, the fire brigade saves someone trapped in a burning building, or a rescue team saves a climber stranded on a mountain rockface. In each case somebody is in acute peril. 'Salvation' means nothing unless there is a situation of grave danger from which a person needs to be rescued...

So let me ask you: have you received the salvation which the gospel proclaims? Have you trusted personally in Christ who once secured and now offers this salvation? Only then shall we be able to say from our experience: 'I am not ashamed of the gospel, for it is the power of God unto salvation to everyone who believes'.

John Stott,
'Salvation Today', a sermon preached in All Souls' Church of England, Langham Place, London, on 7 October 1973. Published in *All Souls' Magazine*, date unknown, pp. 11-15.

Lord save me.

Lord, save me from the sins that separate me from friendship with you, the wilfulness that leads me to stray from your love and your laws, and the selfishness that separates me from being there for others.

Save me from self-despising which separates me from enjoying living with myself, or the pride which prevents me from seeing myself realistically, and the immaturity which is unable to accept others' uniqueness.

Deliver me from bad habits that imprison me in addictive behaviours, laziness which prevents my realising your full potential for me, or workaholism which confuses ends and means.

Rescue me, Lord, from closed-mindedness which prejudices me against receiving a new idea, or the stubbornness which causes me to be unteachable, and any bigotry which exalts my beliefs or my group above others.'

Redeem me, Saviour, from the enticements of the world, the flesh and the devil: the seductions of fame, temptations from lust, or violence which destroys rather than heals.

Thank you, Lord and Saviour, for the good news that if I believe in you, trust you, commit myself to you, I will be saved. Thank you for doing for me what I cannot possibly do for myself. Help me to change any attitudes, beliefs or behaviours that are not pleasing to you and therefore are unwholesome for me and unhelpful for others.

Help me to ask often,
'What must I do to be saved?' 'Day by day, am I being saved?'

A benediction

May God bless you with every good gift from on high. May he keep you pure and holy in his sight at all times. May he bestow the riches of his grace upon you, bring you the good news of salvation, and always fill you with love for everyone...
May the Lord God be your strength, your song, your salvation, the stronghold of your life, your fortress, so that you will never be shaken, and trusting him will not be afraid. Amen.

Notes
1. Quoted in Clyde S. Kilby (ed.), *A Mind Awake: An Anthology of C. S. Lewis*, London: Geoffrey Bles, 1968, p. 133.
2. ibid., p. 131.
3. W. E. Sangster, *How Much Are You Saved?*, Westminster pamphlet no. 11, London: Epworth, 1959, p. 15.

4

What to do with your sins

All have sinned and fall short of the glory of God. If we say that we have no sin, we deceive ourselves, and the truth is not in us. If we confess our sins, he who is faithful and just will forgive us our sins and cleanse us from all unrighteousness.

The Lord is not slow about his promise, as some think of slowness, but is patient with you, not wanting any to perish, but all to come to repentance.

God... commands all people everywhere to repent. Repent, and believe the good news. Remember then what you received and heard; obey it, and repent. Humble yourselves before the Lord, and he will exalt you.

Yet even now, says the Lord, return to me with all your heart... Return to the Lord, your God, for he is gracious and merciful, slow to anger, and abounding in steadfast love, and relents from punishing.

Cast away from you all the transgressions that you have committed against me, and get yourselves a new heart and a new spirit! Turn, then, and live. Repent, therefore, and turn to God so that your sins may be wiped out, so that times of refreshing may come from the presence of the Lord.

(The Lord) does not deal with us according to our sins, nor repay us according to our iniquities. For as the heavens are high above the earth, so great is his steadfast love toward those who fear him; as far as the east is from the west so far he removes our transgressions from us.

Seek the Lord while he may be found, call upon him while he is near; let the wicked forsake their way, and the unrighteous their thoughts; let them return to the Lord, that he may have mercy on them, and to our God, for he will abundantly pardon.

So they (the disciples) went out and proclaimed that all should repent... They should repent and turn to God and do deeds consistent with repentance.

Have mercy on me, O God, according to your steadfast love; according to your abundant mercy, blot out my transgressions. Wash me thoroughly from my iniquity, and cleanse me from my sin. Create in me a clean heart, O God.

Romans 3:23; 1 John 1:8, 9; 2 Peter 3:9; Acts 17:30; Mark 1:15; Revelation 3:3; James 4:10; Joel 2:12-13; Ezekiel 18:31, 32; Acts 3:19, 20; Psalm 103:10-12; Isaiah 55:6, 7; Mark 6:12; Acts 26:20. Psalm 51:1, 2, 10.

A comedian, Dan Leno, used to open his act saying, 'Ah, what is man? Wherefore does he why? Whence did he whence? Whither is he withering?'

Who am I? As our first three chapters disclose, I am a special person made in the image of God, but whose image has been scarred. I am like God, and like the devil. I am good... and bad. I am a delight, but my sins are a horror, both to God and to myself.

How bad am I? There are two opposite errors in some replies to this question. 'Too bad' you might say. Wrong. 'Not bad enough' — again, wrong. Pascal once wrote: 'There are only two kinds of people — the righteous who believe themselves sinners; the rest, sinners who believe themselves righteous'.

We are all are equally guilty — not just those the law calls 'criminals'. Indeed it's people who think they're good enough who are in the greatest peril. Most people in the Bible who were asked to repent were religious people. We cannot offer our righteousness to God (we'll never have enough), only our penitence.

You will sometimes read about the doctrine of 'total depravity' in connection with our sin. This doesn't mean that humans are as bad as they can be, but rather that no part of us has escaped the pollution of sin.

C. S. Lewis explains the old prayer-book phrase about being 'miserable offenders' by analysing the situation of those who don't realise they're miserable. Passengers on two trains speeding towards each other on the same track may be reading magazines, dozing over a drink, or laughing boisterously. They don't feel miserable. But in fact their situation can be described as utterly miserable. Tell them they're miserable and they'll laugh at you.

John Bunyan's classic *Pilgrim's Progress* opens with 'a man clothed with rags standing in a certain place with his face from his own house, a book in his hand and a great burden upon his back'. 'How camest thou by thy burden?' this pilgrim was asked by his companion, Mr Worldly Wiseman. He replied, 'By reading this book in my hand'.

The book, of course, was the Bible, a book with an accurate diagnosis and cure for the human condition. The problem: you are a sinner. Cure: 'Repent!' If you check a concordance, you'll find 'repentance' is an idea mentioned as often in the Old as in the New Testaments (for example Ezekiel 18:31, Luke 13:3, Acts 3:19). Jesus' first recorded preaching was about repentance; so was his last.

So repentance isn't funny, like the little old men in cartoons with sandwich boards shouting 'Repent, the end is nigh!' Or the mourners bench in Charlie Chaplin films. Byron was wrong in his opinion that 'The weak alone repent'.

And the cynic who said

> Christians are people who feel
> Repentance on a Sunday
> For what they did on Saturday
> And intend to do on Monday

could not be more wrong!

Repentance is about radical change. It means coming to your senses, waking up to yourself! It means turning from your sins to God.

Repentance isn't the same as 'doing penance': inflicting pain on yourself isn't the way to go. Christ died for your sins: his sacrifice was sufficient. Repentance is more than feeling sorry, though it includes sorrow. Judas felt remorse for betraying Jesus, but apparently he didn't truly repent. (His greater sin was not to betray our Lord, but to refuse to go to Calvary for a pardon.) Repentance is more than feeling guilty; guilt can be a form of self-hatred. You should hate your sins, not yourself.

And repentance is not superficial. The buck stops with you, the penitent. You can't blame anyone but yourself. Repentance has no room for excuses, putting the blame somewhere else. Sigmund Freud, probably more than anyone else in the twentieth century, has done a lot to help us understand ourselves. He located many of our personality disorders in the early experiences of infancy. These, he said, are repressed into our subconscious and come back later to haunt us. Now this may be true, but it could lead to a 'blame-oriented' approach to life. Many who have never heard of Freud still blame their parents for who they are. Repentance is the opposite of blaming. It's you taking responsibility for who you are and what you've done.

Repentance involves a radical change of heart, and mind, and behaviour. It is a U-turn, not merely a course correction. The story of the prodigal son and the waiting father (Luke 15:11-32) is about repentance. The boy felt sorry for himself, then sorry that he'd wronged his dad, so he decided to go to his father and confess: 'I have sinned against God and against you'. He was instantly forgiven, welcomed back into the family, and his homecoming was the occasion for great rejoicing. There's feasting in heaven, Jesus said, whenever a sinner repents. If you have repented, did you know you caused the angels to throw a party?

The Bible encourages us to confess our sins to God and to another human being (1 John 1:9, James 5:16). Be careful to whom you confess: that person must be able to keep a confidence, and to pray a healing prayer for you.

You are saved from the penalty of your sins (though their effects may linger on). So confess them and forsake them and then don't carry their guilt with you: 'own and disown' them. God has truly, completely forgiven you. It's like being sick, then well: don't keep thinking about your sickness; enjoy your health!

A Christian evangelist was asked, 'How is it that your religion has been around for two thousand years and hasn't influenced more people?' His reply: 'How is it that water has been around for thousands of years and many people are still dirty?'

A final serious word: the refusal to repent is worse than the sin for which one ought to repent. The question really isn't 'Shall I repent?' but 'Shall I repent now, when it may save me?' Jesus had some awesome things to say about one's repentance being one's punishment... So...?

I went back to the New Testament, to the Acts and the epistles, to Peter and Paul, who were the first ones to preach the gospel to a pagan world. What does it mean to preach the Christian gospel to such a world...?

Christ, after his resurrection, said... 'Now that the resurrection is a reality, now that forgiveness of sins is accomplished in this new covenant, go out to all the earth and preach the good news of the forgiveness of sins to all the nations'...

That is good news, to the Masai, to the guilty man cast out of his community, to the sinful son and to the offending family. I do not have to convince them of sin. They know of sin. What they did not know of was forgiveness. It has touched the earth. This is where Christianity parts company from Judaism and from Hinduism and from paganism. Sin is a conquered thing. This is a redeemed world. One wonders if one should dare talk to pagans about sin — apart from Christ, until they know Christ. The job of a missionary, after all, is... to teach the forgiveness of sin.

Vincent J. Donovan,
Christianity Rediscovered, London: SCM, 1985, pp. 61-2.

Jesus describes sinfulness as more than just doing wrong things. When we fail to do what's right, it's as bad as doing wrong. You can be totally law-abiding and not give a thought for anyone else. Sin is basically four things: 1. Failing — in our thinking, saying and action — to do what is right. 2. Trying to find meaning and fulfilment without God's love, relationship and guidance. 3. Rejecting and rebelling against God. 4. Missing out on the full and creative life God intends for us...

(Repentance) begins with being sorry enough to quit the past... It begins with: • changing directions • changing sides • changing what is important to us • changed alliances • changed intentions • changed commitments... There should be changes everywhere — enough for it to be noticeable: • at home • at work • at sport • in relationships • in lifestyle • in attitudes • in thinking.

John Smith,
'When love comes to stay', Care and Communication Concern, 1990, pp. 5, 7.

Sin incriminates. To be a sinner means to be guilty before God. Guilt is that aspect of sin which belongs to the past, and is well expressed in the words from Fitzgerald's *Omar Khayyam*,

> The Moving Finger writes; and having writ
> Moves on: nor all thy piety nor wit
> Shall lure it back to cancel half a line,
> Nor all thy tears wash out a word of it.

As Paul would say, 'the handwriting is against us', and this is something that no merely human means can ever remedy...

The late Archbishop Temple once wrote, 'A great deal too much attention has been given to sins as compared with sin. And so, if it happens that I cannot think of any particular wrong thing that I have done, or any particular good thing that I might have done and neglected, yet still I must ask God to be merciful to me a sinner, for I share the common sin of (humankind) and make myself in a host of ways the centre of the world. I think like a human and not like God.'

James Philip,
Repentance: Its Meaning and Implications, London: the Tyndale Press, 1963, pp. 12-13, 20.

Your intellect says, 'I accept Christ', your emotions say, 'I love Christ', and your will says 'I will follow Christ'. In true repentance all your powers are diverted and channelled through

Christ. It is not just giving mental assent, it is not just an act of volcanic emotion, nor is it an act of will power alone. True repentance is bringing all of our being — mind, heart and will — under the control of Christ.

Billy Graham,
'The Meaning of Repentance', a sermon preached on 'The Hour of Decision', Billy Graham Evangelistic Association, Box 779, Minneapolis, Minnesota 55440, 1967, pp. 8-9.

Repentance must not be mistaken for remorse. It does not consist in feeling terribly sorry that things went wrong in the past; it is an active, positive attitude which consists in moving in the right direction. It is made very clear in the parable of the two sons (Matthew 21:28) who were commanded by their father to go to work at his vineyard. The one said 'I am going', but did not go. The other said, 'I am not going', and then felt ashamed and went to work. This was real repentance, and we should never lure ourselves into imagining that to lament one's past is an act of repentance. It is part of it, of course, but repentance remains unreal and barren as long as it has not led us to doing the will of the father. We have a tendency to think it should result in fine emotions and we are quite often satisfied with emotions instead of real, deep changes.

Metropolitan Anthony of Sourozh,
'Meditation and Worship', in John Garvey (ed.), *Modern Spirituality: An Anthology*, London: Darton, Longman and Todd, 1986, pp. 35-6.

Ignatius sums up as one single and fundamental principle (in other words, his First Principle and Foundation): our end is God; therefore what helps towards God is good, what gets in the way is bad. Things are not good or bad in themselves, but only in the effect they have on our relationship with God. We can recall Augustine's classic, rule-defying pronouncement: 'Love, and do what you will'.

Margaret Hebblethwaite,
Finding God in All Things, London: Fountain Paperbacks, 1987, p. 35.

Repentance is a gift... I do not have to live into fearful defensiveness in relation to my past... I can learn things today that shed a whole new light on yesterday's conclusions, and this is precisely what I hear Jesus encouraging us to do in his call for us to repent and believe the Good News. He is affirming that God is more interested in growth than innocence, in how much we have learned from our mistakes rather than how many mistakes we have made. Is not that the crucial point in the way the father of the prodigal son responded to his return from the far country? He was more concerned about what the lad had gained in terms of self-understanding than about the money and time he had lost in coming to that wisdom.

John Claypool,
'Growing and the Gift of Repentance', a sermon preached in Northminster Baptist Church, 3955 Ridgewood Road, Jackson, Mississippi, on 31 August 1980.

41

Repentance, *metanoia*, is the turning of the mind, and with the mind the imagination, the affections and the will, away from self and sin and towards God. It is within an act of Godward-turning that our self-examination happens. We look towards God in gratitude for his loving-kindness, towards Jesus in his death for our sins, towards our own true self in what it is meant to become. The examining of our consciences will be thorough, and while it means a looking into ourselves it will not be an introspective self-scrutiny, for it will be mingled with the looking up towards God and the exposing of the self towards him. But the preparation will be thorough. It is not a matter of naming those sins which seem to be 'big' or which worry us specially, for it is necessary to confess all the ways in which our attitudes and actions have been contrary to the Christian way. That is important. It is a confession of the whole self, and the attitudes and actions which we may sometimes think to be small may be a decisive part of the self's orientation.

William Ramsay,
Be Still and Know: A Study in the Life of Prayer, London: Collins (Fount paperbacks), 1982, pp. 107-8.

Oh the comfort, the inexpressible comfort
of feeling safe with a person,
Having neither to weigh thoughts
or measure words
but pour them all out just as they are
Chaff and grain together, and
a faithful hand will take them
and sift them,
keep what is worth keeping,
and with the breath of kindness
blow the rest away.

George Eliot

The most noble strategy for dealing with guilt is the way of self-punishment. Do you remember how T. S. Eliot's Celia said, 'I feel I must atone for this'? This is a very deep impulse of the human spirit — to conclude that because a wrong has been done, some price needs to be paid or some equivalent action taken. At least in this approach there is a recognition of the seriousness of the situation and of the individual's responsibility. However, the problem with self-punishment is that one never knows how much is enough; we can spend all our lives scourging ourselves and still feel no sense of absolution. Soren Kierkegaard's father, as a shepherd lad out on the freezing Danish slopes, once cursed God, and the memory of that act of blasphemy haunted the man for the rest of his life. He never stopped punishing himself for this misdeed. He gave lavish sums of money to the church, even lacerated his own body, but he was never able to believe that the debt had at last been paid. Any attempt to design or effect our own atonement is bound to end in uncertainty and failure.

John Claypool,
The Light Within You, Texas: Word, 1983, p. 188.

The practice of confession and absolution is central to the teachings of the Christian church. Throughout the pages of Holy Scripture the reader encounters a variety of forms and procedures reflecting an understanding of and support for confession and forgiveness.

Luther struggled to restore the proper practice of individual confession and absolution to the church... His writings reveal that he allowed... six types of confession: (1) confession in the heart (secret confession); (2) general or public confession in the liturgy; (3) public confession made by an individual before an assembled congregation; (4) reconciliatory confession (based on Matthew 5:23-24); (5) the 'mutual consolation of the brethren'; and (6) private (individual) confession.

From *Counseling and Confession*, Copyright © 1982 Concordia Publishing House, St Louis, MO USA.
Reprinted by permission from CPH.

Confessing one's sins to another human being... makes a public expression of my sorrow... It is an act of humility wherein I accept the authority of the Church as guardian and guide to the holy things of God. I accept my fellow human being as someone better able than myself to make a judgment of where I stand, of my guilt — and of my goodness; and I accept through his word the promised forgiveness of God, who knows me through and through. This practice brings peace of mind and soul, a deeper trust in God, and a facing of the reality of sin in my life as something to be tackled in the future, once it is clear that the past is no more a burden, that guilt does not remain, that there is nothing to hold me back.

Michael Hollings,
Hearts Not Garments, London: Darton, Longman and Todd, 1982, p. 50.

The seven capital sins are pride, covetousness, lust, anger, gluttony, envy and sloth...

What am I proud about? What are my ambitions? What does sex mean for me? Have I shown anger and if so was it constructive? Have I suppressed anger in any areas of my life, and if so is it doing damage? What am I dependent on in food and drink? Have I got professional jealousies, or jealousies in relationships? What am I lazy about?

Or, if we turn our minds to the corresponding positive qualities:

What is the gift of humility? What would it be like to be less concerned with better status and possessions? What would it mean to have a sexual drive directed towards the real purpose of sex? What is the virtue of gentleness? What is best for my health in eating and drinking? What would it be like to desire the well-being and success of others without envy? For what causes would it be good to be able to work tirelessly...?

'God works with those who love him... and turns everything to their good' (Romans 8:28). And St Augustine adds, 'even my sins'.

Margaret Hebblethwaite,
Finding God in All Things, London: Fountain Paperbacks, 1987, pp. 158, 142.

O Lord, our God, grant us the grace to long for you with our whole heart, and that so longing we may seek and find you; and that so finding you we may love you; and that so loving you we may hate those sins from which you redeemed us for the sake of Jesus Christ.

Anselm,
quoted in *Praying with the Saints*, Dublin: Veritas Publications, 1989, p. 12.

Lord, your 'need' is to love, mine to be loved by you. Your 'need' expressed itself in my creation, my being made an object of your love. I am a masterpiece of spiritual, emotional and physical engineering, with a spirit yearning to relate to you, the living God; a soul and mind and heart and will to relating lovingly to others, and a body to relate to a dynamic cosmos.

Your love, Lord, expressed itself ultimately in the life of Jesus, and now in the life of Jesus-in-me.

Lord, when I think back on my sins, my feelings range from sadness (for what might have been) through regret (either that I was found out by others or found out who I was really was myself) to anger (that I could have been so destructive and stupid). Perhaps also fear: what will almighty God do to me for what I've done?

So out of my darkness, sorrow and night, Jesus, I come to you. I receive your gift of forgiveness, and ask for your help to live in the future a life of commitment to yourself and obedience to your word.

I am not worthy to come to you, or belong to your eternal family, Lord. But apparently that's not the point: your invitation is not conditional upon my goodness, but simply upon my acceptance of it.

I accept!

A benediction

May God, who in your conscience has already graciously given you an awareness of your sins, give you also grace to repent, grace to accept his complete forgiveness, and then grace to forgive yourself! Amen.

5
Commitment and cost

We... have been chosen... to be obedient to Jesus Christ.

If you love me, you will keep my commandments. If you continue in my word, you are truly my disciples; and you will know the truth, and the truth will make you free. Everyone then who hears these words of mine and acts on them will be like a wise man who built his house on rock. If any want to become my followers, let them deny themselves and take up their cross and follow me. For those who want to save their life will lose it, and those who lose their life for my sake will find it. For what will it profit them if they gain the whole world but forfeit their life?

The Lord your God you shall follow, him alone you shall fear, his commandments you shall keep, his voice you shall obey, him you shall serve, and to him you shall hold fast.

I have chosen the way of faithfulness; I set your ordinances before me. I run the way of your commandments, for you enlarge my understanding. Teach me, O Lord, the way of your statutes, and I will observe it to the end. Give me understanding, that I may keep your law and observe it with my whole heart. Lead me in the path of your commandments, for I delight in it. Turn my heart to your decrees, and not to selfish gain. See, I have longed for your precepts; in your righteousness give me life. I will keep your law continually, forever and ever. This blessing has fallen to me, for I have kept your precepts.

Teach me your way, O Lord, that I may walk in your truth.

The precepts of the Lord are right, rejoicing the heart; the commandment of the Lord is clear, enlightening the eyes.

I will give them one heart, and put a new spirit within them...

so that they may follow my statutes and keep my ordinances and obey them. Then they shall be my people, and I will be their God.

Do you not know that if you present yourselves to anyone as obedient slaves, you are slaves of the one whom you obey, either of sin, which leads to death, or of obedience, which leads to righteousness? But thanks be to God that you, having once been slaves of sin, have become obedient from the heart to the form of teaching to which you were entrusted.

Now that you have purified your souls by your obedience to the truth so that you have genuine mutual love, love one another deeply from the heart. Like obedient children, do not be conformed to the desires that you formerly had in ignorance. Instead... be holy.

We take every thought captive to obey Christ. For the love of Christ urges us on... he died for all, so that those who live might live no longer for themselves, but for him who died and was raised for them.

1 Peter 1:2; John 14:15; John 8:31-32; Matthew 7:24; Matthew 16:24-26; Deuteronomy 13:4; Psalm 119:30, 32-36, 40, 44, 56; Psalm 86:11; Psalm 19:8; Ezekiel 11:19-20; Romans 6:16-17; 1 Peter 1:22; 1 Peter 1:14-15; 2 Corinthians 10:5; 2 Corinthians 5:14, 15.

Christians throughout history have ranged in commitment from cold to hot. (Even Jesus was tempted — he really was — to be other than a suffering Messiah.) The earliest of his followers were generally (though not exclusively) at the warmer end of the temperature scale. Some went around with Jesus to watch his amazing miracles or get some free food. Others were prepared to risk their lives and reputations for him.

And post-Easter Christians followed someone who had been executed: the prospect of an early or violent death does something to your commitment-level!

A young first-century church, at Antioch, was visited by one of the most committed Christian leaders of the first century, Barnabas. In his first preaching to these new converts he urged them to 'be faithful and true to the Lord with all your hearts' (Acts 11:23). As Australians would say, 'Get fair-dinkum!' Don't be a half-hearted Christian! Be committed!

Commitment involves change, growth, fervour, enthusiasm. 'Enthusiasm' comes from two Greek words — *en* (in) *theos* (God), so the word means 'one possessed by God (or the gods)'. Enthusiasm literally means being full of God.

Christian enthusiasts are concerned above everything else

with what God wants (Matthew 6:33). Being a Christian is the most exciting thing in all the world!

Charles Schwab, the American industrialist who rose from poverty to put the US Steel Corporation together, said 'You can succeed at almost anything for which you have unlimited enthusiasm'. Emerson said, 'Nothing great was ever achieved without enthusiasm'. And here's another quote from my desk calendar: 'Years wrinkle the skin, but lack of enthusiasm wrinkles the soul'. Which reminds me of Thoreau's 'None are so old as those who have outlived enthusiasm'.

Most people get enthusiastic about something, as you will discover at a football grand final, or in a disco, or at a political convention. However, as Billy Graham once said, 'It is very strange that the world accepts enthusiasm in every realm but the spiritual'. Those who have achieved great things for God have been people of infectious zeal and unquenchable enthusiasm.

John the Baptist was one of these. Jesus said he was a bright and shining light, a light that blazed and shone. But John the Baptist had earlier said that Christ would baptise with the Holy Spirit and with fire.

How do we get on fire for God?

The earliest church leaders were people on fire for God. 'We can't help speaking', they said, 'of the things we have seen and heard'. Jeremiah was like that. He could not keep God's message to himself. It was like a fire burning deep within him. He'd tried to hold it back but could not (Jeremiah 20:9).

Generally speaking, we get from those who follow us the level of commitment we expect. Quintilian laid it down as a first principle of rhetoric that the orator who wishes to set the people on fire must himself be burning. Because church-people are in a sense a pastor's employers, there's a temptation for the pastor to soften the prophetic side of ministry, opting to pitch the commitment-level within people's 'comfort zone'. Where ecclesiastical wineskins are bereft of new wine, the church becomes stale, lifeless. There may be order, but as British Anglican David Watson used to say often, it's the orderliness of the cemetery. The oyster may be there, but the pearl has gone.

Now there's another side to all this. 'Dead churches are afraid of enthusiasm': that's true, but enthusiasm has a history that justifies this fear to some extent. 'Enthusiasts' were sometimes people who had plenty of heat but not too much light. They got all excited about minor things. Fanatics are enthusiastic, but such enthusiasm can sometimes lead to stupidity or even violence. Paul said before he was a Christian he was zealous. But his zeal was misdirected: he persecuted the church.

W. B. Yeats in his poem 'The Second Coming' says 'the best lack all conviction' while 'the worst are full of passionate

47

intensity'. We must search for the dividing line between enthusiasm and fanaticism — being inspired by God or the devil. A person without judgment is like a car without brakes; but a person without enthusiasm is like a car without a motor.

The great Presbyterian James Stewart said: 'The supreme need of the church is the same in the twentieth century as in the first: it is people on fire for Christ'.

> O Thou who camest from above
> The pure celestial fire to impart,
> Kindle a flame of sacred love,
> On the mean altar of my heart!

A cold church is like cold butter: it doesn't spread very easily. A selfish church is like a glee club, existing for the benefit of its members rather than those outside it. Other churches through their preaching offer all sorts of goodies like a trouble-free or sickness-free life — which is foreign to the teaching of the New Testament.

So it is possible to become a Christian for the wrong reasons. Faith in Christ is not an insurance policy against 'the slings and arrows of outrageous fortune'. Never forget, Jesus promises you three things: constant trouble, and constant joy, because of his constant presence with you!

Certainly, it is worthwhile to be a Christian for the side benefits, including eternal life! This is expressed in the saying 'You are no fool if you give up what you cannot keep, to gain what you cannot lose!' The prayer by Cardinal Newman sums up this motivation: 'Teach me, dear Lord, frequently and attentively to consider this truth: that if I gain the whole world and lose (you), in the end I have lost everything. Whereas, if I lose this world and gain (you), in the end I have lost nothing'.

But the greatest incentive to complete commitment to Jesus Christ is in response to his love, shown ultimately in his death for us. 'Love so amazing, so divine demands my soul, my life, my all!'

❧

There is strong support among Christians for the notion that an individual is free to do whatever they please, as long as it does not hurt others. Two out of five Christians maintain that such thinking is proper, thus effectively rejecting the unconditional code of ethics and morality as taught in the Bible. Three out of ten Christians agree that nothing in life is more important than having fun and being happy... One out of four believers thinks that the more you have the more successful you are. The fact that the proportion of Christians who affirm these values is equivalent to the proportion of non-Christians who hold similar views indicates how meaningless Christianity has been in the lives of millions of professed believers.

George Barna,
Vital Signs: Emerging Social Trends and the Future of American Christianity, (Westchester, Ill.: Crossway Books, 1984), quoted in Bill Hull, *The Disciple-Making Pastor*, New Jersey: Revell, 1988, p. 21.

A true disciple of Christ is one (who) follows him in duty, and shall follow him to glory. (A true disciple) follows Christ as the sheep after the shepherd, the servant after the master, soldiers after their captain, aiming at the same end that Christ aimed at, the glory of God... All the followers of Christ must deny themselves. It is the fundamental law of admission into Christ's school, and the first and greatest lesson to learn in his school... They take up their cross: (this) should reconcile us to troubles, and take the terror from them; they are what we bear in common with Christ. And many a life is lost for Christ's sake, in doing his work, by labouring fervently for him... by choosing rather to die than to deny him or his truths and ways. Christ's holy religion is handed down to us, sealed with the blood of thousands...

Matthew Henry,
Commentary on the Whole Bible, Peabody, Mass: Hendrickson Publishers, 1991, p. 1698.

The need for devotion to something outside ourselves is even more profound than the need for companionship. If we are not to go to pieces or wither away, we all must have some purpose in life; for no one can live for themselves alone.

Ross Parmenter,
The Doctor and the Cleaning Woman, quoted in Margaret Pepper (ed.), *The Pan Dictionary of Religious Quotations*, London: Pan Books, 1989, p. 95.

A disciple is one who knows God personally, and who learns from Jesus Christ, who most perfectly revealed God... Obedience to God's will is the secret of spiritual knowledge and insight... You will know as much of God, and only as much of God, as you are willing to put into practice.

Eric Liddell,
The Disciplines of the Christian Life, London: Triangle/SPCK, 1986, pp. 27, 28.

But Saint Francis, faithful guardian of the secrets of God, when he judged that Master Bernard was fast asleep, in the deep stillness of night rose from his bed. With face turned to heaven, and hands and eyes lifted to God, in complete surrender and with the warmest devotion he prayed, saying: 'My God, my All'. These words he groaned out to God with copious tears, again and again with solemn devotion until dawn: 'My God, my All' — no more. So said Saint Francis, worshipping God's Majesty, which seemed to stoop to the imperilled world and provide a remedy for the salvation of the poor through his own Son. Enlightened by the spirit of prophecy, and foreseeing the mighty deeds God was about to do through his own Order, and considering in the same spirit's teaching his own insufficiency and poverty of virtue, he was calling on God to do himself what he was unable to do. Without such aid, (all our) frailty is powerless. Hence his words: 'My God, my All'.

E. M. Blaiklock & A. C. Keys (tr.),
The Little Flowers of St Francis, London: Hodder and Stoughton, 1985, pp. 16-17.

Since... Francis, along with his companions, had been called by God to bear the Cross as much as to preach it, he and the pioneers of his Order seemed, as indeed they were, men truly crucified. Bearing the Crucified in dress, food and in all their doings, desiring rather the reproach of Christ than the empty things of the world and its treacherous blandishments, they rejoiced in sufferings and held honour in contempt. They went through the world like pilgrims and strangers carrying nothing with them but Christ...

Thus it happened that, in the early days of the Order, Saint Francis sent Brother Bernard to Bologna, that there he might produce fruit for God... Some children saw him in his unusual and miserable dress, and began to heap insults on him. Brother Bernard, true saint that he was, not only bore them patiently, but even suffered them with deepest joy, because he was a true disciple of Christ who became 'the scorn of the crowd and shame...' For the love of Christ he deliberately placed himself in the market-place of the city, where he could be the greatest object of the people's ridicule. One tugged at his hood from behind, another from the front, one threw dust, another stones. They pushed him this way and that. Bernard endured all this violence joyfully and patiently, without resistance in word or deed. What is more, in order to endure such persecution day after day, he would deliberately return to the same place. Whatever violence was heaped on him by them, he remained calm in spirit and with joyous face...

E. M. Blaiklock & A. C. Keys (eds),
The Little Flowers of St Francis, London: Hodder and Stoughton, 1985, pp. 25-6.

(When) the martyr in Tibet, Kartar Singh... went to preach the gospel the people said: 'Keep quiet, we don't like to hear about Christ'. He was the son of very wealthy people and gave up everything to preach the gospel in Tibet. His experience was that wealth cannot give peace and satisfy the soul, only Christ can satisfy. When I was in Tibet they told me how this man was killed. He was taken to the top of a hill, sewn up for three days in a wet skin and exposed to the sun. When that man told me about the martyrdom of Kartar Singh, I noticed that his face was shining with joy, and I was rather surprised. 'You are telling me something sad and you seem happy.' 'It is not sad — I tell you about his death, but there was no death but life, wonderful life. He was three days in that skin, hungry and thirsty, and when asked: "How do you feel now?" he replied: "I thank God for this great privilege to suffer for him", but he did not suffer, he had such joy that I wish people could realise it, then they would agree with me that to live with Jesus Christ is heaven on earth. The people took sharp iron nails and thrust them into his body, the blood was flowing out of him, but he had such wonderful joy, a joy that cannot be expressed. Everybody left him. He said: "Everyone has left me, but not my Saviour; he is with me, and not only with me but within me. In this skin I am really in heaven. I thank God for this privilege"'.

Sadhu Sundar Singh,
Life in Abundance, Madras: Christian Literature Society, 1986, pp. 41-42.

It may be easy for good Christians to die for Christ: it may be easy to be a martyr to be killed at once, but it is difficult to live for Christ, because if we live for him then we have to die daily. The real secret of life is that we should know how to die daily.

Christianity is not a religion, not a society, but Christianity is Christ himself.

I have seen many seekers after truth who only used their head; the result was agnosticism and atheism. But when they used their heart they found something and were satisfied.

Sadhu Sundar Singh,
Alys Goodwin, *Sadhu Sundar Singh in Switzerland*, Madras: Christian Literature Society, 1989, p. 39.

Each day before I leave my study I ask God to 'wear me like a garment.' My clothes are nothing in themselves — they are inanimate, and when I take them off they can't stand up or walk or do anything on their own. They collapse. I want to be like that in relation to Christ. I want my only animation to be Christ who lives in me, who thinks his thoughts, desires his will, and loves his love through me (see Galatians 2:20).

Richard Halverson,
'Wear me like a Garment', in LaVonne Neff et al. (eds), *Practical Christianity*, Wheaton, Illinois: Tyndale House Publishers Inc, 1988, p. 59.

Therefore it becomes us to spend this life only as a journey towards heaven, as it becomes us to make the seeking of our highest end and proper good, the whole work of our lives; to which we should subordinate all other concerns of life. Why should we labour for or set our hearts on anything else, but that which is our proper end, and true happiness?

Jonathan Edwards,
Ola Elizabeth Winslow (ed.), *Basic Writings*, New York: New American Library, 1966, p. 142.

51

Meister Eckhart in particular keeps on reminding us that we must grasp God in everything... We must be completely detached about all circumstances, external and internal; we must even be detached about detachment. The truly spiritual person does not even seek tranquillity (of whose importance Eckhart elsewhere speaks in emphatic terms), because he is in no way hampered by lack of it. So all possible answers we might give to the question, 'What shall I do to inherit eternal life?' are declared irrelevant and counter-productive; we are given no encouragement at all to entertain our feeling that if only we did not get these headaches, if only we had nicer neighbours, if only we knew how to pray, if only we were more humble, everything would go swimmingly.

Simon Tugwell,
'The Beatitudes' in John Garvey (ed.), *Modern Spirituality: An Anthology*, London: Darton, Longman and Todd, 1985, p. 66.

He (a church official) was one of those grim-looking men who sometimes hold office in the church. (Nobody doubts their integrity, but nobody wants to be like them.) All the lines of his face seemed to run down at acute angles, as though he lived all the while with an unpleasant odour under his nose...

It is an undoubted fact that many people outside the churches think that if they become Christians they will become miserable. They think that life in Christ is less and less rather than more and more. They think that it is giving up most of the things which make glad our hearts... Who could help being radiant with God living in them? The best Christians have surrendered their wills and their minds to Christ.

W. E. Sangster,
The Secret of Radiant Life, London: Hodder & Stoughton, 1957, pp. 58-63. Reprinted by permission of Edward England Books.

Jesus was a deeply serious man. He was tremendously in earnest... He was so serious that there were times when his face was wet with tears. There were times that he sobbed as only the broken-hearted sob. Naturally many have come to think of him as one who could never laugh and whose face was seldom if ever lighted by a smile.

But... in spite of his seriousness — and because of this fact! — he was the most joyful of people. The artists have done Jesus a great injustice by picturing him as one whose life was one long sob. He did sob, but he also sang. He could laugh... In fact he was so glad that many of his day who looked on religion as a bit of a kill-joy did not think that Jesus was religious at all... Those too serious to laugh generally major on minors.

Clovis Chappell,
'If I were young I'd avoid being half-baked', in *If I Were Young*, New York: Abingdon-Cokesbury, 1945, pp. 96-97.

O most merciful Lord, grant to us your grace, that it may be with us and labour with us and persevere with us even to the end. Grant that we may always desire and will that which is most acceptable and dear to you. Let your will be ours and our wills follow yours in everything... Grant to us, above all that can be desired, to rest in you and to have our hearts at peace with you. You are the true peace of the heart and its only rest; outside of you all things are hard and restless.

O Father and God of our risen Lord, like the would-be followers then, we now tend to follow Christ at a distance. It just seems safer that way: no threat of being called fanatic or faint-hearted. O God, empower us to walk close with him, to learn of him, to be like him, to serve with him. From him may we know how to forget self but never forget you. May we learn of him the power of gentleness, the grace of humility, the greatness of servanthood, the freedom found in service to you. O Master, let us walk with you...

William M. Johnson,
in James Cox (ed.), *Ministers Manual*, San Francisco: Harper & Row, 1990, pp. 26, 85.

Hold my faith steady when I cannot see the road ahead. May I always know I am loved. Protect me this day from evils seen or unseen. May I expect little, and so be less prone to be disappointed.

It's a tough decision, Lord. Should I surrender completely to your will? But what will I have to give up? My commercial culture teaches me to think like this, Lord. I pay a price — and what do I get in return? Is the value worth it all?

But then, when I think of your love for me, it's not a question of giving up anything, but rather of living a truly worthwhile life. Any relationship involves surrender of some independence, in return for the great benefits of friendship, a listening ear, a reassuring touch when things go wrong, the promise of companionship into the future...

Help me, Lord, to believe the testimony of thousands through the centuries: once we are really committed to you, sacrifice is not an issue. No one can outgive God. And after all, when I gave myself to you, I promised you everything. I promised to be yours to the end.

May I see the superficiality of merely being religious. Help me to do what is right because I love you, not to earn your love. Help me to serve you from gratitude for all you have given to me, rather than for any reward. You sacrificed your life for me: may I learn to hate the things that cost you your life. May I sacrifice whatever will hinder your grace operating through me.

Save me from the disillusionment of trusting anyone or anything but you.

Teach us, good Lord, to serve you as you deserve, to give and not to count the cost, to fight and not to heed the wounds, to toil and not to seek for rest, to labour and to look for no reward save that of knowing that we do your will, through Jesus Christ our Lord.

Ignatius Loyola,
quoted in *Praying with the Saints*, Dublin: Veritas Publications, 1989, pp. 46-7.

A benediction

May the Lord bless and strengthen you; may you always remain faithful to him who gave you life and his life; who loves you. May you freely choose to offer him everything — your love, your obedience, your relationships, your time, talents and possessions, even your own life. For the glory of Jesus Christ our Master. Amen.

*God is
on your
side*

6
Meet your new Father

Ah Lord God! It is you who made the heavens and the earth by your great power and by your outstretched arm! Nothing is too hard for you.

You know no God but me, and besides me there is no saviour. I am the first and I am the last; besides me there is no god.

Holy, holy, holy is the Lord of hosts; the whole earth is full of his glory.

He who is the blessed and only Sovereign, the King of kings and Lord of lords. It is he alone who has immortality and dwells in unapproachable light, whom no one has ever seen or can see; to him be honour and eternal dominion.

Every generous act of giving, with every perfect gift, is from above, coming down from the Father of lights, with whom there is no variation or shadow due to change.

The beloved of the Lord rests in safety.

Happy are you, O Israel! Who is like you, a people saved by the Lord, the shield of your help, and the sword of your triumph!

I led them with cords of human kindness, with bands of love. I was to them like those who lift infants to their cheeks. I bent down to them and fed them.

It is I who answer and look after you. I am like an evergreen cypress; your faithfulness comes from me.

The Lord, your God, is in your midst... he will rejoice over you with gladness, he will renew you in his love; he will exult over you with loud singing.

God is love, and those who abide in love abide in God and

God abides in them. Although you have not seen him, you love him; and even though you do not see him now, you believe in him and rejoice with an indescribable and glorious joy.

Love the Lord, all you his saints. The Lord preserves the faithful, but abundantly repays the one who acts haughtily.

Be strong, and let your heart take courage, all you who wait for the Lord.

But to all who received him, who believed in his name, he gave power to become children of God, who were born, not of blood or of the will of the flesh or of the will of man, but of God.

Ask, and it will be given you; search, and you will find; knock, and the door will be opened for you. For everyone who asks receives, and everyone who searches finds, and for everyone who knocks, the door will be opened. Is there anyone among you who, if your child asks for bread, will give a stone? Or if the child asks for a fish, will give a snake? If you, then, who are evil, know how to give good gifts to your children, how much more will your Father in heaven give good things to those who ask him!

And my God will fully satisfy every need of yours according to his riches in glory in Christ Jesus.

He will feed his flock like a shepherd; he will gather the lambs in his arms, and carry them in his bosom, and gently lead the mother sheep.

For all who are led by the Spirit of God are children of God. For you did not receive a spirit of slavery to fall back into fear, but you have received a spirit of adoption. When we cry, 'Abba! Father!' it is that very Spirit bearing witness with our spirit that we are children of God, and if children, then heirs, heirs of God and joint heirs with Christ — if, in fact, we suffer with him so that we may also be glorified with him. For I am convinced that neither death, nor life, nor angels, nor rulers, nor things present, nor things to come, nor powers, nor height, nor depth, nor anything else in all creation, will be able to separate us from the love of God in Christ Jesus our Lord.

May the Lord direct your hearts to the love of God and to the steadfastness of Christ.

Jeremiah 32:17; Hosea 13:4; Isaiah 44:6; Isaiah 6:3; 1 Timothy 6:15-16; James 1:17; Deuteronomy 33:12; Deuteronomy 33:29; Hosea 11:4; Hosea 14:8; Zephaniah 3:17; 1 John 4:16; 1 Peter 1:8; Psalm 31:23, 24; John 1:12-13; Matthew 7:7-11; Philippians 4:19; Isaiah 40:11; Romans 8:14-17, 38-39; 2 Thessalonians 3:5.

Who is God? And who is God for me? There are many ways, many theologies, many systems-of-words which have tried to answer these, the most important questions humans have ever asked.

Some of these theologies concentrate on God's essence (who he is); others on his activity (what he does); others still on his relationship with his human creatures (who he is for us). All fail to capture adequately the grandeur, the creativity, and the love of the God who has revealed himself in history to his people, through the Scriptures, in nature, in our consciences, in the events of the world, in our own lives, but ultimately in the life of Jesus Christ. Here we will simply look at three attributes of God: his greatness, his goodness, and his generosity.

1. *God is great.* All of the Christian saints affirm, with so many of the Psalmists, 'Great is the Lord'. He is the sovereign ruler of the universe. All power and authority belong to him. He is not a passive spectator.

He is great in his 'being', beyond our comprehension or definition (any definition claiming to be adequate would be an idol of the mind).

He is great in wisdom. He is the one unto whom 'all hearts are open, all desires known, and from whom no secrets are hidden'.

So our prayer to him must begin with worship, with adoration. Some of the great hymns can help us: 'Great God of wonders...'; 'Jesus, thou joy of loving hearts...'

As one person lay dying of cancer he wrote: 'All too often our faith is earth-bound and we find it hard to believe that God can do anything that our minds cannot explain. It is only as we spend time worshipping God, concentrating on the nature of his person, especially his greatness and his love, that our faith begins to rise'. (David Watson, *Fear No Evil*, London: Hodder & Stoughton, 1984, p. 59).

So adoration and worship are therapeutic!

But we must add an important footnote here. The God who is incarnated in Jesus is the kind of God who, when he wants to show himself in our world, does so in weakness and poverty.

2. *God is good.* He is 'for us'. When we call on him in the day of trouble, he will care for us (Psalm 50:15). As we read the biblical drama we find that he either delivers us from trouble, or in trouble. He is always there for us. He will never leave us or forsake us.

However, we are not to treat God as a lawyer or doctor, only going to him when we've got a problem. Some of us want our adolescent independence too soon! God is our father, and like little children we ought to learn to enjoy our father's company in all the events of our lives. When a little girl said, 'God's my best friend!' she was uttering something that is at the heart of true spirituality.

He should become everything to us ('What could be greedier', remarks St Augustine, 'than a person for whom God is not

59

enough?') and everything we do should be done for his glory. We should want him to accomplish in our lives 'all things according to the counsel of his will' (Ephesians 1:11). When we really believe God is good, it is easier to pray 'not my will but yours...'

3. *God delights to give gifts.* There are thirty texts in the New Testament describing prayer as asking. Our Father delights to give gifts to us. Indeed, he is the 'God of surprises' who delights to give before we ask. Christian thought calls this aspect of God's character 'prevenient grace' (*Grace* — God's giving freely out of his love for us; *prevenient* — from the Latin 'to go before'). We will notice these gifts all the time if we have developed the habit of living gratefully. True lovers think in terms of giving gifts to one another.

In a very real sense, of course, God's best gift to us is himself. Our response? As the great commandment puts it, we are to love the Lord our God with all our heart, mind, soul and strength. This is not the same as 'getting religion' — even the Christian religion; it is actively seeking and loving God himself.

Brother Lawrence was a lame, clumsy man who went to a monastery to atone somehow for his disabilities. He was put to work washing floors and kitchen pots and pans. In the midst of all this he 'practised the presence of God'. When he was dying, his friends asked what he was thinking about. He replied, 'I am doing what I shall do through all eternity — blessing God, praising God, adoring God, giving him the love of my whole heart'.

Charity, says the anonymous author of *The Cloud of Unknowing*, 'is nought else but love of God for himself above all creatures'.

'I love you, Lord, not doubtingly but with absolute certainty. Your Word beat upon my heart until I fell in love with you and now the universe and everything in it tells me to love you...' (Augustine)

The Masai called their god Engai. Well, that is no more strange-sounding than our gods. The god invoked by the pope to bless the troops of Mussolini about to embark on the plunder of Ethiopia, and the god invoked by an American cardinal to bless the 'soldiers of Christ' in Vietnam, and the god of French glory, and the German god of Hitler were no more the High God of Scripture than is 'Diana of the Ephesians' or Engai of the Masai of Eastern Africa.

Vincent J. Donovan,
Christianity Rediscovered, London: SCM, 1985, p. 46.

I have always been 'surprised' by life.

And as I believe that God is life, just as he is light and love, I have come to the conclusion that it is God himself who has 'surprised' me on my journey.

God is surprise. God is novelty. God is creativity...

I don't know how it happened to you, but I know how it happened to me.

God arrived in my heart like a huge parable. Everything around me spoke to me of him.

The sky spoke to me of him, the earth spoke to me of him, the sea spoke to me of him. He was like a secret hidden in all things, visible and invisible. He was like the solution to all problems. He was like the most important person who had ever entered my life and with whom I should have lived for ever...

The Good News is this: that God is God, that God is the God of the Impossible, he is the God who can make Sarah's barren womb fruitful and separate the waters of the Red Sea.

He is a living God. He is a God who guides. He is a God who raises from the dead. He is an Eternal God. He is a God who wants me in his Kingdom for ever.

Carlo Carretto,
The Desert in the City, London: Fount Paperbacks, 1983, pp. 9, 25-26, 58.

Something in us wants to insist on having (both) God and health, God and riches, God and honour, God and long life... But God is so infinitely much more than these other things that in the end the 'and' bit does not add anything. All that is good and that belongs to our eternal joy is included in God, for God is all in all.

Margaret Hebblethwaite,
Finding God in All Things, London: Fount Paperbacks, 1987, p. 39.

Perceiving, as other mortals have not perceived, the burning love of God, the saint gives God love for love. He cannot help it. Certainly, it is not the fruit of labour. Having seen the love of God, his own love leaps in response. His heart is drawn out of him and lost in God's immensity.

No mortal can love as God loves, but the saint loves with all that there is of him... It is by love that the saint becomes free — free of that aweful self-centredness which is the mark of most mortals... It is by love that we come to freedom, and there is no other way.

W. E. Sangster,
The Pure in Heart, London: Epworth, 1954, pp. 242-3.

He had always been governed by love, without selfish views; and having resolved to make the love of God the end of all his actions, he had found reasons to be well satisfied with his method. He was pleased when he could take up a straw from the ground for the love of God, seeking him only, and nothing else, not even his gifts...

'I did not engage in a religious life but for the love of God, and I have endeavoured to act only for him; whatever becomes of me, whether I be lost or saved, I will always continue to act purely for the love of God. I shall have this good at least, that till death I shall have done all that is in me to love him.'

Brother Lawrence,
The Practice of the Presence of God: the best rule of a holy life, being conversations and letters of Brother Lawrence, Epworth, n.d., pp. 6-7.

O God, I love thee, I love thee —
Not out of hope of heaven for me
Not fearing not to love and be
In the everlasting burning.
Thou, thou, my Jesus, after me
Didst reach thine arms out dying,
For my sake sufferedst nails and lance,
Mocked and marred countenance,
Sorrows passing number,
Sweat and care and cumber,
Yea and death, and this for me.

And thou couldst see me sinning:
Then I, why should not I love thee,
Jesus, so much in love with me?
Not for heaven's sake; not to be
Out of hell by loving thee;
Not for any gains I see;
But just the way that thou didst me
I do love and I will love thee:
What must I love thee, Lord, for then?
For being my king and God. Amen.

Translated from the Latin by Gerard Manley Hopkins

(A fearful person said, 'I fear lest I should be cast into hell'. Another anxious person said, 'I dread lest I should be deprived of the joy of heaven...) A third was very happy and contented. (He was asked) 'What is the secret of your joy and peace?' He said, 'My constant prayer to God is that he may grant me to love him with heart and soul, and may serve and worship him by love alone. Should I worship him from fear of hell, may I be cast into it. Should I serve him from desire of gaining heaven, may he keep me out. But should I worship him from love alone, may he reveal himself to me, that my whole heart may be filled with his love and presence'.

Sadhu Sundar Singh,
The Spiritual Life, Christian Literature Society, 1926/1986, pp. 13-14.

'...When thoughts come, welcome them, and when they do not flow freely, simply rest back and love, and grant Me the shared joy of being loved by you. For I, too, by my very nature, am hungry with an insatiable hunger for the love of all of you, just as your love reaches out at your highest moments to all the people about you. So child, I, even I, God, whom people have foolishly feared and flattered for my gifts, I want love and friendship more than I want grovelling subjects. So while we love each other, child, My share is as keen as yours.'

Frank Laubach,
Letters by a Modern Mystic, London: Lutterworth, 1957, p. 30.

Thou knowest not what, saving that thou feelest in thy will a naked intent unto God... this darkness and this cloud... hindereth thee, so that thou mayest neither see him clearly by light of understanding in thy reason, nor feel him in sweetness of love in thy affection. And therefore shape thee to bide in this darkness as long as thou mayest, evermore crying after him whom thou lovest. For if ever thou shalt see him or feel him as it may be here, it must always be in this cloud and in this darkness... Smite upon that thick cloud of unknowing with a sharp dart of longing love.

'The Cloud of Unknowing',
quoted in Michael Cox, *Handbook of Christian Spirituality*, New York: Harper & Row, 1985, p. 139.

When the next step comes, you do not take the step, you do not know the transition, you do not fall into anything. You do not go anywhere, and so you do not know the way by which you got there or the way by which you come back afterward. You are certainly not lost. You do not fly. There is no space, or there is all space: it makes no difference.

The next step is not a step... And here all adjectives fall to pieces. Words become stupid. Everything you say is misleading — unless you list every possible experience and say: 'That is not what it is'. 'That is not what I am talking about.'

What it is is freedom. It is perfect love. It is pure renunciation. It is the fruition of God... It is freedom living and circulating in God, who is Freedom. It is love loving in Love. It is the purity of God rejoicing in his own liberty.

Thomas Merton,
New Seeds of Contemplation, Copyright © 1961 by The Abbey of Gethsemani, Inc. Reprinted by permission of New Directions Pub. Corp.

To the few who are converted, goodness is pleasant, and needs no sanctions. It needs no authority, for it has been verified by experience. But when people have to be coerced into goodness it is plain that they do not care for it.

Walter Lippmann,
'A Preface to Morals', *Time*, 1964, p. 188.

The gravest question any of us face is whether we do or do not love the Lord... Our Lord told his disciples that love and obedience were organically united, that the keeping of his sayings would prove that we loved him, and the failure or refusal to keep them would prove that we did not. This is the true test of love... Not sweet emotions, not willingness to sacrifice, not zeal, but obedience to the commandments of Christ. Love for Christ is a love of willing as well as a love of feeling...

If we would turn from fine-spun theological speculations about grace and faith, and humbly read the New Testament with a mind to obey what we see there, we would easily find ourselves, and know for certain the answer to the question that troubled our fathers and should trouble us: Do we love the Lord or no?

A. W. Tozer,
'Love's Final Test', *The Life of Faith*, 20 October 1960.

'Marvellously close, God, help me to keep thinking of You all day today, as love crowding gently as the ether, warm as the sunlight, into every nook and cranny of my thoughts, words, looks, acts — love pressing in, and oozing out, floating like perfume out to others.'

'O Love that wilt not let me go,
I rest my weary soul in Thee;
I give thee back the life I owe,
That in thine ocean depths its flow
May richer, fuller be.'

'My child, this makes Me happy. Now let love flow out to My world of needy people all about you. Despise not one of the least. Do not see colour or clothes, just souls and My children. Do not hear titles or languages, just hear Me speak through them. I call from behind every eye, I float upon every wave of speech and song and sigh. See Me in people, for I seek to make them grow in Christlike love.'

Frank Laubach,
Learning the Vocabulary of God: A Spiritual Diary, London: Lutterworth, 1956, pp. 59-60.

In Graham Greene's novel *The Heart of the Matter*, Scobie is torn between love for his wife and his mistress, and decides to commit suicide. Sitting in his car he holds a very moving conversation with God, acknowledging that he is guilty before God and that he can no longer face the altar. 'You'll be better off when you lose me once and for all. You'll be at peace when I'm out of your reach', he tells God.

God replies... 'You say you love me, yet you'll do this to Me — rob Me of you for ever. I made you with love. I've wept your tears... and now you push me away, put me out of your reach. I am as humble as any other beggar. Can't you trust me as you'd trust a faithful dog? I've been faithful to you for 2000 years... Can't you trust me to see that the suffering isn't too great?'

Ivor Bailey,
'Live and Let Love', a sermon preached from Maughan Church, Adelaide, 9 July 1972.

I no longer want to build empires,
to ascend thrones,
or to be number one in my little kingdom.
I want to love you,
and to respond to your love for me
by communicating such love to others.
This is what I want, O Lord,
but you know my soft spots, my hang-ups.
May the victory be yours today, O Lord.
In Jesus' name. Amen.

Leslie F. Brandt,
A Book of Christian Prayer, New York: Kingsway, 1978, p. 10.

O merciful God, grant that I may always do your will perfectly in all things. May it be my wish to work only for your honour and glory. May I rejoice in nothing except what leads to you. May I wish nothing that leads away from you. May all passing things be as nothing in my eyes. May all that is yours be dear to me and may you, my God, be dear to me above all things. May I wish for nothing apart from you. May all joys have no importance for me apart from you. May all effort and work delight me when it is for you.

Thomas Aquinas,
cited in *Praying with the Saints*, Dublin: Veritas Publications, 1989, p. 65.

No soul can have rest until it finds created things are empty. When the soul gives up all for love, so that it can have him that is all, then it finds true rest.

For he is endless and has made us for his own self only, and has restored us by his blessed Passion, and keeps us in his blessed love. And he does all this through his goodness.

God of goodness, give me yourself, for you are enough for me and I may ask nothing that is less, that may be full worship to you. And if I ask anything that is less, I am always wanting — *but only in you I have all.*

Julian of Norwich,
Showings, Chapter 5, quoted in Margaret Hebblethwaite, *Finding God in All Things*, London: Fount Paperbacks, 1987, p. 48.

O you Omnipotent goodness, you care for us all as if each of us were your only concern, and you look after each of us as if we were all one person...!
Eternal truth, truth of love, love of eternity! That's what you are, my God, and that's why day and night you form the breath of my being. When I first knew you, you lifted me up and I realised there was something to see, but I wasn't quite capable of seeing it. My vision was too weak to stand the radiance of your glory, and I trembled with a combination of love and dread. I seemed to be a long way from you, in a far country, listening to your voice as it spoke to me from above, 'I am the real food. Grow up and feed on me. But you will never change me into yourself as your digestion changes its food; rather you will be changed into my likeness.'

Augustine,
Sherwood E. Wirt, *The Confessions of Augustine in Modern English*, Grand Rapids: Zondervan, 1977, pp. 46, 95-96.

Lord, I am your child. In some mysterious sense, my Father, you are hungry for my love. Your love is mediated through words and the Word, through sunsets and rain and the whispering trees, soft shadows on the water. I was created for friendship with you, my Creator. I was redeemed for friendship with you, my Saviour. I am cared for friendship with you, my ever-present Friend. Lord, it's not a self-improvement course I want, but you.

We taste thee, O thou living Bread,
And long to feast upon thee still.
We drink of thee the fountainhead,
And thirst our souls from thee to fill.

I have tasted a little of your goodness, Lord, and it has both satisfied me and made me hunger for more. My desire is to desire you more. Give me a gift of love — for you and for others. And to journey towards the final self-forgetfulness — to be absorbed into you forever.

A benediction
Keep yourselves in the love of God, as you wait for our Lord Jesus Christ in his mercy to give you eternal life. May God's grace be with all those who love our Lord Jesus Christ with undying love. Amen.

Jude 21, Ephesians 6:24

7

If God is like Jesus, nothing is too good to be true

For a child has been born for us, a son given to us; authority rests upon his shoulders; and he is named Wonderful Counsellor, Mighty God, Everlasting Father, Prince of Peace.

Look, the virgin shall conceive and bear a son, and they shall name him 'Emmanuel', which means, 'God is with us'.

I am the way, and the truth, and the life. No one comes to the Father except through me. I am the bread of life... I am the light of the world... I came from God and now I am here. I did not come on my own, but he sent me. I am the gate. Whoever enters by me will be saved... I came that they may have life, and have it abundantly. I am the good shepherd... I know my own and my own know me... I lay down my life for the sheep.

The Father loves the Son and has placed all things in his hands. Whoever believes in the Son has eternal life. Indeed, just as the Father raises the dead and gives them life, so also the Son gives life to whomever he wishes. The Father judges no one but has given all judgment to the Son, so that all may honour the Son just as they honour the Father. Anyone who does not honour the Son does not honour the Father who sent him. Very truly, I tell you, anyone who hears my word and believes him who sent me has eternal life, and does not come under judgment, but has passed from death to life. Very truly, I tell you, the hour is coming and is now here, when the dead will hear the voice of the Son of God and those who hear will live. For just as the Father has life in himself, so he has granted the Son also to have life in himself.

To all who received him, who believed in his name, he gave power to become children of God.

Grace and truth came through Jesus Christ... These are written so that you may come to believe that Jesus is the Messiah, the Son of God, and that believing you may have life in his name... He is the image of the invisible God, the firstborn of all creation; for in him all things in heaven and on earth were created, things visible and invisible, whether thrones or dominions or rulers or powers — all things have been created through him and for him.

God put this power to work in Christ when he raised him from the dead and seated him at his right hand in the heavenly places, far above all rule and authority and power and dominion, and above every name that is named, not only in this age but also in the age to come.

Jesus Christ is the same yesterday and today and forever.

I believe that you are the Messiah, the Son of God, the one coming into the world.

Those who love me will keep my word, and my Father will love them, and we will come to them and make our home with them.

Isaiah 9:6; Matthew 1:23; John 14:6; John 6:35; John 8:12; John 8:42; John 10:9-15; John 3:35, 36; John 5:19-26; John 1:12, 17; John 20:31; Colossians 1:15-16; Ephesians 1:20-21; Hebrews 13:8; John 11:27; John 14:23.

Ask almost anyone, anywhere, which individual has done most to change the course of history, and the answer will almost invariably be, 'Jesus of Nazareth'.

Who was this Jew from an ancient, frontier province of the Roman Empire who has left such an indelible mark upon the earth? Well, first let's get one thing straight: the man Jesus actually lived, and the histories describing his life (mainly the four gospels in the New Testament) are regarded by the overwhelming majority of scholars — Christian or not — as reliable.

And he was a real person: an extrovert who enjoyed the company of others, but who also spent hours and days and weeks in solitary prayer; an angry man who would not tolerate hypocrisy and injustice, but also a tender, compassionate friend of the downtrodden; a brilliant teacher and debater, but also 'down-to-earth'; a man who was tempted in every way others are, but, his friends asserted, remained sinless; a man who was truly masculine (prepared to take the fight up to his enemies) and also in touch with the feminine in his personality (there is no woman in the gospels who was ever his enemy).

But Jesus said he was more than a man: he claimed divinity. Now that's not odd: psychiatrists counsel many people who have delusions of grandeur. But this man was different: he was not a 'nut-case'. In fact, he comes across to his contemporaries and to us as a very-well-put-together person indeed.

Now if Jesus was God, a lot follows. He was God's Word that caused the cosmos to come into being; he is God's Life that holds everything together; he will be the Resurrector and Judge of the living and the dead. He offers us eternal life, and a deep peace, and forgiveness of our sins, and trouble. You'd better not ignore him.

Athanasius, a great church father, said that when Jesus became one of us he did not subtract deity but rather added humanity. Jesus wasn't less than God, but became something in addition to God, a human being. Byron the poet put it succinctly: 'If ever a man were God or God were man, Jesus was both'.

What was he like? Artists depict him with a sad, pained expression, or with piercing eyes, or with a 'lean and hungry look' or as a wan, 'pale Galilean'. The gospels give us a picture of a sometimes joyful, sometimes weeping, sometimes compassionate, sometimes angry person, a brilliant debater with intellectuals but also someone who was fearless in the company of the powerful, but tender with the down-trodden.

Jesus is Lord. What does that mean? For the first Christians who lived under the rule of the Roman Empire, the statement 'Jesus is Lord' was a fast ticket to trouble. The empire already had one Lord — Caesar — and he didn't want to share his sovereignty with some prophet from a far-off Eastern colony.

To say Jesus is Lord means he's the boss. He has the right to give orders. Your response and my response is either to rebel or obey: we make that decision every hour of every day of our lives. So being a Christian isn't just doing what's right: it's doing what Jesus the Lord wants you to do.

'Turn your eyes upon Jesus, look full in his wonderful face; and the things of earth will grow strangely dim in the light of his glory and grace.' This old gospel song is still very meaningful. When you 'surrender' to Christ, you do not cease to be a fully-functioning person. You are still fully active. You choose to do his will, not because you are forced to, but because you want to. You realise his will is 'good, pleasing and perfect' (Romans 12:2). Surrender to Christ is the only way to a complete, full life.

When the great theologian Karl Barth was asked 'What's the best thought you've ever had?' he would customarily reply, 'Jesus loves me, this I know for the Bible tells me so'. That's the best motivation of all for following Jesus. 'Jesus loves even me!'

Nineteen wide centuries have come and gone and today He is the centrepiece of the human race and the leader of the column of progress. I am far within the mark when I say that all the armies that ever marched and all the navies that ever were built, and all the parliaments that ever have sat, and all the kings that ever reigned put together have not affected human life upon this earth as powerfully as has that one solitary life, Jesus of Nazareth.

Anon,
quoted in Bill Bright, *A Handbook for Christian Maturity*, San Bernadino, California: Here's Life Publishers, 1982/1990, p. 28.

A man who was merely a man and said the sort of things Jesus said would not be a great moral teacher. He would either be a lunatic — on a level with the man who says he is a poached egg — or else he would be the devil of hell. You must make your choice. Either this man was, and is, the Son of God: or else a madman or something worse. You can shut him up for a fool, you can spit at him and kill him as a demon; or you can fall at his feet and call him Lord and God. But let us not come with any patronising nonsense about his being a great human teacher. He has not left that open to us. He did not intend to.

C. S. Lewis,
Mere Christianity, New York: Macmillan, 1960/1978, p. 56.

Deity is not an easy term to define... But it is not impossible to imagine a line which separates God from all God's creatures, so that on one side is God, and on the other is everything less than God. If we ask on which side of this line Jesus Christ is to be found, the answer given by all the New Testament writers is 'God's side'. They differ in their terminology and their habits of thought. They are writing independently. They are not simply copying from one another... Nowhere in the New Testament do we find any such thought as that Jesus is like one of the angels, or that he can be fully explained in purely human terms. With one accord the New Testament writers insist that Jesus must be thought of as God in the fullest sense... This is all the more remarkable in view of their convinced monotheism.

At the same time the early church did not waver in its thought that Jesus was a man. It is not easy to hold this in conjunction with his deity... How these two... are related, or even how they could co-exist in one person, we do not know. The evidence does not indicate that Jesus was partly God and partly man, that he did some things as God and others as man. Rather he was one person, albeit a person with divine and human characteristics.

Leon Morris,
The Lord from Heaven, London: Inter-Varsity Fellowship, 1958, p. 109.

I say, the acknowledgement of God in Christ
Accepted by thy reason, solves for thee
All questions in the earth and out of it.

Robert Browning,
'A Death in the Desert', quoted in Margaret Pepper (ed.) *The Pan Dictionary of Quotations*, London: Pan
Books, 1989, p. 76.

Apart from Christ we know neither what our life nor our death
is; we do not know what God is nor what we ourselves are.

Blaise Pascal,
Pensées, quoted in Margaret Pepper (ed.) *The Pan Dictionary of Quotations*, London: Pan Books, 1989,
p. 77.

The much-maligned doctrine of the Trinity is an assertion that,
appearances to the contrary withstanding, there is only one
God.

Father, Son, and Holy Spirit mean that the mystery beyond
us, the mystery among us, and the mystery within us are all the
same mystery. Thus the Trinity is a way of saying something
about us and the way we experience God.

Frederick Buechner,
Wishful Thinking, London: Collins, 1973, p. 93.

After the severe storms and floods which Holland suffered in
1952... the dyke had to be strengthened one Sunday. The
pastor... found himself in a religious difficulty. Should he call out
the people of the parish... and set them to work if it meant
profaning the sabbath? Should he, on the contrary, abandon
them to destruction in order to honour the sabbath? He...
summoned the church council to consult and decide. The
discussion went as one might suppose. We live to carry out God's
will. God, being omnipotent, can always perform a miracle with
the wind and waves. Our duty is obedience, whether in life or in
death. The pastor tried one last argument, perhaps against his
own conviction: Did not Jesus himself, on occasion, break the
fourth commandment and declare that the Sabbath was made
for (humankind, not humankind for the Sabbath)? Thereupon a
venerable old man stood up: 'I have always been troubled,
pastor, by something that I have never yet ventured to say
publicly. Now I must say it. I have always had the feeling that our
Lord Jesus was just a bit of a liberal.'

Ernst Kasemann,
Jesus Means Freedom, London, SCM Press, 1972, p. 16.

Jesus does not offer an opinion for he never uttered opinions. He
never guessed; he knew, and he knows... To accept Christ is to
know the meaning of the words 'as he is, so are we in this world.'
We accept his friends as our friends, his enemies as our enemies,

his ways as our ways, his rejection as our rejection, his cross as our cross, his life as our life and his future as our future...

A. W. Tozer,
in Harry Verploegh (comp.), *Signposts: A Collection of Sayings from A. W. Tozer*, Wheaton, Illinois: Victor Books, 1988, pp. 23, 25.

Christianity began with an encounter. Some people, Jews, came into contact with Jesus of Nazareth. They were fascinated by him and stayed with him. This encounter and what took place in Jesus' life and in connection with his death gave their own lives meaning and significance. They felt that they were reborn, understood and cared for. Their new identity was expressed in a new enthusiasm for the kingdom of God and therefore in a special compassion for others... in a way that Jesus had already showed them. This change in the direction of their lives was the result of their real encounter with Jesus, since without him they would have remained as they were, as they told other people later (see 1 Corinthians 15:17). This was not something over which they had taken the initiative; it had happened to them.

This astonishing and amazing encounter which some people had with Jesus of Nazareth, a man from their own race and religion, becomes the starting point for the view of salvation found in the New Testament. This means that grace and salvation, redemption and religion, need not be expressed in strange, 'supernatural' terms; they can be put into ordinary human language, the language of encounter and experience, above all the language of picture and image, testimony and story, never detached from a specific liberating event...

Edward Schillebeeckx,
in Robert Schreiter (ed.), *The Schillebeeckx Reader*. Foreword copyright © 1984 by Edward Schillebeeckx. Editor's preface and commentaries copyright © 1984 by Robert Schreiter. Reprinted by permission of The Crossroad Publishing Company.

We have an interesting problem in Spanish with the word *lord*. Lord is *señor*, the same word we use for mister. (So) Señor Lopez runs the gas station on the corner, Señor Rodriguez drives a city bus, and Señor Jesuscristo listens to your prayers.

The result in Spanish is that we have lost the 'lord' concept. To call Jesus the Lord (Señor) doesn't really say anything very strongly.

But since I have come among English-speaking people, I have found that you have the same problem, even though you have two separate words, mister and lord, in your language... The Bible presents Jesus as King, as Lord, as the maximum authority. Jesus is at the very centre.

Juan Carlos Ortiz,
Disciple, Carol Stream, Ill.: Creation House, 1975, pp. 11, 12.

A ship's captain was once guiding his vessel along a rocky coast on a cloudy night. He peered ahead and saw a faint light. He ordered his signalman to send this message by radio: 'Alter your course ten degrees south'.

Soon a message came back: 'Alter your course ten degrees north'.

The captain was a little disgusted. He sent a second message: 'The captain says, "Alter your course ten degrees south!"'

A second message came back: 'Seaman Third Class Jones says, "Alter your course ten degrees north"'.

This sent the captain into full-scale fuming. 'Alter your course ten degrees north; this is a battleship!' he thundered.

One more reply came back: 'Alter your course ten degrees north; this is the lighthouse'.

Our modern world is full of voices shouting orders into the night, telling others how to live, what to do, how to change. And there is one Voice whose directions seem opposite to the rest... He is the one voice who knows what he's talking about. He is the Light of the world. He is the authority on this treacherous coastline. He is Lord.

Dean Merrill,
'Jesus is Lord', in LaVonne Neff et al. (eds), *Practical Christianity*, Wheaton, Illinois: Tyndale House Publishers Inc., 1988, p. 139.

Picture a gloved hand. The glove is a limp piece of leather until the hand moves into the glove and begins to mobilise it. When the hand does something, the glove could say, 'I just picked up my coffee cup', but it really is not the glove doing it. In a sense, Jesus' living in us is like the hand in the glove. Jesus Christ clothes himself and uses me for his purpose. I want to allow the indwelling Christ to mold me and use me and bend me any way he pleases as long as he accomplishes his will.

Luis Palau,
'The Indwelling Christ', in LaVonne Neff et al. (eds), *Practical Christianity*, Wheaton, Illinois: Tyndale House Publishers Inc., 1988, pp. 149-150.

Arise, shine, for your light has come. The glory of the Lord is risen upon us...

Great beyond all question is the mystery of our religion; Christ was manifested in the body, vindicated in the spirit, seen by angels.

Christ was proclaimed among the nations, believed in throughout the world, glorified in heaven...

Jesus, you are the good shepherd, you are willing to die for the sheep. You are the good shepherd; as the Father knows you and you know the Father, in the same way you know your sheep, and your sheep know you; you are willing to die for us.

The Father loves you because you are willing to give your life; no one takes your life from you; you give it up of your own free will; you are the good shepherd.

Jesus is the good shepherd who understands our frailty, and knows each one of us by name.

A New Zealand Prayer Book, Auckland: Collins, 1989, pp. 114, 107, 128-129.

Almighty, ever-living God, our Father, you enlighten all who come into the world. You have given the human race Jesus Christ our Saviour: born of a woman and to die on a cross. In him we see you as you really are. Your Holy Spirit comes into our lives to confirm your reality and teach us your truth.

Jesus fulfilled your will; he was a model of humility; he loved us, even giving his life for us.

Father, Son and Holy Spirit, fill my heart with the light of your gospel, that my thoughts may please you, and my love be sincere.

Help me to bear witness to you by following Jesus' example of suffering and make me worthy to share in his resurrection.

Guide my mind by his truth and strengthen my life by the example of his death, that I may live in union with you in the kingdom of your promise. Amen.

A benediction

Grace to you and peace from God our Father and the Lord Jesus Christ. Amen.

Philippians 1:2

Further reading

Bill Bright, *A Handbook for Christian Maturity*, Josh McDowell, *The Resurrection Factor, Evidence That Demands a Verdict, More Evidence That Demands a Verdict*, Josh McDowell and Bart Larson, *Jesus, a Biblical Defense of his Deity* (all published by Here's Life Publishers, Inc., San Bernadino, California).

8
What Easter is all about

Surely he has borne our infirmities and carried our diseases; yet we accounted him stricken, struck down by God, and afflicted. But he was wounded for our transgressions, crushed for our iniquities; upon him was the punishment that made us whole, and by his bruises we are healed.

He was oppressed, and he was afflicted, yet he did not open his mouth; like a lamb that is led to the slaughter and like a sheep that before its shearers is silent, so he did not open his mouth. By a perversion of justice he was taken away... For he was cut off from the land of the living, stricken for the transgression of my people.

Pilate said to them, 'Then what should I do with Jesus who is called the Messiah?' All of them said, 'Let him be crucified!' Then he asked, 'Why, what evil has he done?' But they shouted all the more, 'Let him be crucified...!' After twisting some thorns into a crown, they put it on his head. They put a reed in his right hand and knelt before him and mocked him, saying, 'Hail, King of the Jews...!' At that moment the curtain of the temple was torn in two, from top to bottom. The earth shook, and the rocks were split. Now when the centurion and those with him, who were keeping watch over Jesus, saw the earthquake and what took place, they were terrified and said, 'Truly this man was God's Son!'

He went to Pilate and asked for the body of Jesus; then Pilate ordered it to be given to him. So Joseph took the body and wrapped it in a clean linen cloth and laid it in his own new tomb. So they went with the guard and made the tomb secure by sealing the stone.

Christ... suffered for you, leaving you an example, so that you should follow in his steps... When he was abused, he did not return abuse; when he suffered, he did not threaten... He bore our sins in his body on the cross... by his wounds you have been healed.

For there is one God; there is also one mediator between God and humankind, Christ Jesus, himself human, who gave himself a ransom for all — this was attested at the right time...

They took him down from the tree and laid him in a tomb. But God raised him from the dead; and for many days he appeared to those who came up with him from Galilee to Jerusalem, and they are now his witnesses to the people. And we bring you the good news that what God promised to our ancestors he has fulfilled for us.

Do not be afraid; I know that you are looking for Jesus who was crucified. He is not here; for he has been raised, as he said. Suddenly Jesus met them and said, 'Greetings!' And they came to him, took hold of his feet, and worshipped him. Then Jesus said to them, 'Do not be afraid; go and tell my brothers to go to Galilee; there they will see me'.

Christ died for our sins in accordance with the Scriptures... he was buried, and was raised on the third day... He appeared to Cephas, then to the twelve. Then he appeared to more than five hundred brothers and sisters at one time, most of whom are still alive, though some have died. Then he appeared to James, then to all the apostles. Last of all... he appeared also to me.

If for this life only we had hoped in Christ, we are of all people most to be pitied. But in fact Christ has been raised from the dead, the first fruits of those who have died... As all die in Adam, so all will be made alive in Christ. We know that the one who raised the Lord Jesus will raise us also with Jesus.

God has fixed a day on which he will have the world judged in righteousness by a man whom he has appointed, and of this he has given assurance to all by raising him from the dead. If you confess with your lips that Jesus is Lord and believe in your heart that God raised him from the dead, you will be saved. Blessed be the God and Father of our Lord Jesus Christ! By his great mercy he has given us a new birth into a living hope through the resurrection of Jesus Christ from the dead.

Isaiah 53:4, 5, 7, 8; Matthew 27:22-23, 29, 51, 54, 58-60, 66; 1 Peter 2:21-24; 1 Timothy 2:5-6; Acts 13:29-33; Matthew 28:5, 6, 9, 10; 1 Corinthians 15:3-8, 19, 22; 2 Corinthians 4:14; Acts 17:31; Romans 10:9; 1 Peter 1:3.

Most early Christians were Jews who were used to celebrating religious festivals at various times in the year (Passover, Tabernacles, Pentecost, etc.). So Christians were encouraged to follow the great events of our Lord's life at various times in the year. We begin the 'Christian Year' with Advent as we prepare for Christ's coming. Advent also completes the cycle by reminding us of Christ's second coming to judge the world. The Christmas festival celebrates the Incarnation of God in Christ, when 'the Word became flesh'. Some churches commemorate the coming of the Wise Men at Epiphany (January 6); others the baptism of Jesus. Lent reminds us of Jesus' temptation and sufferings, preparing the way for the celebration of the triumphant entry into Jerusalem on Palm Sunday and the contemplation of his passion and death on the cross on 'Good Friday'. Easter is the celebration of Christ's resurrection. Then we have Ascension Sunday. Pentecost, seven weeks after Easter, is the anniversary of the coming of the Holy Spirit. (It is sometimes called Whitsunday, the Sunday on which baptismal candidates were dressed in white.) Last of all Trinity Sunday recalls the key doctrine of our faith: there is one God, in three Persons — Father, Son and Holy Spirit.

In the forty-day season of Lent (forty-six if you include Sundays) we take a spiritual inventory. Moses, Elijah and Jesus fasted for forty days, so from the fourth century, the church has observed Lent as a time of inner examination, prayer, fasting and almsgiving. Fasting is more than 'giving up candy for God'. It is the sharpest way we know of making ourselves pray, and pray more intensely. For Jesus and his disciples, this was a time of tension, a time of expectancy and excitement. In Lent, we prepare ourselves to experience the mighty meaning of the Cross. Lent begins with Ash Wednesday, when in some churches ashes are put on people's foreheads to remind them of their mortality: 'Remember you are dust, and to dust you shall return'. Lent comes from the Old English *lencten*, the 'lengthening' of the days of Spring. Lent anticipates new life. It's when 'the daffodils come before the swallow dares', to quote one of Shakespeare's loveliest lines.

Beyond the triumphant entry into Jerusalem, Jesus weeping over that city, his anger at the exploitation of the poor as he overturned the Temple money-changers' tables, his anguish in Gethsemane, the mockery of a trial... Jesus the Son of God is crucified on a cross between two criminals. And they call that Good Friday.

Good Friday? Yes, for three reasons: reasons associated with the three greatest needs humans have — to be loved, to be forgiven, and to find meaning in the face of their inevitable death.

(1) When Jesus died he was demonstrating that the God who was his Father entered our life and loved us even to the point of death. The death of Jesus, says Bonhoeffer in *Letters and Papers from Prison* is the ultimate symbol of the suffering of God in the life of the world. God allows himself to be edged out of the world and on to a cross. Only a powerless and suffering God can really help us... God did not come to save us by an act of terror so that we would be cowed into belief, but by a great act of love. Abelard, a twelfth century philosopher and theologian, believed the cross primarily demonstrates the greatness of the love of God, a love that should move us away from our sin and to love God in return. God so loved, that he gave (John 3:16). The Son of God, says Paul, loved me and gave himself for me (Galatians 2:20). Our response? Obedient love — even if we suffer too (1 Peter 2:21).

(2) There's a theme running through the Bible which is somewhat foreign to Westerners, that of animal sacrifices for human sins. John the Baptist recognised Jesus as 'the lamb of God who takes away the sin of the world' (John 1:29, 36). Exodus, Leviticus and Numbers describe how animals can 'bear the sins' of humans. These animal sacrifices (for example of bulls and goats) were repeatable, but, says Hebrews, Christ was offered once to bear the sins of many (Hebrews 9:28). Jesus thought of himself as the Suffering Servant (see Isaiah 53) offering his life as a sacrifice, as a ransom for others' sins (for example Mark 10:45). Anselm, an eleventh century Archbishop of Canterbury, argued that sin is an insult to the majesty of God, and at the cross God's honour was 'satisfied'. The Protestant Reformers emphasised more our sin breaking God's holy law. We deserved to incur the penalty — death (Romans 6:23) — but Christ died in our place, paying the penalty and setting us free. We are so important to God that what is destroying us is of ultimate concern to him, and he acts to offer a way out of our misery. We are invited to repent, turn from our sins, and be forgiven, because we have been pardoned!

(3) Gustav Aulen, a Swedish theologian (*Christus Victor*) says the cross is mainly about a cosmic drama in which God in Christ does battle with the forces of evil and defeats them. Jesus' death on the cross not only demonstrates God's amazing love for us and saves us from our sins, but it also saves us from death and all the evil powers as well. Through his death he destroyed the one who has the power of death, that is, the devil, and frees us from

the fear of death (Hebrews 2:14, 15; see also Colossians 2:13-15, 2 Timothy 1:10).

The three traditional theories of the Atonement, a demonstration of love, the bearing of penalty, and victory over evil may have had more appeal to earlier ages than our own... Australian New Testament scholar Leon Morris has suggested that today we might also see the cross addressing problems of futility and frustration (see Romans 8:20, Hebrews 2:8-9); sickness and death (Isaiah 53:4, Matthew 8:17); ignorance (Jeremiah 17:9, 1 Timothy 2:4); loneliness (Genesis 2:18, Mark 15:34, Romans 8:38-39); and selfishness (Luke 9:23, Galatians 2:10, Romans 6:4).

Aleksander Solzhenitsyn, the Russian dissident, was working twelve hours a day at hard labour. He had lost his family and had been told by the doctors in the Gulag that he had terminal cancer. One day he thought, 'There is no use going on. I'm soon going to die anyway'. Ignoring the guards, he dropped his shovel, sat down, and rested his head in his hands.

He felt a presence next to him and looked up and saw an old man he had never seen before, and would never see again. The man took a stick and drew a cross in the sand in front of Solzhenitsyn. It reminded him that there is a Power in the world that is greater than any empire or government, a Power that could bring new life to his situation. He picked up his shovel and went back to work. A year later Solzhenitsyn was unexpectedly released from prison and went to live in the United States.

Good Friday? Yes. When God's human creatures are bad, God is good. When we are at our worst, God is at his best...!

The French thinker, August Comte, once told Thomas Carlyle that he was going to start a new religion to replace Christianity. 'Very good', replied Carlyle, 'all you have to do is to be crucified, rise again, and get the world to believe that you are still alive. Then your new religion will have a chance'.

Easter is the annual celebration of the resurrection of Christ, and is the most important date in the Christian year. In the early church the Easter celebration included the lighting of a candle, prayer, readings from Scripture, and the joyful celebration of the Lord's Supper. It was also a common time for baptisms, with resurrection life symbolised by white robes. Over the centuries some pagan spring customs have been added, including Easter eggs and rabbits!

The death and resurrection of Christ are the key events and doctrines of the Christian faith. In an early creed (1 Corinthians 15:3ff.) Paul reports several eyewitness accounts to substantiate his claim that if the resurrection had not occurred, the whole Christian faith is false (verse 14) and ineffective (verse 17), Christian preachers are wasting their time (verse 14), our sins aren't forgiven after all (verse 17), we die without hope (verse 18), we are the most miserable of people (verse 19), and so without resurrection let's 'live it up' for tomorrow we die (verse 32).

The dominant note in the celebration of Easter is joy. 'Make people laugh and you open heaven to them', says a rabbinical proverb. 'The risen Christ makes life into a constant celebration', writes the fourth century bishop and theologian Athanasius. Some Greek Orthodox Easter worship services include the Rite of Laughter: 'Now let us laugh. Let us worship God by laughing together...!'

Easter turns despair into hope. The American playwright Eugene O'Neill lived tragically, and shortly before his death he wrote poignantly, 'I can partly understand how God can forgive humans, for we are so weak and ignorant. What I can't understand is how he can ever forgive himself?' We have each, in our darkest moments, probably wondered the same thing. But Easter, if it has any message for us at all, says that human tragedy is never ultimate. He who vacated the tomb is alive, and has not vacated his throne! All powers-that-be will become powers-that-have-been (1 Corinthians 2:6). Easter reminds us that God is in control of the universe. The Easter-event is about a God who loves eternally, individually and sufficiently.

All we are called to do is to be what we are created to be. We need only be human, a simple matter of being in relationship with God and other human beings. Further, the story that calls us together and forms us is one of a God who is in relentless pursuit of us and of the divine dream that those relationships might grow and thrive and that we might indeed have life. Up to a point Ash Wednesday is supposed to make us uncomfortable, as we contemplate our sinful condition. However, it need be ultimately uncomfortable only inasmuch as we insist on cherishing death and refusing to acknowledge our continuing life in God.

Byron L. Rohrig,
'The Most Uncomfortable Day of the Year' *Christian Century*, 25 February 1987, p. 181.

Jesus always valued and cherished life as the astonishing gift that it is, and there was nothing of the suicide's disdain for life that drove him 'to set his face toward Jerusalem'. Yet neither did he make an idolatry of continued existence no matter what. He sensed that good as life was, there were some things of even greater value... He literally 'sweat blood' in grappling with all the factors here...

I still remember driving into a village high in the Swiss Alps and seeing a larger-than-life statue of an Alpine mountain guide. He had the traditional pointed hat on his head with a feather sticking up, a rope on his shoulder, and hobnail boots on his feet. His finger was pointed to the highest peak in evidence and his head was thrown back over his shoulder as if he were calling to others behind him. And the inscription underneath said: 'Follow me. I have been there before'. This is what Jesus invites us to do in relation to our future, and I cannot think of a better resource for the journey that gets better and better and harder and harder as we go along. How wise we would be to accept that invitation and join forces with him immediately and forever!

John Claypool,
'Palm Sunday and Heightened Responsibility', unpublished sermon, preached 8 April 1979.

Greetings also to you,
brothers and sisters of the people
Who brought forth the Redeemer.
Let no one try to find blame in others.
Let all of us recognise
Our own guilt in these events...

Prologue to the Oberammergau Passion Play, addressing the Jewish people.

The late Dr Albert Mollengen of Virginia Seminary was on a driving trip across the South. Somewhere in Tennessee he stopped for a meal at a diner. As he was in the men's room washing his hands, another man stepped up to wash at the next sink. The other man turned to him and said, 'Have you been saved?' Startled, Mollengen turned and responded, 'Why, yes.' Undaunted, the other pressed him by asking, 'When?' With certainty, Dr Mollengen looked deeply into the man's eyes and replied, 'On Good Friday'.

Kenneth Swanson,
Uncommon Prayer, New York: Ballantine, 1987, pp. 70-1.

The death of Christ is the central moment in the whole event to which Christian faith and devotion look back... (It has represented) all the values and meanings realised within the Christian community, providing universal Christianity with its most characteristic symbol. And it has always been remembered as... significant beyond our understanding, pointing us to heights incalculably beyond our reach and making us aware of depths in our existence which we know we shall never sound or probe. No wonder the sun was hidden 'from the sixth hour... until the ninth'. It is significant that... both the death of Christ and the Resurrection took place in darkness — events too sacred to be gazed on, too full of portent to be plainly seen.

John Knox,
The Death of Christ, London: Collins/Fontana, 1967, p. 11.

Perhaps the most horrifying experience of all (for Elie Wiesel in Nazi death camps) was when the guards first tortured and then hanged a young boy, 'a child with a refined and beautiful face', a 'sad-eyed angel'. Just before the hanging Elie heard someone behind him whisper, 'Where is God? Where is he?' Thousands of prisoners were forced to watch the hanging (it took the boy half an hour to die) and then to march past, looking him full in the face. Behind him Elie heard the same voice ask, 'Where is God now?' 'And I heard a voice within me answer him: "Where is he? Here he is — he is hanging here on this gallows".'

Cited in John Stott,
The Cross of Christ, Leicester: Inter-Varsity Press, 1986, p. 335.

The opposition to him grew, the opposition of sin, of those who would not let God be God. God, in Christ, had the power to eliminate all opposition (Matthew 26:53). God, in Christ, does not eliminate his enemies. He protests against their injustice and their hypocrisy, and uncovers their deceit, but he does not distance himself from them. God, in Christ, takes the pain of their sinfulness upon himself. It is as though all the accumulated power of evil, the hatred, greed and cruelty of humanity had joined forces and hurled itself at God, in Christ. 'He became sin for us', Paul says.

In Christ, who is God, human sin and God's goodness meet in the same person... Christ absorbs the pain in himself and prays, 'Father forgive them'. When human sin had done its worst, God, in Christ, replies with the blood and water from his pierced side. God's love is greater than human hatred and has won a victory for ever. This is the triumph and joy of the cross.

Gerard W. Hughes,
God of Surprises, London: Darton, Longman and Todd, 1985, p. 129.

God was in Christ, reconciling the world. Just as the flame which flashes out from a volcano momentarily reveals the elemental, unceasing fires burning at the earth's heart, so the love that leapt out on one crowning day of history in the sheer flame of the cross disclosed what God's inmost nature is for ever. Jesus... made himself a sacrifice when he poured out his soul unto death: but in the deepest sense, the sacrifice was God's. It was God who made the offering, God who paid the price, God who 'having loved his own who were in the world, loved them to the end'.

James Stewart,
A Man In Christ, London: Hodder and Stoughton, 1962, p. 239. Reproduced by permission of Hodder & Stoughton Ltd/New English Library Ltd.

At the Nuremberg war trials a witness gave evidence about his war experiences. He had lived for some time in a Jewish cemetery in Wilna, Poland. He'd miraculously escaped the Nazi gas chambers by hiding in the cemetery. There were also others who had made the cemetery their secret hiding place. One day, in an open grave, a woman gave birth to a baby boy. The old Jewish 80-year old grave digger assisted in the birth. When the newborn baby uttered his first cry, the devout old grave digger said, 'Good God, have you finally sent Messiah to us? For who else than the Messiah himself can be born in a grave?' After three days he saw the baby sucking his mother's tears as she had no milk to offer him.

Yes, the Messiah was born to die, and died a lonely death, having drunk to the bitter dregs the cup of human tears.

Evil is such a powerful force that not even deity grapples with it apart from the shedding of blood.

Daryl Grigsby,
'The Gospel Blues,' in *The Other Side*, 94 (July 1979), p. 62.

'Father forgive them, they know not what they do.' Blindness was their besetting trouble... Unlike physical blindness that is usually inflicted upon individuals as a result of natural forces beyond their control, intellectual and moral blindness is a dilemma which we inflict upon ourselves by the tragic misuse of our freedom and our failure to use our minds to their fullest capacity... Light has come into the world... Jesus was right about those who crucified him. They knew not what they did. They were inflicted with a terrible blindness. The cross... symbolises a strange mixture of greatness and smallness, of good and evil. As I behold that uplifted cross I am reminded not only of the unlimited power of God, but also of the sordid weakness of humans. I am reminded not only of Christ at his best, but of humanity at its worst. We must see the cross as the magnificent symbol of love conquering hate and of light overcoming darkness. But in the midst of this glowing affirmation, let us never forget that our Lord and Master was nailed to that cross because of human blindness. Those who crucified him knew not what they did.

Martin Luther King,
Strength to Love, London: Hodder and Stoughton, 1964, pp. 32-3.© The Estate of Martin Luther King, Jr.

There's no point in going out of your way to look for suffering, to invent sacrifices, to wear hair-shirts, if you aren't willing to embrace the cross which the Father has judged to be the right one for you. Never forget: this was no ready-made one. The Father made it to measure for your shoulders.

Dom Helder Camara,
A Thousand Reasons For Living, London: Darton, Longman and Todd, 1981, p. 115.

Under the cross we all stand empty-handed. We have nothing to offer except the burden of our guilt and the emptiness of our hearts... Here is where the godless are justified, enemies are reconciled, prisoners are set free, the poor are enriched, and the sad are filled with hope. We discover ourselves, therefore, under the cross both as children of the same freedom of Christ and as friends in the same fellowship of the Spirit. The nearer we come to Christ's cross, the nearer we come to each other. How can our divisions and our enmities be maintained in the light of his bitter suffering and death?

Jurgen Moltmann,
The Open Church: Invitation to a Messianic Lifestyle, London: SCM, 1978, p. 84.

What then must I do now? I will go and sit before the Cross. I will attend to it. I will be concentrated, and unhurried, and let it speak to me.

I take, O cross, thy shadow for my abiding place...

Yes, I must abide here. Here is cleansing, security, and renewal. Here the past is dealt with, and the future secured, and all the present — peace. Here I take strength for service, patience in waiting, and healing for any wounds that come...

W. E. Sangster,
They Met At Calvary, London: Hodder and Stoughton, 1956, p. 128. Reprinted by permission of Edward England Books.

If he died but did not rise,
Speak to me not of triumph but disaster.
If he rose but did not die,
Worship with me a ghost but not our Master.

It is almost impossible to over-emphasise the closeness of Christ's death and resurrection in the Scriptures... Without the cross, the resurrection would be a piece of make-believe, an imaginary triumph over sin after an imaginary death. Equally, without the resurrection, the cross is nothing but a ghastly, unredeemed and unredeeming tragedy.

Peter de Rosa,
Jesus who became Christ, London: Fountain/Collins, 1974, p. 200.

After the crucifixion we see a company of hopeless, frightened, disappointed men, terrified that they would be involved in the same fate... and with nothing but the desire to escape back to Galilee and to get back to their old jobs and forget... Seven weeks later Pentecost came and we see these same men filled with a blazing hope and confidence, with a courage which defied the Sanhedrin and mob alike. Every effect must have an adequate cause. And the only possible explanation of this astonishing change is that the disciples were firmly convinced that Jesus was alive.

William Barclay,
Crucified and Crowned, London: SCM Press, 1961, p. 160.

(The resurrection) is not a belief that grew up within the church; it is the belief around which the church itself grew up, and the 'given' upon which its faith was based... Now (the disciples) were new men in a new world, confident, courageous, enterprising, the leaders of a movement which made an immediate impact and went forward with an astonishing impetus. Clearly something had changed these men. They said it was a meeting with Jesus. We have no evidence with which to check their claim. To propose an alternative explanation, based on some preconceived theory, is of dubious profit.

C. H. Dodd,
The Founder of Christianity, London: Collins/Fontana, 1973, pp. 169, 176.

There are three common features (in the resurrection appearances of Jesus): Those to whom Christ appears are portrayed as being in a negative mood of some kind or other... terrified... sad and disillusioned... distraught... afraid... in doubt... In the pain (is revealed) our poverty and our need of God. If we can acknowledge and be still in our poverty, Christ will show himself to us in his glory. Second... is the slowness to recognise that it is the risen Christ... He enters our consciousness, closed through fear of ourselves and our fear of other people, and says to us 'Peace be to you'. The power of his resurrection gives us hope in a situation where before we felt it was hopeless, gives us courage to face a task when before we wanted to run away, gives us the ability and strength to be open and vulnerable when before we could think of nothing but our own protection and security. A final feature... is that those to whom Christ appears are commissioned to go and tell others.

Gerald W. Hughes,
God of Surprises, London: Darton, Longman and Todd, 1985, pp. 134-5.

With respect to resurrection faith, sheer reason and good sense alone fail to prove decisive. Nor are they final. One has belief in the risen Christ without fully understanding the resurrection. It is like believing in someone's love. You say a lot, although you can say very little conclusively... There is a time to fall silent like those friends of Gandalf (in Tolkien's *The Lord of the Rings*) when the old man quite unexpectedly returned: 'Between wonder, joy and fear they stood and found no words to say'. Christ's resurrection remains far more than the sum of any or all descriptions of it. At some point we find no words to say. Then we can do no more than pay silent homage to the awesome nature of this resurrection from the dead, the beginning of God's new creation.

85

Gerald O'Collins,
The Easter Jesus, London: Darton, Longman & Todd, 1973, pp. 137-138.

As the years pass, swifter than a weaver's shuttle, may we bury what must be buried, grieve and move on, with the alacrity of God who, when Christ had lain in the bonds of death for three days, said 'Enough of that', and raised him from the dead.

Peter Fribley and James Cox (eds)
Ministers Manual (Doran's), San Francisco: Harper & Row, 1990, p. 41.

Saviour, hanging on the cross, declaring God's love to us, you are forgiveness. Beside you hangs a thief, beneath you waits Mary the forgiven, and all around watch those many people to whom you give new life and hope. To us you give new life and hope. Forgiven sinners become your body and your Church; may the reconciliation we share bring your gospel to all the world.

Eternal God, by your power we are created and by your love we are redeemed; guide and strengthen us by your Sprit, that we may give ourselves to your service and live this day in love to one another and to you.

Jesus, you know rejection and disappointment; help us if our work seems distasteful; help us to decide what best to do, what next to do, or what to do at all.

Give us courage and cheerfulness to go the second mile, and all the miles ahead. Amen.

A *New Zealand Prayer Book*, Auckland: Collins, 1989, p. 129-30.

My dear Saviour, let me ask Thee
since Thou art nailed to the cross
and since Thou sayest Thyself: It is finished!
Am I now set free from death?
May I, through Thy suffering and death,
inherit heaven?
Has salvation come for all the world?
True, Thou canst not speak for pain,
yet Thy head Thou bowest
And tacitly Thou sayest: Yes!

Chorus (*Chorale*):

Jesus, Thou Who wert dead, now livest forever; in my last agony nowhere will I turn but to Thee Who hast redeemed me. O my beloved Lord! Give me only that which Thou hast won, more I do not desire.

Aria and chorus from J. S. Bach, *St John Passion*

'Yes' and 'no' are little words, Lord, but they are very powerful. The Son of God said 'yes' and submitted himself to the joys and pains of our life. Mary said 'yes' and submitted to the mystery of bearing the incarnate God. Jesus said 'yes' and submitted to Gethsemane and arrest and trial and death on a cross.

But Jesus also invites us to say 'No.' If we will come after him we will deny ourselves, take up our cross and follow him. This is the only way of saying 'Amen' or 'Yes' to him. To deny ourselves is to love him, and our neighbour. To die to self is to live for you, Lord God, and for others.

Remind me, Lord, that life is only lent to us. So may Lent and the Cross be truly Life to me. I truly and earnestly repent of my sins.

A benediction
God, you call us to serve you with all the strength we have; you are faithful to those you call; may Jesus' resurrection raise us if we stumble, the Christlight beckon us if we lose our way, and we shall have strength once more to walk with you to the cross.

Preserve us, O God, while waking, and guard us while sleeping, that awake we may watch with Christ, and asleep may rest in your peace. Amen.

A New Zealand Prayer Book, Auckland: Collins, 1989, p. 132.

9

The Holy Spirit: the Father's special gift to you

God is spirit, and those who worship him must worship in spirit and truth.

If you then... know how to give good gifts to your children, how much more will the heavenly Father give the Holy Spirit to those who ask him! No one can enter the kingdom of God without being born of... Spirit. What is born of flesh is flesh, and what is born of the Spirit is spirit. Do not be astonished that I said to you, 'You must be born from above'. The wind blows where it chooses, and you hear the sound of it, but you do not know where it comes from or where it goes. So it is with everyone who is born of the Spirit.

Do not take your holy Spirit from me... I will ask the Father, and he will give you another Advocate, to be with you forever. This is the Spirit of truth. But the Advocate, the Holy Spirit, whom the Father will send in my name, will teach you everything, and remind you of all that I have said to you. When he comes, he will prove the world wrong about sin and righteousness and judgment.

No one can say 'Jesus is Lord' except by the Holy Spirit. In him you also, when you had heard the word of truth, the gospel of your salvation, and had believed in him, were marked with the seal of the promised Holy Spirit.

Jesus, full of the Holy Spirit, returned from the Jordan... The two went down and prayed for them that they might receive the Holy Spirit. Then Peter and John laid their hands on them, and they received the Holy Spirit . Be filled with the Spirit, as you sing psalms and hymns and spiritual songs among yourselves, singing and making melody to the Lord in your hearts, giving thanks to God the Father at all times and for everything in the name of our Lord Jesus Christ.

My proclamation (was) not with plausible words of wisdom, but with a demonstration of the Spirit and of power, so that your faith might rest not on human wisdom but on the power of God. For the law of the Spirit of life in Christ Jesus has set you free from the law of sin and of death. The letter kills, but the Spirit gives life. Do not grieve the Holy Spirit of God, with which you were marked with a seal for the day of redemption.

The Spirit of the Lord is upon me, because he has anointed me to bring good news to the poor. He has sent me to proclaim release to the captives and recovery of sight to the blind, to let the oppressed go free, to proclaim the year of the Lord's favour.

Now concerning spiritual gifts... there are varieties of gifts, but the same Spirit... To each is given the manifestation of the Spirit for the common good. To one is given through the Spirit the utterance of wisdom, and to another the utterance of knowledge... to another faith..., to another gifts of healing..., to another the working of miracles, to another prophecy, to another the discernment of spirits, to another various kinds of tongues, to another the interpretation of tongues... We have gifts that differ according to the grace given to us: prophecy, in proportion to faith, ministry... teaching... exhortation... generosity... (leadership)... (compassion).

All these are activated by one and the same Spirit... For just as the body is one and has many members... so it is with Christ. For in the one Spirit we were baptised into one body — Jews or Greeks, slaves or free — and we were all made to drink of one Spirit.

Do not believe every spirit, but test the spirits to see whether they are from God... Be strong in the Lord and in the strength of his power. Put on the whole armour of God, so that you may be able to stand against the wiles of the devil... Fasten the belt of truth... put on the breast-plate of righteousness... proclaim the gospel of peace... take the shield of faith... the helmet of salvation, and the sword of the Spirit, which is the word of God. Pray in the Spirit at all times.

The Spirit is the truth. The Spirit gives life. God did not give us a spirit of cowardice, but rather a spirit of power and of love and of self-discipline. The Spirit helps us in our weakness. Where the Spirit of the Lord is, there is freedom. The fruit of the Spirit is love, joy, peace, patience, kindness, generosity, faithfulness, gentleness and self-control.

John 4: 24; Luke 11:13; John 3:5-8; Psalm 51:11; John 14:16, 17, 26; John 16:8; 1 Corinthians 12:3; Ephesians 1:13; Luke 4:1; Acts 8:15, 17; Ephesians 5:18-20; 1 Corinthians 2:4-5; Romans 8:2; 2 Corinthians 3:6; Ephesians 4:30; Luke 4:18-

19; 1 Corinthians 12:1-10; Romans 12:6-7; 1 Corinthians 12:11-13; 1 John 4:1; Ephesians 6:10-18; 1 John 5:6; John 6:63; 2 Timothy 1:7; Romans 8:26; 2 Corinthians 3:17; Galatians 5:22.

The Holy Spirit is God in action. He has sometimes been described as the 'third person in the Trinity'. Notice we used 'he' — the Holy Spirit is not an 'it' or a thing (although the Bible describes his operations as being like the wind, unpredictable or even mysterious). The English language used to say 'Holy Ghost', but the Spirit is not a 'spook' either.

He is like Jesus, who is like God: he can think, will and feel — that is, he possesses all the attributes of any personality: intellect, emotion and will. He can be grieved and he can be quenched or stifled and ignored.

The Holy Spirit 'inspires' people to say what God wants them to say (or to write those things down). So prophets and Scripture are 'inspired' by the Spirit.

The Spirit guides us into the truth about Jesus, about ourselves and our sinfulness — and its consequence, judgment — and gives us the 'big picture' and God's will for the future (John 16:8-13).

When you become a Christian, the Holy Spirit enters your life, and he will never leave you. In a sense, he's a guest: you've let him in the front door. It's now an exciting (and sometimes scary) process letting him take control of every room in your home. (Perhaps you could imagine these rooms, invite him in, and talk about what he discovers there!).

He helps us to pray (Romans 8:26), to communicate to others about Christ (Mark 13:11), to love (Galatians 5:22), and to do what is right (1 John 2:27).

So be filled with the Spirit (Ephesians 5:18). You get drunk with wine by choosing the sort you want, imbibing it, and ingesting it. Then your behaviour exhibits some changes according to how much and how often you drink (changing — and eventually controlling — you). So with the Spirit, says Paul. But in one sense you don't get more of the Spirit; he gets more of you.

How am I filled with the Holy Spirit? First you must desire him — hungering and thirsting for what is right (Matthew 5:6). This involves confession of your sins (1 John 1:9). Then ask him to fill you: if you ask for anything according to his will, he'll hear you (1 John 5:14, 15). Thank him for filling you, and by faith live moment by moment, hour by hour, day by day in his power and under his direction.

He wants to change you, though your basic temperament remains the same. Paul, for example, was a very aggressive person before his conversion but the Spirit redirected all that emotional energy towards more positive ends. Being 'filled with the Spirit' simply means being controlled by him.

Are you supposed to 'feel' anything when the Spirit comes into your life? Yes and no. Some do, some don't. Some have a 'peak experience' — for a few it's quite powerful. For others it's quite a matter-of-fact transaction. The Spirit operates uniquely in each of us. Remember, he's like the wind — sometimes a hurricane, sometimes a gentle breeze.

Indeed, Paul and Luke describe receiving the Spirit in different ways. For Paul 'receiving' the Spirit makes us God's children (Romans 8:15). For Luke 'receiving' the Spirit gives us power (Acts 1:8). However, Paul also writes about receiving the Spirit with accompanying miracles (Galatians 3:1-5). Christians today generally follow either Luke or Paul on this point — the Pentecostals like Luke, the evangelicals Paul. In the early church, 'Spirit' and 'Word' went hand in hand. Let us combine both Luke and Paul — allowing the Spirit to make us holy, give us wisdom and endue us with power. Throughout the world, where 'signs and wonders' accompany the proclamation of the good news the church is dynamic and alive. However the great need for those young churches is Bible teaching — but without losing their enthusiasm. More of that later.

About miracles: some Christians expect a 'miracle a day'; others confine them to the pages of their Bibles! Jesus did promise that his followers would perform the same miracles he did — even greater ones (John 14:12). His power is still the same. But note that biblical miracles clustered around just four historical periods — the creation, Moses and the Exodus, the prophets Elijah and Elisha, and Jesus and the apostolic era. There were always a few miracles at other times (for example those in the Book of Daniel). Does God still heal miraculously? Certainly, and we should pray for that possibility. But today no one has a gift of healing like Jesus' or Paul's. No one can heal anyone at any time. Sometimes Paul healed everyone in a city. But no faith healer I have heard of has a gift like that today. Some of them build hospitals: if they had Paul's gift they might be emptying them!

Christians sometimes get nervous about spiritual gifts they don't fully understand, especially if they sense the Holy Spirit nudging them to be the channel of such a gift. It is important to remember that the Spirit doesn't offer white-elephant gifts. His presents are not useless, like the thing you took home from the last Christmas party. We are wise not to turn up our noses at his gifts, for he knows what he is doing. And the church is waiting to benefit from our gift-offerings...

Stay open-minded. Don't fall for Cornford's Law, which says

'Nothing should ever be done for the first time'. Instead, opt for the perspective of Charles Schulz, creator of Peanuts: 'Life is like a ten-speed bicycle. Most of us have gears we never use'.

If we could scan a congregation with God's radar, we would probably spot dozens of unused gifts — spiritual capacities lying dormant in the lives of many Christians. Meanwhile, the whole church is poorer.

When the Spirit's power invades a fisherman like Simon Peter or a shoe salesman like D. L. Moody, or a young American who's only done a couple of years in Bible colleges like Billy Graham, they can be very effective evangelists indeed. 'Correct' doctrine, homiletically-sound sermons, professional techniques all have their place, but throughout the world the churches that are open to the Lord's power working among them are alive. Churches that have shunned this dimension for a rationalistic faith are declining everywhere.

Introducing his *Letters to Young Churches*, J. B. Phillips states, 'The great difference between present-day Christianity and that in these letters, is that, to us, it is primarily a performance; to them it was a real experience. We reduce the Christian religion to a code... a rule of heart and life. To these it was quite plainly the invasion of their lives by a new quality of life altogether'.

❧

All the great figures in Acts are people of the Spirit. Filled with the Spirit, Peter addressed the Sanhedrin (4:8). When there was a need for new workers, the instruction was to seek out seven men of honest report and full of the Spirit (6:3). Stephen was full of faith and the Holy Spirit (6:5)... Paul was filled with the Holy Spirit at the beginning of his ministry for Christ (9:17, 13:8). Barnabas was a good man, full of the Holy Spirit and faith (11:24). The criterion by which the early church judged a person was that person's relationship to the Holy Spirit... It is even said of Jesus himself that God anointed him with the Holy Spirit and with power (10:38)... Had it not been for the guidance of the Spirit, the church might well have remained nothing more than a sect of Judaism... The real test of a church lies not in the statistics which an ecclesiastical yearbook can convey, but in the presence or absence of the Spirit.

William Barclay,
The Promise of the Spirit, London: Epworth, 1960, pp. 55ff.

One of the marks of the Spirit's moving amongst us is that 'we hear the sound thereof'. This is the indisputable evidence of the Spirit. When the wind is blowing, it makes its presence felt. You hear its sound... When the Spirit of God stirs up a church or an individual or a community, there are palpable evidences of his working. Even the unbeliever becomes aware that something is going on. (The effects can be seen. The sound can be heard...) The hard supercilious pagan world of Greece and Rome professed itself indifferent to the gospel; but it could not deny that wherever Christ's people went strange things kept happening... The world, says the Book of Acts, saw the evidences: it 'took knowledge of them that they had been with Jesus'.

James S. Stewart,
The Wind of the Spirit, Eastbourne: Victory Press, 1975, pp. 14-5.

People receive the Holy Spirit, in Luke's meaning of the term, in different ways. Some people receive the Spirit more or less spontaneously, while for others the response is quite conscious and deliberate; some experience dramatic manifestations of the Spirit, while with others the manifestations are more subdued. The way in which people receive the Spirit will be determined, to some extent, by the situation and by the person (his or her personality type, age, station in life, church environment). More important than the particular way we receive the Spirit, however, is what we do after having received.

It's like the difference between a big church wedding and a small family wedding. The kind of wedding you have doesn't determine the kind of marriage you'll have. What's important is how you live out the reality of married life.

Larry Christenson,
'Receiving the Holy Spirit' in LaVonne Neff et al. (eds), *Practical Christianity*, Wheaton, Illinois: Tyndale House Publishers, 1988, p. 164.

Notice that Luke equates being 'filled with the Spirit' with moral qualities, goodness and faith (Acts 11:24). Being 'Spirit-filled' does not refer to a special experience, as such, although we ought to be open to whatever experiences of the Spirit the Lord has for us. Sometimes, in Acts, people spoke in tongues when 'filled with the Spirit'; but Acts often speaks of people filled with the Spirit with no reference, explicit or implicit, to tongues (4:8,31; 6:3,5; 7:55; 9:17; 11:24; 13:9, 52). 'If being Spirit-filled without glossolalia was the lot of some, then, it may be God's path for some now' (J. I. Packer). However, you can't be 'Spirit-filled' without exhibiting fruits of the Spirit such as goodness and faith. They are the inevitable proofs of the Spirit's presence in our lives.

Rowland Croucher,
Your Church Can Come Alive, Melbourne: JBCE, 1990, p. 57.

Leonard Ravenhill tells a story about a group of tourists visiting a picturesque village. When they came to an old man by a fence, one of the tourists asked, 'Were any great people born in this village?'

The old man leaned on his cane and replied, 'Nope, only babies.'

Nobody starts out great. God has no instant giants of faith. The most gifted Christian you know began tentatively, serving the Lord with butterflies inside, not sure if he or she would ever make an impact for the kingdom of God. But availability turned into ability. The Holy Spirit's gifts were welcomed and then released to help change the world.

Dean Merrill,
'Why Does a Church Need Spiritual Gifts?' in LaVonne Neff et al. (eds), *Practical Christianity*, Wheaton, Illinois: Tyndale House Publishers, 1988, pp. 167-8.

I've spoken in tongues as part of my devotional life for about thirty-four years, and I can assure you the practice does not give you warts, make your hair fall out, or fry your brain. In fact, it doesn't even require working up a sweat (despite what you may have seen or heard about in some religious meetings).

It is simply an alternate way of communicating with God — a Route B that bypasses the usual patterns of stringing words together from a learned vocabulary... It is an unleashing of speech from deep within, speech that carries feelings, needs, concerns, and praises heavenward in a mystical way.

Might speaking in tongues simply be a form of 'right-brain praying'? We don't know...

There are documented cases of hearers in various parts of the world being surprised by a language they knew but the speaker didn't — which is what happened on the Day of Pentecost. A Brazilian visitor to our church approached my father during the prayer time and said, 'Excuse me, but who's praying in Portuguese here?' The two men walked to the altar area to investigate, and the visitor singled out my (fourteen-year old) cousin. She had studied no foreign language...

Not all churches are comfortable with (tongues), and the Holy Spirit does not force it upon them. He is gentle as a dove...

We may never fully understand tongues in the sense of being able to draw a schematic diagram of how they occur. But our faith was not made for scientific analysis. We serve a God bigger than our minds, a God who regularly surprises us, a God whose ways are not always our ways — and would we want it any differently?

Dean Merrill,
'What About Speaking in Tongues?' in LaVonne Neff et al. (eds), *Practical Christianity*, Wheaton, Illinois: Tyndale House Publishers, 1988 pp. 172-3.

In the Nicene Creed the Holy Spirit is linked to prophetic utterance. While prophetic speech is more often linked in the Old Testament to oracles pertaining to the public or political sphere, this is generalised in the early Christian community to include all instances of address which summon the hearer into renovation and enhancement of authentic life — (an) appropriate, truthful, and liberating speech. The capacity to speak in ways which loosen the bonds of brokenness and invite the other into new and richer life is a... gift of the Holy Spirit...

Thomas Aquinas understood the Holy Spirit in terms of friendship. In this view the Holy Spirit befriends us and conveys to us the love of God. Thus the Spirit, like a friend, draws us near to all our secrets, never betraying us but gently summoning us to richer and fuller life.

T. W. Jennings,
'Holy Spirit, Doctrine of, and Pastoral Care', in Rodney J. Hunter, (ed.), *Dictionary of Pastoral Care and Counseling*, Nashville: Abingdon, 1990, p. 526.

The one who has been taught by the Holy Spirit will be a seer rather than a scholar. The difference is that the scholar sees and the seer sees through; and that is a mighty difference indeed.

A. W. Tozer,
in Harry Verploegh (comp.), *Signposts: A Collection of Sayings from A. W. Tozer*, Wheaton, Illinois: Victor Books, 1988, p. 102.

In the biblical cosmology, there is an invisible realm populated by demonic and angelic beings. The Bible says that Satan himself can appear as an angel of light. We live in a rationalistic age that both scoffs at the notion of the devil and is at the same time obsessed with the occult in popular culture. For people of faith, the best advice comes from British apologist G. K. Chesterton, who said we can make two mistakes about the devil: the first is to deny he exists, and the second is to pay any attention to him.

Kenneth Swanson,
Uncommon Prayer, New York: Ballantine, 1987, p. 179.

O God, forasmuch as without thee we are not able to please thee; mercifully grant that thy Holy Spirit may in all things direct and rule our hearts.

Book of Common Prayer, Collect for Nineteenth Sunday after Trinity, quoted in Margaret Pepper, *The Pan Dictionary of Religious Quotations*, London: Pan Books, 1989, p. 238.

Let us pray (in the Spirit who dwells within us). Father of light, from whom every good gift comes, send your Spirit into our lives with the power of a mighty wind, and by the flame of your wisdom open the horizons of our minds. Loosen our tongues to sing your praise in words beyond the power of speech, for without your Spirit we could never raise our voice in words of peace or announce the truth that Jesus is Lord, who lives and reigns with you and the Holy Spirit, one God, for ever and ever.

Daily Mass Book,
Brisbane: The Liturgical Commission, 1991, p. 209.

Father God, I need your life and your power. For too long I have been in control of my life. I have sinned against you, against others, and against myself. Thank you for forgiving my sins.

Please take control of my life. Fill me with your Holy Spirit, as you have promised — and done with so many others when they asked.

Thank you for fulfilling your promise in me. I accept your Spirit in all his fullness into my life, and will be sensitive to his will for me. I accept whatever gifts he brings, whatever truths he teaches, whatever directions he offers. May I live in the power of your Spirit, exult in the joy of your Spirit, pray with the words your Spirit suggests, and relate to others with his love. Amen.

A benediction
May the Holy Spirit indwell you to give you life in all its fullness, teach you the way of truth and holiness, empower you to serve and obey the living God, spread love within your being and from you to others, and lead you in the way everlasting. Through Jesus Christ our Lord. Amen.

J. I. Packer,
Keep in Step with the Spirit, Leicester: Inter-varsity Press, 1984, pp. 205-6.

Further reading
David Watson, *One in the Spirit*, London: Hodder and Stoughton, 1973, and *I Believe in the Church*, London: Hodder and Stoughton, 1978; C. Peter Wagner, *How to Have a Healing Ministry Without Making Your Church Sick*, Ventura: Regal Books, 1988, and *The Third Wave of the Holy Spirit*, Ann Arbor: Servant Publications, 1988; Rowland Croucher, 'Charismatic Renewal: Myths and Realities', *GRID*, World Vision of Australia (Box 399C Melbourne, Australia 3001).

Discuss
Write for the GRID article mentioned above, and discuss the twenty issues there.

10

Every Christian should be a good theologian

God chose what is foolish in the world to shame the wise; God chose what is weak in the world to shame the strong.

The gifts that he gave were that some should be... teachers, to equip the saints for the work of ministry, for building up the body of Christ, until all of us come to the unity of the faith and of the knowledge of the Son of God, to maturity... We must no longer be children, tossed to and fro and blown about by every wind of doctrine, by people's trickery, by their craftiness... But speaking the truth in love, we must grow up. Do not be children in your thinking; rather, be infants in evil, but in thinking be adults. Therefore let us go on... leaving behind the basic teaching about Christ, and not laying again the foundation... Do your best to present yourself to God as one approved by him, a worker who has no need to be ashamed, rightly explaining the work of truth.

I want their hearts to be united in love, so that they may have all the riches of assured understanding and have the knowledge of God's mystery, that is, Christ himself, in whom are hidden all the treasures of wisdom and knowledge. As you therefore have received Christ Jesus the Lord, continue to live your lives in him, rooted and built up in him and established in the faith, just as you were taught, abounding in thanksgiving. So if you have been raised with Christ, seek the things that are above, where Christ is, seated at the right hand of God. Set your minds on things that are above, not on things that are on earth.

Let the word of Christ dwell in you richly; teach and admonish one another in all wisdom; and with gratitude in your hearts sing psalms, hymns, and spiritual songs to God. And whatever you do, in word or deed, do everything in the name of the Lord Jesus, giving thanks to God the Father through him.

The sower sows the word. These are the ones on the path where the word is sown : when they hear, Satan immediately comes and takes away the word that is sown in them. And these are the ones sown on rocky ground: when they hear the word, they immediately receive it with joy. But they have no root, and endure only for a while; then, when trouble or persecution arises on account of the word, immediately they fall away. And others are those sown among the thorns: these are the ones who hear the word, but the cares of the world, and the lure of wealth, and the desire for other things come in and choke the word, and it yields nothing. And these are the ones sown on the good soil: they hear the word and accept it and bear fruit, thirty and sixty and a hundredfold.

O that my ways may be steadfast in keeping your statutes! Then I shall not be put to shame, having my eyes fixed on all your commandments. I will praise you with an upright heart, when I learn your righteous ordinances.

Blessed are you, O Lord; teach me your statutes. With my lips I declare all the ordinances of your mouth. I delight in the way of your decrees as much as in all riches. I will meditate on your precepts, and fix my eyes on your ways. I will delight in your statutes; I will not forget your word. Open my eyes, so that I may behold wondrous things out of your law. My soul is consumed with longing for your ordinances at all times. Make me understand the way of your precepts, and I will meditate on your wondrous works. Put false ways far from me; and graciously teach me your law. I run the way of your commandments, for you enlarge my understanding. Teach me, O Lord, the way of your statutes, and I will observe it to the end. Give me understanding, that I may keep your law and observe it with my whole heart. Lead me in the path of your commandments, for I delight in it. See, I have longed for your precepts; in your righteousness give me life. I shall walk at liberty, for I have sought your precepts. I revere your commandments, which I love, and I will meditate on your statutes. Teach me good judgment and knowledge, for I believe in your commandments. Your hands have made and fashioned me; give me understanding that I may learn your commandments. I will never forget your precepts, for by them you have given me life. Your word is a lamp to my feet and a light to my path. I incline my heart to perform your statutes forever, to the end. I am your servant; give me understanding, so that I may know your decrees. Your righteousness is an everlasting righteousness, and your law is the truth. Your decrees are righteous forever; give me understanding that I may live. My eyes are awake before each watch of the night, that I may meditate on your promise.

1 Corinthians 1:27; Ephesians 4:11-15; 1 Corinthians 14:20; Hebrews 6:1; 2 Timothy 2:15; Colossians 1:2-3; 2:6-7; 3:1-2, 16-17; Mark 4:14-20; Psalm 119:6-7, 12-16, 18, 20, 27, 29, 32-25, 40, 45, 48, 66, 73, 93, 105, 112,125,130, 135,142, 144,148.

You are about to do a 'crash course' in the subject Bible college and seminary curricula call theology. (If you have not read many books about Christianity, and a quick skim of this chapter turns you off, skip it and come back to it later.)

'Theology' comes from two Greek words — *theos*, God, and *logos*, word, thought. Theology is about God, and how God's will is to be done on earth as it is in heaven. 'Every Christian is called to be a theologian' (Karl Barth): it isn't a specialised, abstract discipline reserved for academics (Luke 10:21). Indeed the best theology doesn't come from 'top down' (from the dogma of 'authorities' Mark 1:22), but is done from bottom up: theology is about life.

Because God is beyond our finite understanding, our questions will always outnumber our answers, so we come to this task not as proud know-alls but as humble and teachable learners.

Everything we do, individually or as churches, has a theological dimension. Theology is about ultimate reality. Theology helps us to know who we are, to discover our identity. It aids our understanding of the church's and our denomination's roots, and to reflect on how the past relates to the issues we face today. Good theology also studies the faith stories of others, and helps us understand what God is doing in their histories.

Every church should be a miniature theological seminary (Elton Trueblood). It is amazing that church leaders may be highly skilled in their profession or trade, but still be in kindergarten theologically. As one layman said, 'We are better trained in our secular jobs than in the great ideas of our faith'. Pastors are the churches' resident 'professional theologians'. Their role as teachers is to make theologians of every Christian.

There is a lot of bad theology around, and bad theology can lead to bad behaviour — bigotry, greed, self-interest, sexual immorality, ignoring or rationalising injustices, etc. Here are eight tests of a 'good theology':

1. *Christological.* Good theology begins with 'The Lord our God, the Lord is One' (Deuteronomy 6:4) and quickly adds

'Jesus is Lord' (Romans 10:9, 1 Corinthians 12:3). Jesus is both fully divine and fully human. Western Christians have been more preoccupied with Christ's divinity: he is 'very God of very God'; third world theology with his humanity: God's solidarity with suffering 'nonpersons'. A good theology agrees with Jesus' emphases — particularly about love and justice.

2. *Biblical.* Scripture is the written record of what God has said and done (and is still saying and doing). So Bible study — alone and with others — is crucial if we are to find the will of God for our lives. Scripture is like a deep mine: and we've still only scratched the surface: 'the Lord has yet more truth' to be mined, if we dig with humility!

3. *Covenantal.* Theology is a community's response to God's grace. Covenants start with God (for example Genesis 6:18, Exodus 6:4-5) and his desire: 'I will be your God, and you shall be my people' (Genesis 17:7, 2 Corinthians 6:16-18, Revelation 21:2-3). The redeemed community celebrates the covenant in worship, and 'keeps' the covenant through loving obedience.

4. *Evangelical.* Theology is 'good news for the poor': the poor in spirit, who hunger and thirst for what is right (Matthew 5:3, 5); the hungry and oppressed poor, whom the Lord will feed and console (Luke 6:20-25). Jesus believed his theology was authentic because it was 'good news proclaimed to the poor' (Luke 7:22). When Paul had his version of the good news 'checked out' by the apostles in Jerusalem, they — and he — were concerned about 'remembering the poor' (Galatians 2:10).

5. *Confessional.* If your theology is worth anything, it is worth giving away! Every Christian is to be a witness (Luke 24:48; Acts 1:8), confessing what he or she has experienced of Christ, even though this may result in suffering or persecution (Matthew 10:38) — even martyrdom (Acts 22:20, Revelation 2:13, 17:6). 'A Christian is someone who's met one.' There is no such thing as secret discipleship: either secrecy kills the discipleship or discipleship kills the secrecy (Richard Glover).

6. *Contextual.* Good theology is done within the context of our real life in the world: we must develop a 'theology of everyday life'. In particular, it ought to be prophetic, offering a critique of social and political reality. For example there's the old question of theodicy: *Si Deus, unde malum?* If there is a God where does evil come from? Today, less abstractly, *Si malum, unde Deus?* If this be evil, where is God? Where is God, when fathers and mothers watch their children dying of malnutrition? When people are chained body and soul to unjust structures? When the water and air are polluted, the forests shrinking, the earth

ravaged? A good theology will save the church from identifying too closely with the surrounding social order. It cannot be a racial church, or a class church, or a male church, or a national church (Galatians 3:28; cf. also Romans 10:12, 1 Corinthians 12:13). And a good theology will also concern itself with the whole creation, fallen and yet-to-be-redeemed (Romans 8:19ff.) from the ravages of 'natural' and human exploitation.

7. *Empirical.* Good theology works in our experience! 'Is anything too hard for the Lord?' (Genesis 18:14) may be the key statement of the whole Bible. God who delivered his people 'with mighty deeds' from the distresses of sin, oppression, sickness, and sometimes even death (Psalm 103:1-7) is a God whose power is still the same today (Isaiah 50:2, 59:1).

More importantly, a good theology (or, better, the grace of God at work in our lives) produces more love, joy, peace — the 'fruit of the Spirit'. And when Jesus promised us his peace (John 14: 27) he was serious. Hence the importance of spiritual theology or spirituality, alongside systematic, moral and other theologies. Spiritual theology teaches us that 'everything is grace' (Karl Rahner). It helps open our eyes in childlike wonder and surprise to see all of life as 'gift'. Such theology helps us to be grateful (Ephesians 5:20) and 'graceful': it sees primarily the goodness of God in creation and the image of God in humankind, as well as our 'fallenness'. A theologian, said Evagrius Ponticus in the 4th century, 'is one whose prayer is true'. But good theology is more than 'mystical'; it is also reconciling, forgiving, peacemaking.

8. *Eschatological.* Eschatology (from the Greek *eschatos,* 'last') is the study of the 'last things'. The future belongs to God, not the Bomb or a disappearing ozonosphere. Good theology is hope-full: what God has done for people in the past (particularly when they cried out in their distress and God acted), God will continue to do! So even in our despair we trust 'the God of hope' (Romans 15:13) whose kingdom is surely coming. How are we redemptively involved in this process? Through loving justice, practising mercy, and living in a humble relationship with God, says Jesus (Matthew 23:23; cf. Micah 6:8).

Ultimately Christ is the unifying person and factor in all our thinking and reflecting and doing. He is the One who holds this fragmented, sin-scarred universe together and in whom everything will become united. Only this conviction will help us to be 'joyful in hope' and 'patient in trouble' (Romans 12:12) as all things 'fit into a pattern for good' (Romans 8:28) for those who love God.

101

Theology is the study of God and his ways. For all we know, dung beetles may study humans and their ways and call it humanology. If so, we would probably be more touched and amused than irritated. One hopes that God feels likewise.

Frederick Buechner,
Wishful Thinking, London: Collins, 1973, p. 91.

There are certain words that frighten people. 'Theology' is one of them. Some people regard theology as something extremely dry and remote from Christian living. Others regard the word with suspicion... This attitude arises very largely through ignorance of the simple meaning of theology... The term embraces the whole body of Christian doctrine and if we understand it this way we may be less frightened by theology...

There is therefore no need to be alarmed at theology: to understand it will make for intelligent Christian faith and living. At the heart of every doctrine of Holy Scripture we are brought to the very heart of God — the God who was in Christ reconciling the world to himself... This is the God who reveals himself in holy scripture, and this God is our God for ever and ever.

G. C. D. Howley,
'Christian Theology', *The Witness*, (Glasgow), September 1956, p. 183.

The supreme goal of theology: so to know about God that you know him, and so to know him that you reflect him.

Michael Green,
'The Theologian' in John Eddison (ed.), *'BASH': A Study in Spiritual Power*, Basingstoke, Hants UK: Marshalls, 1983, p. 93.

God is unconditional love and forgiveness. To me (this) belief is more than a theological proposition which one accepts in the mind. It is rather a basic assumption by which one lives and does one's work... We know so little about God apart from Jesus, the human face of God, in whom he has said all we need to know, while leaving many things ambiguous. Human existence is surrounded by mystery, often painful mystery, but out of the heart of it, God has spoken to his Son. I have come to believe profoundly in that unconditional love of God. There is nothing I can do to make him love me more; there is nothing I can do to make him love me less.

Tom Keyte,
The Chronicles of a 'Luckie Fellowe', Melbourne: self-published, 1991, pp. 161-2.

Jesus taught that we should love God with our minds, and the capacity to analyse statements, detect hidden presuppositions, and distinguish the primary from the secondary are all important intellectual benefits which theological study, when rightly approached, will yield. The modern student who is prepared to have his or her mind stretched while remaining faithfully humble before the Lord has nothing to fear from an academic study of the Bible. It will not inevitably confuse one's mind or cool one's love. (It is sometimes forgotten that Wesley felt his heart 'strangely warmed' after listening to an intellectual preface to a theological commentary on the most doctrinal of the New Testament epistles!). And on the positive side, one's preaching and teaching will increase in value as one's knowledge of Scripture deepens, because true theology is as inextricably bound up with proclamation as the gospel is involved in the total message of the Bible. It was not with any desire to belittle academic study that the theologian James Denney wrote: 'I have not the smallest interest in a theology that cannot be preached'.

David Field,
Approach to Theology, London: Inter-varsity Press, 1969, pp. 6-7.

God's Word alone is and should remain the only standard and rule, to which the writings of no one else should be regarded equal, but to it everything should be subordinated.

Martin Luther,
quoted in John Warwick Montgomery, 'Current Religious Thought', *Christianity Today*, 24 March 1978, p. 57.

While we deliberate, he reigns; when we decide wisely, he reigns; when we decide foolishly, he reigns; when we serve him in humble loyalty, he reigns; when we serve him self-assertively, he reigns; when we rebel and seek to withhold our service, he reigns — the Alpha and the Omega which is, and which was, and which is to come, the Almighty.

Archbishop William Temple,
quoted in a *Christianity Today* editorial, 27 September 1968, pp. 36-7.

If there were no God, there could be no such word as 'responsible'. No criminal need fear a judge who does not exist; nor would there be any need to worry about a law that had not been passed... There is someone to whom we are accountable; otherwise the concept of responsibility could have no meaning.

It is precisely because God is, and because we are made in his image and accountable to him, that theology is so critically important. Christian revelation alone has the answer to life's unanswered questions about God and human destiny...

As one not wholly unacquainted with Greek thought, I state it as my belief that but one of Isaiah's eloquent chapters, or David's inspired Psalms, contains more real help than all the output of the finest minds in Greece during the centuries of her glory...

The secret of life is theological, and the key to heaven as well.

We learn with difficulty, forget easily and suffer many distractions. Therefore we should set out hearts to study theology. We should preach it from our pulpits, sing it in our hymns, teach it to our children, and make it the subject of conversation when we meet with Christian friends.

A. W. Tozer,
'There is no Substitute for Theology', *The Life of Faith*, 6 April 1961, pp. 281-2.

There are three obvious functions that good theology can perform. First, it edifies the church, which is founded on, and lives by, the word of God... The function of theology is to keep the church's memory fresh and to rouse it from forgetfulness with respect to important features of God's revelation. Second, theology is summoned to preserve the truth, because the church is always in danger of losing it. In this world, where evil powers are abroad, the truth is never safe, and we are charged with guarding the gospel (2 Timothy 1:14). One thing that worried Paul was the possibility that Satan might deceive the church by his cunning and lead it astray from a pure devotion to Christ (2 Corinthians 11:13). We stand in constant danger of twisting or losing the truth of God. Third, theology is the art of communicating the gospel in all its richness... If we would just display the beauty of God and the gospel, and show it for what it is — the pearl of greatest price — hungry souls would be attracted to it. Biblical answers are relevant to contemporary questions; the work of theology is to show how they are.

Clark Pinnock,
'Why Do We Need Theology?' *Canadian Baptist*, June 1981, p. 44.

Imagine a line punctuated by five types of theology. At one end, the first type is simply the attempt to repeat a traditional theology or version of Christianity... At the other extreme, the fifth type gives complete priority to some modern secular philosophy or worldview, and Christianity in its own terms is only valid in so far as it fits in with that... Type two gives priority to the self-description of the Christian community... 'faith seeking understanding.' It insists that... Christianity itself continually needs to be rethought and that theology must engage seriously with the modern world in its quest for understanding... Type three comes exactly at the middle of the line. It is a theology of correlation. It brings traditional Christian faith and understanding into dialogue with modernity, and tries to correlate the two in a wide variety of ways... The fourth type uses a particular... modern philosophy... as a way of integrating Christianity with an understanding of modernity.

David Ford,
'Introduction to Modern Christian Theology' in David Ford (ed.), *The Modern Theologians: An Introduction to Christian theology in the twentieth century*, Oxford: Basil Blackwell, 1989, pp. 2-3.

Few current terms are less precise than 'theological pluralism'...
The term gains prestige from the fact that our society is
pluralistic. Should not Christian theology, then, grant 'equal
rights' to all shades of doctrinal opinion...?

One is reminded of the Indian who had to follow poorly
marked trails through the forest. He had to depend upon
marking a tree every hundred yards or so in order to return
home. An enemy who wished to cause him to get lost did not
obliterate the marks: he merely marked all the trees.

Harold B. Kuhn,
'The Liberal Charade', Christianity Today, 29 August 1975, p. 51.

The West has its own theological formulations derived from its
own cultural background... Yet in Asia the historical and cultural
background is quite different... and demands careful attention
from Asian Christians to their own cultures in order to make the
gospel relevant to their life situation.

Some of the issues we are facing today are communism,
poverty, overpopulation, hunger, suffering, war, demon
possession, bribery, cheating, idolatry, ancestor worship, caste
system, secularism, and the resurging Asian religions of
Buddhism, Islam and Hinduism. Asian theologians must...
produce an Asian theology that wrestles with these problems.

The task... is threefold: (to) search the Scriptures and provide
guidelines to the grass-root churches on key controversial issues
such as Christian responses to socio-political situations in
Asia... Secondly, (to) encourage the Asian church to adopt a
holistic approach to ministry by caring for the needs of society...
Thirdly, (to) emphasise that the priority of the church is
evangelism and mission in this vast continent which has only 3%
Christian population (but) 60% of the world's population.

Bong Rin Ro,
'Theological Trends in Asia', Themelios, Jan/Feb, 1988, p. 57.

Black theology... is a conscious attempt to do theology from
within the experience of black oppression. The very fact that it
calls itself 'black' shows that it is fully aware of starting from the
particular context of black experience... The theology that
comes from and serves the interests of white people, not
surprisingly, does not call itself white theology because it is not
conscious of its limited context.

Similarly the Latin American theology of liberation is a
conscious attempt to do theology in the revolutionary situation
of Latin America — dependence crying out for liberation. The
context... is the experience of poverty, powerlessness and
domination, of being totally dependent culturally, economically,
politically and psychologically upon the so-called developed
nations...

105

Feminist theology... is the experience of being a woman in a man's world; the experience of being oppressed as a woman... Other theologies are for the most part thoroughly masculine but they never say that. They naturally don't call their theology a male chauvinist theology.

Cultural theology — African theology would be a form of this (and) starts from the context of African culture...

Institute of Contextual Theology, *Whose Theology?*, Johannesburg, South Africa: Institute for Contextual Theology, 1985, pp. 5-6.

Anyone's first reaction to the 'good news' should be to find it bad news, because the condition of receiving the good news is change (what the Bible calls *metanoia*, 'conversion'). To be told that we need to change is to be told that we are presently unsatisfactory...

The source of our discomfort is not third world Christians trying to put us down. It is not they who are giving us a bad time; rather the Bible is giving us a bad time. They have not created a new biblical message to make us feel guilty; they are only calling attention to the old biblical message we have camouflaged for centuries in order not to feel guilty...

The great hope, surely, is that we can begin to be liberated from some of the false gods — the Bible calls them 'idols' — that have held us in captivity.

Robert McAfee Brown,
Unexpected News: Reading the Bible with Third World Eyes, Philadelphia: Westminster Press, 1984, pp. 157-60.

The choice... is not to retreat to a hermetically sealed 'pure' biblical theology that is relevant only when it confirms prior ideological commitments. Rather, the only responsible choice... is to forge a theology that is committed to seeking harmony between Scripture and present obedience.

Martyn Newman,
Liberation Theology is Evangelical, Clifton Hill, Victoria: Mallorn Press, 1990, p. 94.

I was trained in seminary to reflect on religion from the top down — from dogma and theology down to practical programs — and learned in Christ the King (parish church) to work with religion from the bottom up — from human problems and needs to religious responses...

I suspected (and would later prove) that it is the religion of daily experience and not the religion of propositional theology which has the greater impact on our behaviour.

(There is) a firm Catholic conviction that God reveals Himself/Herself through the whole of creation as well as through the official teachings of the tradition. Everything is grace, as Karl Rahner has put it. For some things to be a

'Sacrament' with a capital S all things must be a sacrament with a small s; for God to lurk in the official acts of the Church, S/He must also lurk in all the objects and events and persons of creation.

Andrew M. Greeley,
Confessions of a Parish Priest, New York: Pocket Books, 1987, pp. 245, 404.

A tall skyscraper could not stand against the wind unless it were built so that it could sway. An ocean liner, if it could not bend with the waves, would be broken by them. Flexibility is not the antithesis of structure, but the condition of preserving it in a changing world. Quite evidently, then, the Church... precisely because it has a mission to every time and culture, must be able to adapt its message and its structures. If dogma were inflexible it would be brittle; but because dogma has an inbuilt elasticity, it can and will survive.

Avery Dulles,
The Survival of Dogma: Faith, Authority and Dogma in a Changing World. Copyright © 1971 by Avery Dulles. Reprinted by permission of The Crossroad Publishing Company.

Philosopher Alfred North Whitehead perceptively stated that 'religions commit suicide when they find their inspiration in their dogmas'... All faith statements... involve a tension between mystery and meaning. Too often (we) subordinate mystery in search of meaning.

Carnegie Samuel Calian,
Today's Pastor in Tomorrow's World, Philadelphia: Westminster Press, 1982, p. 59.

I have known pert young ministers fresh from (theological) college bring forth new things in such a way as to cause the utmost distress to faithful Christians, who were living by the Word of God long before the minister was born. After all, we are not saved by knowing that Isaiah 53 was almost certainly not written by Isaiah; and it may well be that the deaf old granny in the front row knows more than you will ever understand of what it means that the Lord hath laid on him the iniquity of us all.

Stephen Neill,
On the Ministry, London: SCM Press, 1952, p. 86.

It behoves all of us to be accepting of others. Those whose thinking is rooted in 'simplicity this side of complexity' must not be too harsh with others who enjoy 'complexity the other side of simplicity'. Ideally, we are all moving towards 'simplicity the other side of complexity', but we need to be patient with one another on the way there... So our aim in wrestling with theological issues is to be both radical and conservative, in fellowship both evangelical and ecumenical, in attitudes espousing both truth and love, and in spirituality given both to reflection and action. We must develop a 'Christian mind' on the big issues of our day, but also learn to 'fold the wings of the intellect' and open our hearts to God as well...

Sometimes in our questioning we have lost the 'sure word of the Lord'. But sometimes, too, in our resistance to change we have not listened to the wind of the Spirit.

Rowland Croucher,
Recent Trends Among Evangelicals, Heathmont, Victoria: John Mark Ministries, 1991, pp. 40-1.

Lord God, what impertinence that we humans should create an academic subject called 'theology'. All of life is theology. There is no place where you are not present, nothing about which you are unconcerned. We know you a little because you have revealed a little of yourself to us, but you have infinitely more to teach us about yourself. Give us a hunger and a thirst to know more of you, and knowing more to love you more, and loving you more to obey you in this world (not some other world), and love the people you cause to cross our path (rather than merely loving humanity in the abstract).

Lord, please give me humility to realise that I know so very little; grace to listen to others, who have learnt other things about you; courage to relearn some things I learnt wrongly, or partially; conviction when I put what I learn into preaching, diligence when I put what I learn into practice.

God, we praise you: Father all-powerful, Christ Lord and Saviour, Spirit of love. You reveal yourself in the depths of our being, drawing us to share in your life and your love. One God, three Persons, be near to the people formed in your image, close to the world your love brings life.

Daily Mass Book,
Brisbane: The Liturgical Commission, 1991, p. 217.

A benediction
May God who is light illumine your way, May God who is truth enlighten your mind. May God who is love enrich your heart. May God who is grace fill you with his joy through Jesus Christ our Lord. Amen.

Further reading
(1) See article on David Tracy in Martin E. Marty & Dean G. Peerman (eds) *A Handbook of Christian Theologians*, 1984, pp 677ff. (2) James D. Smart, *The Rebirth of Ministry*, 1960, and *The Teaching Ministry of the Church*, 1964; Carnegie Samuel Calian, *Today's Pastor in Tomorrow's World*, 1982. (3) Article 'Hermeneutics' in *The New Dictionary of Theology*, IVP, 1988. (4) See E. J. Yarnold, 'Sacramental Theology' in Alan Richardson and John Bowden (eds) *A New Dictionary of Christian Theology*, SCM, 1983, p. 516. (5) J. Metz, *Theology of the World*, 1969. (6) J. Moltmann, *The Church in the Power of the Spirit*, 1977, p. 106. (7) Walter Brueggemann et al., *To Act Justly, Love Tenderly, Walk Humbly*, 1986. See also the booklets published by the Institute for Contextual Theology, Johannesburg, South Africa (available from A.C.R., 154 Elizabeth St, Sydney, 2000). Or, part 2 'Towards an Evangelical Theology of Social Justice' in Rowland Croucher, *Recent Trends Among Evangelicals*, John Mark Ministries, 1991. (8) David Steindl-Rast, *Gratefulness, the Heart of Prayer*, 1984. Rowland Croucher (ed.), *Still Waters, Deep Waters: Meditations and Prayers for Busy People*, Albatross/Lion, 1987 (9) Matthew Fox, *Original Blessing: Creation-centred Spirituality*, 1983; *Creation Spirituality*, 1991. (10) Kenneth Leech, *True Prayer: An Introduction to Christian Spirituality*, 1980. (11) J. Moltmann, *Theology of Hope*, 1967.

Strength for the journey

11

Understanding the Bible

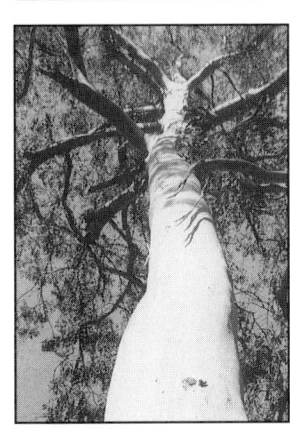

There was an Ethiopian (who) had come to Jerusalem to worship and was returning home; seated in his chariot, he was reading the prophet Isaiah. So Philip... asked, 'Do you understand what you are reading?'

Our beloved brother Paul wrote to you according to the wisdom given him... In his letters there are some things (that are) hard to understand, which the ignorant and unstable twist to their own destruction, as they do the other scriptures.

By faith we understand that the worlds were prepared by the word of God, so that what is seen was made from things that are not visible.

The Lord exists forever; your word is firmly fixed in heaven.

My word that goes out from my mouth shall not return to me empty, but it shall accomplish that which I purpose, and succeed in the thing for which I sent it.

The law is holy, and the commandment is holy and just and good... Your word is a lamp to my feet and a light to my path... You have known the sacred writings that are able to instruct you for salvation through faith in Christ Jesus. All scripture is inspired by God and is useful for teaching, for reproof, for correction, and for training in righteousness, so that everyone who belongs to God may be proficient, equipped for every good work.

Be strong and very courageous, being careful to act in accordance with all the law that my servant Moses commanded you; do not turn from it to the right hand or to the left, so that you may be successful wherever you go. This book of the law shall not depart out of your mouth; you shall meditate on it day and night, so that you may be careful to act in accordance with all that is written in it. For then you shall make your way prosperous, and then you shall be successful. Hold to the standard of sound teaching that you have heard from me, in the faith and love that are in Christ Jesus. Guard the good treasure entrusted to you, with the help of the Holy Spirit living in us.

Their delight is in the law of the Lord, and on his law they meditate day and night. They are like trees planted by streams of water, which yield their fruit in its season, and their leaves do not wither. In all that they do, they prosper... I treasure your word in my heart, so that I may not sin against you.

No prophecy of scripture is a matter of one's own interpretation, because no prophecy ever came of human will, but men and women moved by the Holy Spirit spoke from God. The Advocate, the Holy Spirit, whom the Father will send in my name, will remind you of all I have said to you... He will guide you into all the truth... and will declare to you things that are to come.

In Christ God was reconciling the world to himself, not counting their trespasses against them, and entrusting the message of reconciliation to us. You have heard of this hope before in the word of the truth, the gospel that has come to you. To us the message of this salvation has been sent. Let the word of Christ dwell in you richly; teach and admonish one another in all wisdom. Pursue righteousness, godliness, faith, love, endurance, gentleness. Fight the good fight of the faith; take hold of the eternal life, to which you were called and for which you made the good confession in the presence of many witnesses. Keep the commandment without spot or blame until the manifestation of our Lord Jesus Christ.

Finally, beloved, whatever is true, whatever is honorable, whatever is just, whatever is pure, whatever is pleasing, whatever is commendable, if there is any excellence and if there is anything worthy of praise, think about these things. Keep on doing the things that you have learned and received and heard and seen in me, and the God of peace will be with you.

Acts 8:27-30; 2 Peter 3:16; Hebrews 11:3; Psalm 119:90; Isaiah 55:11; Romans 7:12; Psalm 119:105; 2 Timothy 3:15-17; Joshua 1:7-8; 2 Timothy 1:13-14; Psalm 1:3-4; Psalm 119:11; 2 Peter 1:21; John 14:26; John 16:13; 2 Corinthians 5:19; Colossians 1:6; Acts 13:26; Colossians 3:16; 1 Timothy 6:11-12, 14; Philippians 4:8-9.

The most important thing about being a Christian is your friendship with Jesus Christ. In any friendship you talk and listen to one another. God speaks to us in many ways: primarily through the life and ministry of his living Word, Jesus Christ, and secondarily through his written word in the Scriptures. So one of the most important keys to spiritual growth is a regular diet of Bible!

The Bible is the authoritative guide for all we believe and do: for faith and practice. It is the inspired and trustworthy record of the mighty acts and teachings of God in the history of his people Israel, and fulfilled in the life, teachings and saving work of Jesus Christ.

The Bible is actually a library of sixty-six books. The Old Testament has thirty-nine books, written and collected over more than a thousand years. This was the 'Bible' for the early Christians. The New Testament, written after Jesus' life and teaching, comprises twenty-seven books, written between about AD 50 and 100 about the life and teaching of Jesus. During the first three centuries these books came to be used alongside the Old Testament. Some books of the Bible are mainly poetry, others history, others comprise ancient laws, others what we would call sermons. Each book reflects the personality and emphases of its author/s: there is a wonderful unity-in-diversity about the library we call the Bible!

Many try to read the Bible from Genesis, but they soon get bogged down somewhere in Leviticus. The best place to start reading the Bible is the beginning of the New Testament. The ministry and teaching of Jesus is the key to the whole Bible, so get to know him first! Perhaps read through to the end of Romans, then go back to the Old Testament and read Genesis, then perhaps the first twenty-four Psalms, then stories like Ruth, Esther, Jonah. Then maybe you could study Ephesians, James, 1 Peter; then go back to Deuteronomy. After that, finish the rest of the New Testament.

Get an easy-to-read, modern translation, like the *New Revised Standard Version* (which uses non-sexist language) or the *Good News Bible*. Buy a couple of books to help you understand the Bible's background. Ask your pastor about a good one-volume Bible introduction (like the *Lion Handbook to the Bible*) commentary (for example *Harper's Bible Commentary*), dictionary (like the IVP *New Dictionary of Theology*). Ask someone in Scripture Union for the best daily Bible reading notes for your background and age. Or begin with a more serious devotional book like *Still Waters Deep Waters* (Albatross, edited by Rowland Croucher).

But once we begin to read the Bible, all sorts of questions will arise. In the film *Ghandi*, the Indian was walking down a narrow street with a young clergyman. About to be accosted by some white youths, the clergyman was in favour of turning back. 'I thought your Bible said that if you were struck on one cheek, you should turn the other cheek', said Ghandi. 'I always took that rather figuratively', replied the clergyman. 'I think Jesus may well have meant it literally', said Ghandi...

Hermeneutics is about understanding and interpreting the Bible. This isn't always easy, as your Bible was translated from languages which you probably don't speak at home! It is difficult sometimes to get an exact parallel of thought from one language to another. (A missionary Bible translator in Northern Australia wanted to teach Aborigines the song 'Jesus loves me'. To get the word for 'me' he pantomimed, pointing repeatedly to himself. Much later he learned that they had all been singing 'Jesus loves the hairs on my chest'!).

Interpreting the Bible isn't easy for another reason: some of our modern questions (for example about abortion or genetic engineering or the morality of contraception or nuclear pacifism) aren't addressed specifically in the Bible. But the broad principles which can guide us in making individual choices in these complex areas are all there.

The rich and the poor read from the same Bible, but read it differently. We all bring our cultural and ideological biases to Scripture. Poor Latin Americans find the Exodus story full of meaning and promise: oppressors misuse their power against the poor, God is concerned about it and rescues the powerless. I once preached from the Bible about social justice to a conference of Australian Aborigines. Those with dark skins said it was wonderful. The missionaries said it was dangerous... Blacks in South Africa see the God of the Bible as a friend in their distress; hard-line Afrikaaners justify apartheid from the same Bible.

How can we be more sure of understanding the Bible better? Here are five guidelines: (1) Pray: ask the Spirit of God who inspired these human authors to guide you to understand what they wrote. (2) Ask: What did these words originally mean? The Bible was written in Hebrew or Aramaic (most of the Old Testament) and Greek (New Testament). Those languages, like most others, were rich in figures of speech, especially similes (for example 'white as snow', 'death-like silence'), and metaphors (I will build my church, Joseph is a fruitful bough). (3) Note the type of literature: prose or poetry; prophecy ('the Lord says') or apocalyptic (prophetic visions/preaching especially in the midst of cataclysmic events, for example the visions of Daniel or Revelation); parables (stories which teach one main truth) or allegories (where every detail has some significance); principle (for example plucking out your eye or cutting off your hand, Matthew 5:28, 30; or forgiving 'seventy seven times', Matthew 18:22: what's Jesus really saying?) or precept. (4) Study each text or sentence within its context: who is speaking? to whom is it addressed? what is the main theme of the whole book or passage? what is the cultural/ geographical/ historical background? (5) Let scripture interpret scripture: if something is obscure, ask: how does this idea square with the teachings of Jesus and of the whole Bible?

When you preach or teach from the Bible, there are usually three elements involved: *exegesis* (what does this part of Scripture actually say? What would it have meant to the original writer or hearer?), *exposition* (what does it mean now?) and *application* (how does it apply to our lives here, today?).

Finally three important principles: (1) When you read the phrase 'the Word of God' in the Bible it means much more than printed words on a page. The Word of God is his life-giving and powerful communication with his creatures in all sorts of ways — ultimately in the person of Jesus, the living Word of God. (2) Don't believe anything about the Bible which the Bible doesn't assert about itself. For example, if you want to believe that the original documents (before scribes started copying them and making mistakes) were without error, that's fine, but don't make a doctrine out of it, because the Bible itself doesn't spell it out in those terms. That said, you can be sure that the modern Bibles are trustworthy: the documents translators use are thoroughly checked. (3) Most importantly, if you want to understand what Christ and the Scriptures are really saying, you must want to obey him and them (John 7:17).

The scribes tended to speak in footnotes. When Jesus spoke, he spoke as if his words need no authority other than that he said them... (he claims) the sovereign right to interpret and to restate the Law, without reference to anyone else's verdict or opinion... Jesus did not only speak in 'the style of deity'; he claimed to be the unique revelation of God... In Jesus there is fully displayed the mind of God.

William Barclay,
By What Authority?, London: Darton, Longman and Todd, 1974, pp. 7, 8, 102, 107.

In Scripture, the Lord represents himself in the same character in which... he is delineated in his works... In every part of Scripture we meet with descriptions of his paternal kindness and readiness to do good, and we also meet with examples of severity which show that he is the just punisher of the wicked... We must diligently heed both to the reading and hearing of Scripture, if we would obtain any benefit from the Spirit of God.

John Calvin,
Institutes of the Christian Religion, translated by Henry Beveridge, London: James Clarke & Co., 1957, pp. 87, 85.

The interpretation of Scripture must be within the Church (2
Peter 1:20, 21; 3:16)... The individual is not on one's own, (he or
she) is within the Church. There is a real sense in which it is true
that one cannot have God to be one's father unless one has the
church to be one's mother.

William Barclay,
By What Authority? London: Darton, Longman and Todd, 1974, p. 121.

Of the three classical canons of authority — reason, tradition
and scripture — evangelicals have always affirmed that
scripture is 'God's word in human words' and therefore is always
our primary and supreme authority for all matters of faith and
conduct. Although reason and tradition may have been
illumined and guided by the Holy Spirit, they have a secondary
and subordinate place to scripture. Why? Because this was
Christ's view of scripture. John Stott puts it simply: 'The
conservative view of scripture... is Christ's view of scripture. He
endorsed the Old Testament, made provision for the New
Testament, and because of Christ we accept the authority of the
book.

Rowland Croucher,
Recent Trends Among Evangelicals, Melbourne: John Mark Ministries, 1991, p. 16.

A story is told about a Rabbi who once entered heaven in a
dream. He was permitted to approach the temple of Paradise
where the great sages of the Talmud, the Tannaim, were
spending their eternal lives. He saw that they were just sitting
around tables studying the Talmud. The disappointed Rabbi
wondered, 'Is this all there is to Paradise?' But suddenly he
heard a voice, 'You are mistaken. The Tannaim are not in
Paradise. Paradise is in the Tannaim'.

Abraham Heschel,
'The Sigh' in John Garvey (ed.), *Modern Spirituality, An Anthology*, London: Darton, Longman and Todd,
1985, p. 12.

Our understanding of the function of Scripture must be carried
out in the light of the particular situation in which we find
ourselves. The word of God enters this situation through
preaching or private reading. There we meet a God who has
entered into a unique relationship with a particular people at a
special time, a people who are in many ways like those I know.

William A. Dyrness,
'How Does the Bible Function in the Christian Life' in Robert K. Johnston, (ed.), *The Use of the Bible in
Theology: Evangelical Options*, Atlanta: John Knox Press, 1985, p. 168.

I (cannot) ignore the influence of culture upon me as an
interpreter. Obviously we are influenced by our place in history
in a thousand respects. Yet this is the reason we must not
succumb to it but must instead take measures to ensure that

bias does not overcome God's truth. Precisely because we tend to be prejudiced (what people politely call 'having pre-understanding') we have to be self-critical and take action against the danger of Scripture-twisting. There is a hermeneutical circle, but it need not be a vicious one. What we need to do is to strive for such interpretation of the Bible which anyone reading the text can see even if he or she does not come with the opinions we hold ourselves. Perfect objectivity is not something we can achieve, but it is an ideal we can strive for by consciously opening ourselves to criticism and correction both by God, speaking through the text, and by the convictions of others.

Clark Pinnock,
'How I Use the Bible in Doing Theology' in Robert K. Johnston, (ed.), *The Use of the Bible in Theology: Evangelical Options*, Atlanta: John Knox Press, 1985, p. 30.

(I have) five convictions. (1) By entering into the expressed mind of the inspired writers I do in fact apprehend God's own mind. What Scripture says, God says... (2) Since all sixty-six books come ultimately from the mind of our self-revealing God, they should be read not just as separate items... but also as parts of a whole. They must be appreciated not only in their particular individuality of genre and style, but also as a coherent, internally connected organism of teaching. (There is a) truly amazing unity of viewpoint, doctrine and vision (in) this heterogeneous library of occasional writings. (3) Biblical teaching, like the law of the land, must be applied to the living of our lives... Interpretation has to be imperative, self-involving, and thus (to use an abused word) existential in style. (Our) ears must always be open to what Bultmannites call decision, what most Anglo-Saxons call commitment, and what the Bible itself calls repentance, faith, worship, obedience, and endurance. (4) (We must read Scripture) as God's witness to his saving grace in Christ and God's call to sinners to believe and respond. (5) I must be ready to give account of my interpretative encounters with Scripture not just to my human and academic peers but to God himself.

James I. Packer,
'In Quest of Canonical Interpretation' in Robert K. Johnston, (ed.), *The Use of the Bible in Theology: Evangelical Options*, Atlanta: John Knox Press, 1985, pp. 43-4.

Now if I doubt poor Adam's rib,
Or hint that Samson told a fib,
Or if I question Noah's ride,
Or ask how Jonah lived inside,
I'm answered rather bitterly
That I must take it literally.
But if I quote what Christ did say
About giving one fine coat away

Or turning round the other cheek
Or that this earth is for the meek,
I'm also answered bitterly
I must not take it literally.

Source unknown

The Bible is so rich and diverse a religious document that you can find support for almost any position if you ignore the context or isolate certain parts of it to the exclusion of all the rest. Even the atheist can point to the words 'There is no God,' in Psalm 14:1. Of course the whole verse reads 'Fools say in their hearts, "There is no God,"' but if you take a 'Yellow Pages' approach to Scripture, almost anything can be supported.

John Claypool,
'The Secret is Collaboration', unpublished sermon preached on 11 March 1979.

In religion,
What damned error but some sober brow
Will bless it and approve it with a text,
Hiding the grossness with fair ornament?

William Shakespeare,
The Merchant of Venice, Act 3, Scene 2.

'How the Bible uses me when I do theology' (is a title that) would have meshed directly with my experience of the Bible during the forty years since my conversion. How often in modern contexts has my heart echoed the protest of John Rogers, the Reformation martyr, against the alleged inertness of the biblical text: 'No, no, the Bible is alive!'

James I. Packer,
'In Quest of Canonical Interpretation' in Robert K. Johnston, (ed.), *The Use of the Bible in Theology: Evangelical Options*, Atlanta: John Knox Press, 1985, p. 37.

Jesus taught mostly through stories (Matthew 13:35)... Religion finds its origin and its raw power in the imaginative dimension of the personality. In religion, experience, image (symbol or metaphor, if you will) and story precede propositional and theological reflection. Why then do we not more often use story... to transmit our religious heritage? Why not more religious novels, films, TV series?

Andrew M. Greeley,
Confessions of a Parish Priest, New York: Simon & Schuster, 1987, p. 80.

As a translator... I was dealing with material which was startlingly alive, and I could not really be overmuch bothered whether Matthew 'borrowed' part of his Gospel story from Mark, or whether he and Mark shared a common source of written or spoken information which the critics call 'Q'. I know it is a shock to us today, and perhaps especially if we are professional writers and conscious of the laws of copyright, but it was not in the least strange in the first century A.D. to say that a gospel was 'according to Matthew', even though it might contain sentences which were not written by Matthew at all... What seems to have happened, and in this I think all Christian scholars agree, is that the first three evangelists wrote down what had previously been an oral tradition...

I doubt very much whether any of (the New Testament writers of the epistles) had any idea he was writing 'Holy Scripture'. For the most part, it was 'ad hoc' writing: a particular situation, or even the behaviour of a particular person or group, called for the writing of the letter...

The Spirit of truth does not contradict himself... our eyes are opened and we see how much more deeply relevant (the faith of the New Testament) is to our modern days than we thought. So we do not gain but lose if we dismiss what was written by the inspiration of the same Spirit as folk-tale or myth. He will certainly lead us into all truth... (and we must not) attempt to modify the wisdom of God to fit the cleverness of the twentieth century...

In translating the Greek of the New Testament into modern English, I made every effort to correct any bias of which I was conscious. When I came to compare it with the writings which were excluded from the New Testament by the early 'Fathers', I can only admire their wisdom.

J. B. Phillips,
Ring of Truth: A Translator's Testimony, London: Hodder and Stoughton, 1967, pp. 59-60, 29, 93, 95.

...Jesus Christ, whom the Testaments regard, the old as its hope, the new as its model, and both as their centre.

Blaise Pascal,
Pensées, No. 739, quoted in Elton Trueblood, *A Place to Stand*, New York: Harper & Row, 1969, p. 42.

Thank you, Lord, for the treasury of truth you have preserved for us in your Holy Word. Without its light we would stumble in the darkness; without its guidance we would lose our way; without its commands we would live carelessly; without its central focus on Jesus we would be led into all kinds of error.

Help me — in fellowship with others who are similarly seeking you — to understand your truth, your guidance, your commands.

May I be disciplined in reading these sacred pages every day. Help me to find a few others to study the Bible with me. Bless organisations like the Bible Societies, Scripture Union, and *Wycliffe Bible Translators who are doing their best to get the Bible into the hands of as many as possible.*

A benediction
May the Word of the creative God in nature enrich you with its beauty and power; may the convicting Word of the Lord in your conscience guide you in his way; may God's Word through history help you put your faith in One who is the same yesterday today and forever; may the ministry of Jesus through others sustain and comfort you; may God's Word in the Scriptures enlighten your mind and strengthen your will to obey him in all things; above all, may your commitment to God's living Word, Jesus Christ, lead you into eternal life. Amen.

Further reading
Robert McAfee Brown, *Unexpected News: Reading the Bible with Third World Eyes*, Philadelphia: Westminster Press, 1984.

12
Prayer: friendship with God

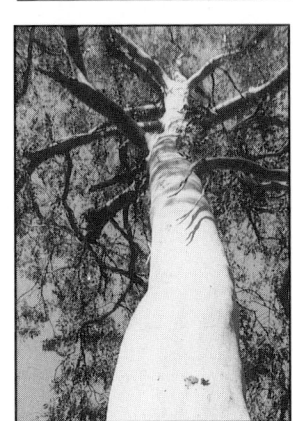

Be still, and know that I am God!

Wait for the Lord; be strong, and let your heart take courage; wait for the Lord! For God alone my soul waits in silence, for my hope is from him...

He was praying in a certain place, and after he had finished, one of his disciples said to him, 'Lord, teach us to pray, as John taught his disciples'. He said to them, 'When you pray, say: Father, hallowed be your name. Your kingdom come. Give us each day our daily bread. And forgive us our sins, for we ourselves forgive everyone indebted to us. And do not bring us to the time of trial'.

Whenever you pray, go into your room and shut the door and pray to your Father who is in secret; and your Father who sees in secret will reward you.

Then when you call upon me and come and pray to me, I will hear you. Call to me and I will answer you, and will tell you great and hidden things that you have not known.

He makes me lie down in green pastures; he leads me beside still waters; he restores my soul. He leads me in right paths for his name's sake.

Before they call I will answer, while they are yet speaking I will hear. When the righteous cry for help, the Lord hears, and rescues them from all their troubles.

Do not worry about anything, but in everything by prayer and supplication with thanksgiving let your requests be made known to God. Devote yourselves to prayer, keeping alert in it with thanksgiving. Pray in the Spirit at all times in every prayer and supplication. To that end keep alert and always persevere in supplication for all the saints.

Pray without ceasing.

Again, truly I tell you, if two of you agree on earth about anything you ask, it will be done for you by my Father in heaven. For where two or three are gathered in my name, I am there among them.

Psalm 46:10; Psalm 27:14; Psalm 62:5; Luke 11:1-4; Matthew 6:6; Jeremiah 29:12; Jeremiah 33:3; Psalm 23:2-3; Isaiah 65:24; Psalm 34:17; Philippians 4:6; Colossians 4:2; Ephesians 6:18; 1 Thessalonians 5:17; Matthew 18:19-20.

How we pray is who we are. Prayer is friendship with God. Our prayer is the best measure of the integrity of our Christian life. Jacques Ellul gives us the clue in a powerful chapter he calls 'The Only Reason for Praying' in his *Prayer and Modern Man*. According to the Bible, he says, the only reason to pray is that God commands us to pray. The biblical prayers are often very direct and frank (for example 2 Kings 19:15-19, 2 Samuel 7:18-29). Sometimes there is a sense of the awesome majesty and power of God (Isaiah 6:5, Job 42:1-6). Others are mystical (Ezekiel 1:4-28); many of the Psalms are lamentations — cries to God 'from the depths' to be healed, to be set free, to be saved. Some biblical prayers are very brief — even one word ('*maranatha*', 'our Lord, come', which is the oldest Christian prayer — 1 Corinthians 16:22, see also Revelation 22:20). The prayers of the Bible often arise out of crisis and conflict, leading us to faith, hope and confidence in God.

Prayer covers all the events of our lives, so there are many different ways to pray. Sometimes we are still, knowing within the depths of our being that he is God. At other times, we have to work hard at prayer: it 'is not a gentle pastime', as the Dutch Roman Catholic catechism puts it. The masters of prayer teach us:

• Pray as you can, not as you can't. There is no 'instant' holiness. Prayer is hard work. It is the work of a lifetime — the longest journey is the journey inward — but we begin afresh every morning. You are unique, so your relationship with God will be unique, and therefore your prayer will be unique.

• Ask yourself: 'What is my desire?' (Mark 11:24). What do you want? Do you want God to take possession of you? Prayer is, essentially, the soul's sincere desire... Prayer is an acknowledgment of our willingness to be changed, our readiness to be surprised.

Jesus taught two parables about prayer, one about a sleepy

neighbour and another about an unjust judge (Luke 11:5-13; 18:1-8). The main point he made was about the importance of earnest desire in prayer. We ought always to pray, and never to faint, or give up. Someone has said that when we faint we fall back on nothing, but when we pray we fall forward on God. And yet even if your desire is only tentative and flickering, our Lord never 'snuffs out the smouldering wick' (Matthew 12:20). Write down what you are really after in your life.

● Prayer is a gift. Like love, it is a gift experienced every day, fresh from one who loves us. Prayer is not a bag of spiritual techniques. Paul says God gives us the Holy Spirit to help us (Romans 8:26-27). The Spirit prays in us, for us, through us, and with us. Prayer is not just what we do, but what God wants to do through us. So prayer is not merely seeking God. Rather, it is allowing him to find us.

● The main aim of prayer: to know God, through love. Knowing God — or anyone else — is much more than knowing about him. In her beautiful book Poustinia, Catherine de Hueck Doherty talks about 'folding the wings of the intellect and opening the door of the heart' in God's presence. This is 'affective knowledge', a knowing that leads to loving and responds to our being loved.

●There are three kinds of prayer: spoken (adoration, confession, thanksgiving, supplication, intercession), contemplative ('thinking of God with love' as Charles de Foucauld expressed it), and meditative, reflecting on Scripture or life's events in God's presence. Bonhoeffer advocated half an hour's silent meditation on Scripture every morning. This was not 'Bible study' as such, but the discipline of being 'under the Word'.

As our prayer deepens, many of the saints tell us, we find ourselves needing fewer words.

● Find a quiet, regular place and time each day for prayer. If possible, guarantee that you will be unhurried and uninter-rupted. Your 'quiet time' may sometimes be short — but a short time with a friend is better than no time at all.

For many it's difficult to find silence in our noisy world, or solitude in our crowded cities. But you must keep trying. Turn a corner of your house into an 'oratory'. Pull off the road under some trees. Walk along a deserted beach. Put in a telephone answering machine. Your quest, as Carlo Carretto suggests, is to make your own desert. Remember, if you are too busy to pray, you are too busy.

● Prayer is also living and working. All of our life, our thoughts, our words, our actions, our motives, are lived in the presence of

125

our God. Père de Caussade talked inspiringly of 'the sacrament of the present moment'.

Sometimes, however, our work negates our prayer. Remember how Isaiah expressed the Lord's message: 'When you lift your hands in prayer, I will hide my eyes from you. Though you offer countless prayers, I will not listen... Pursue justice and champion the oppressed' (Isaiah 1:15-17).

Prayer is not an escape from reality. In prayer we 'love the world' as God does — the world of people. He or she who is not listening to the heart-cry of another, is not listening to God either — and God is not listening to them.

So be encouraged! Prayer is hard — but so is everything else in this life that is worthwhile. There is no short cut to true spirituality.

But prayer is essentially a simple process — even a child-like one. We come empty-handed to our heavenly Father, humble, and poor. And, over time, we gradually discover that God inhabits more and more the centre of our lives, as Augustine put it, 'more intimate to us than we are to ourselves'.

● Prayer is a corporate activity. The apostolic Christians prayed together from the start. The Holy Spirit was poured out on a group at prayer (Acts 1:14). They continued to spend a lot of time in prayer together (Acts 2:42). Paul prayed constantly with his co-missioners (Colossians 1:9; 1 Thessalonians 1:2; 2 Thessalonians 1:11) and asked others to join him in disciplined prayer (Romans 15:30). James (5:16) tells us to 'confess your sins to one another and pray for one another, so that you will be healed'.

Praying together is one of the richest experiences Christians can have with each other.

Sometimes prayer meetings are large; they are church-wide. These can be powerful occasions, but only where there is a strong sense of community. In Western nations such intimate 'belongingness' on a larger scale is quite rare, so there has been a worldwide movement towards smaller prayer-groups. This is good. Such 'growth groups', 'prayer cells' — call them what you will — should do three things: Scripture reading, meditation and study; sharing of our personal concerns with one another; then prayer. That is, we listen to God, listen to each other, then speak to God the things have arisen in the other two encounters. The 'mix' of Bible, sharing and prayer will vary from group to group, and from time to time in one group. What is important is that all three occur in all groups all the time.

Finally, a modern paraphrase of some advice from Julian of Norwich: Pray inwardly, even if you do not enjoy it. It does good even though you think you are doing nothing. For when you are dry, empty, sick, or weak, at such a time your prayer is most pleasing to God, though you find little enough to enjoy in it.

Sometimes prayer is simple. Sometimes it seems impossible. Sometimes the life of prayer is fulfilling and refreshing. Other times it's dry and lifeless.

Paul Wallis,
Rough Ways in Prayer, London: Triangle SPCK, 1991, p. xi.

The most important discovery of my life of prayer... Do you want to know what it is? That prayer takes place in the heart, not in the head.

Carlo Carretto,
The Desert in the City, London: Fount Paperbacks, 1983, p. 23.

The primary reason not to pray has to do with control. There is a strong need inside every human being to be in control. People who have an extreme desire to control their environment try to think through an adequate response to every possible contingency that might arise from any given situation. They want no surprises and are often successful in achieving their goals. People like this are not likely to entrust their well-being to another person, because that means giving up control. Consequently, these people are very unlikely to pray. Genuine prayer flows out of an acknowledgement of inability and finitude. Genuine prayer means giving up control of our destiny to God...

I need to pray, yes, and not just because I so often feel inadequate and am looking for help. I need to pray because I know the emptiness inside of me can only be filled by God. I need to pray because I know that it is only in prayer that I begin to become fully human. I need to pray because I was created to be in relationship with God. I need to pray because in prayer heaven and earth meet, and the reality of God's Kingdom, the future reality of redemption, wholeness, and joyous love, breaks into my present brokenness.

Kenneth Swanson,
Uncommon Prayer, New York: Ballantine, 1987, pp. 42, 85.

The Bible pray-ers prayed as if their prayers could and would make an objective difference. The apostle Paul gladly announced that we are 'co-labourers with God' (1 Corinthians 3:9); that is, we are working with God to determine the outcome of events...

Moses was bold to pray because he believed he could change things, even God's mind. In fact, the Bible stresses so forcefully the openness of our universe that, in an anthropomorphism hard for modern ears, it speaks of God constantly changing his mind in accord with his unchanging love (Exodus 32:14, Jonah 3:10).

Richard Foster,
Celebration of Discipline, Sevenoaks: Hodder & Stoughton, 1980, p. 32.

Whatever else it may or may not be, prayer is at least talking to yourself, and that's in itself not always a bad idea.

Talk to yourself about your life, about what you've done and what you've failed to do and about who you are and who you wish you were and who the people you love are and the people you don't love too. Talk to yourself about what matters most to you, because if you don't, you may forget what matters most to you.

Even if you don't believe anybody's listening, at least you'll be listening.

Believe Somebody is listening.

Frederick Buechner,
Wishful Thinking, London: Collins, 1973, p. 71.

We want to know not how we should pray if we were perfect, but how we should pray being as we now are... It is no use to ask God with factitious earnestness for A when our whole mind is in reality filled with the desire for B. We must lay before him what is in us, not what ought to be in us.

C. S. Lewis,
'Prayer' in John Garvey (ed.), *Modern Spirituality: an Anthology*, London: Darton, Longman and Todd,
1985, p. 86.

The head is not a very good place for prayer. It is not a bad place for starting your prayer. But if your prayer stays there too long and doesn't move into the heart it will gradually dry up and prove tiresome and frustrating. You must learn to move out of the area of thinking and talking and move into the area of feeling, sensing, loving, intuiting. That is the area where contemplation is born and prayer becomes a transforming power and a source of never-ending delight and peace.

Has it ever occurred to you that Jesus, that master in the art of prayer, would take the trouble to walk up a hill in order to pray? Like all great contemplatives he was aware that the place in which we pray has an influence on the quality of our prayer.

Anthony de Mello,
Sadhana, pp. 13, 24, quoted in Margaret Hebblethwaite, *Finding God in All Things*, London: Fountain
Paperbacks, 1987, pp. 60, 223.

Sir Thomas Browne solemnly pledged himself, whenever in any quiet place, to give himself to prayer. He never passed a church of any denomination without lifting up his heart on behalf of the minister and people who worshipped there. He never left the home of a patient without a silent petition for the sufferer and for all sufferers everywhere. When he met handsome men and comely women, he prayed that their souls might be made as beautiful as their bodies. And when he met deformed or unsightly people, he prayed that their outward ugliness might be compensated by inner graces.

F. W. Boreham,
The Tide Comes In, London: Epworth Press, 1958, p. 19.

Is not listening to the pulse of wonder worth silence and abstinence from self assertion? Why do we not set apart an hour of living for devotion to God by surrendering to stillness?

About a hundred years ago, Rabbi Isaac Meir Alter of Ger pondered over the question of what a certain shoemaker of his acquaintance should do about his morning prayer. His customers were poor people who owned only one pair of shoes. The shoemaker used to pick up their shoes at a late evening hour, work on them all night and part of the morning, in order to deliver them before their owners had to go to work. When should the shoemaker say his morning prayer? Should he pray quickly the first thing in the morning, and then go back to work? Or should he let the appointed hour of prayer go by and, every once in a while, raising his hammer from the shoes, utter a sigh: 'Woe unto me, I haven't prayed yet!'? Perhaps that sigh is worth more than the prayer itself.

We too, face this dilemma of wholehearted regret or perfunctory fulfilment. Many of us regretfully refrain from habitual prayer, waiting for an urge that is complete, sudden and unexampled. But the unexampled is scarce, and perpetual refraining can easily grow into a habit. We may even come to forget what to regret, what to miss...

We do not refuse to pray. We merely feel that our tongues are tied, our minds inert, our inner vision dim, when we are about to enter the door that leads to prayer. We do not refuse to pray; we abstain from it. We ring the hollow bell of selfishness rather than absorb the stillness that surrounds the world, hovering over all the restlessness and fear of life — the secret stillness that precedes our birth and succeeds our death...

We do not step out of the world when we pray; we merely see the world in a different setting...

Prayer is the way to master what is inferior in us, to discern between the signal and the trivial, between the vital and the futile, by taking counsel with what we know about the will of God, by seeing our fate in proportion to God.

Prayer is no panacea, no substitute for action. It is, rather, like a beam thrown from a flashlight before us into the darkness.

The idea of prayer is based upon the assumption of (our) ability to accost God, to lay our hopes, sorrows and wishes before him...
Prayer is not a soliloquy. But is it a dialogue with God? Do (we) address him as person to person? It is incorrect to describe prayer by analogy with human conversation; we do not communicate with God. We only make ourselves communicable to him. Prayer is an emanation of what is most precious in us toward him, the outpouring of the heart before him. It is not a relationship between person and person, between subject and subject, but an endeavour to become the object of his thought.

Abraham Heschel,
in John Garvey (ed.), *Modern Spirituality: an Anthology*, London: Darton, Longman and Todd, 1985,
pp. viii, 8, 9, 11, 13.

Meditation is an activity of thought, while prayer is the rejection of every thought. According to the teaching of the eastern Fathers, even pious thoughts and deepest and loftiest theological considerations, if they occur during prayer, must be considered as temptation and suppressed; because, as the Fathers say, it is foolish to think about God and forget that you are in his presence. All the spiritual guides of Orthodoxy warn us against replacing this meeting with God by thinking about him. Prayer is essentially standing face to face with God, consciously striving to remain collected and absolutely still and attentive in his presence, which means standing with an undivided mind, an undivided heart and an undivided will in the presence of the Lord; and that is not easy...

In *The Way of a Pilgrim*, a village priest gives some very authoritative advice on prayer: 'If you want it to be pure, right and enjoyable, you must choose some short prayer, consisting of few but forcible words, and repeat it frequently, over a long period. Then you find delight in prayer.' The same idea is to be found in the *Letters of Brother Lawrence*: 'I do not advise you to use multiplicity of words in prayer; many words and long discourses being often the occasions of wandering'.

Theophane the Recluse says: 'You ask yourself, "Have I prayed well today?" Do not try to find out how deep your emotions were, or how much deeper you understand things divine; ask yourself: "Am I doing God's will better than I did before?" If you are, prayer has brought its fruit, if you are not, it has not, whatever amount of understanding or feeling you may have derived from the time spent in the presence of God'.

Metropolitan Anthony of Sourozh,
'Meditation and Worship', in John Garvey (ed.), *Modern Spirituality: an Anthology*, London: Darton,
Longman and Todd, 1985, pp. 30, 32, 33.

Archbishop John (Maximovich), Russian bishop in Shanghai, in Western Europe, and finally in San Francisco (d. 1966)... It was his custom each year to visit Holy Trinity Monastery at Jordanville, N.Y. As he left, after one such visit, a monk gave him a slip of paper with four names of those who were gravely ill. Archbishop John received thousands upon thousands of such requests for prayer in the course of each year. On his return to the monastery some twelve months later, at once he beckoned to the monk, and much to the latter's surprise, from the depths of his cassock Archbishop John produced the identical slip of paper, now crumpled and tattered. 'I have been praying for your friends', he said, 'but two of them' — he pointed to their names — 'are now dead and the other two have recovered'. And so indeed it was.

Kallistos Ware,
'The Spiritual Father in Orthodox Christianity' in John Garvey (ed.), *Modern Spirituality: an Anthology*,
London: Darton, Longman and Todd, 1985, pp. 55-6.

Every bearer of the word of God was a (person) of prayer: Abraham, Moses, David, Solomon. Each one has bequeathed us both a style of prayer, prayers which can turn directly to our own use, and also a model of the relationship with God, which is unique and yet available to each person. To read the Bible is to read prayers...

Jacques Ellul,
Prayer and Modern Man, New York: Seabury, 1979, pp. 108-9.

Here are some guidelines (in praying for others): 1. Set aside a specific time... each day. 2. One specific place for prayer is the ideal... 3. Prepare by quieting your heart and mind. It helps to reread some of the great Scripture passages on intercession (for example Isaiah 59:16; Romans 8:26-39; Ephesians 1:17-23; Hebrews 7:14-28). 4. See the person for whom you are praying as being in the presence of Jesus with his light shining around and through that person... See the person as Jesus does. If emotions need healing, see them as becoming stable; if there are body ailments, see them as becoming whole... 5. Be objective about the person and the problem... God's power is what matters, not our feelings. Our sense of weakness can be his strength. 6. Listen. God speaks to us most often by planting a thought in our minds. Do not be discouraged if nothing comes through right away. Keep listening. Keep asking for his ideas, his help, his guidance. 7. Write down what you hear... 8. Peace and joy in your spirit are often given you as the sign that the prayer is being answered.

Leonard E. LeSourd (ed.),
Intercessory Prayer, London: Hodder & Stoughton, 1990, pp. 24, 25. Reproduced by permission of
Hodder & Stoughton Ltd/New English Library Ltd.

131

Contemplative prayer is the prayer of the heart, imagination and will, where the lips and mind are both at rest. It is a simple gazing, looking at the Lord in wordless prayer, seeking to be one with him. It is 'communing with your own heart ... and being still' (Psalm 4:4b).

When Jean Vianney asked a peasant what he did as he sat alone in church he replied, 'I just look at him, and he looks at me'.

In our modern preoccupation with achieving 'results', working hard, late and long, we have lost the one thing necessary: to sit at Jesus' feet looking at him and listening to him. In the Carmelite tradition, such prayer has been given various names: the prayer of recollection (Teresa of Avila), prayer of simplicity (Bossuet), prayer of silence, prayer of loving attention, and prayer of the heart.

Rowland Croucher,
Recent Trends Among Evangelicals, Melbourne: John Mark Ministries, 1991, p. 75.

The well-known Australian Baptist theologian, Principal G. H. Morling used to have a sermon he called 'A Robe of Healing'. His text was Mark 5:31 — 'Who touched Me?' — and he made the point that 'the woman touched his robe, his vesture... Nature may be thought of as his vesture. The world of nature is a cloak of God. William Carey prayed in the open air. Nature is a garment of the Most High. And we can touch God if we're sensitive'.

However, nature mysticism is a means, not an end. It is meant to draw us beyond nature into a relationship with a loving Creator, Provider and Redeemer ('panentheism' as Baron von Hugel called it — seeing in all created things God's energies — not 'pantheism' which identifies creation with God). There is also the danger of nature mysticism being escapist; so rather than 'loving' nature, we should do as Jesus instructed and consider it. We might not be poetic, like Keats or Wordsworth, or praise God as St Francis did (with birds in his hair) for sun and moon, fire and water, wind and weather, flowers and grass. However we can all learn to see more, with newly-opened eyes, in the magnificent world God has given to us.

Rowland Croucher,
Recent Trends Among Evangelicals, Melbourne: John Mark Ministries, 1991, pp. 71-3.

There is a deep joy in praying together, an added vitality, a plus difficult to define. It is rather like the difference between eating your meal alone and sharing in a party feast. Eating together is not the same as eating in solitude; the something more is the company, the fellowship. So it is with prayer.

Stephen Winward,
Teach Yourself to Pray, London: Hodder & Stoughton, 1976, p. 86. Reproduced by permission of Hodder & Stoughton Ltd/New English Library Ltd.

Thomas Merton said, 'If you want a life of prayer, the way to get it is by praying'. So how does one begin a life of prayer? Dom Chapman said it is best to pray as you can, not as you can't. Begin with what you know about prayer and use that as the basis for beginning a relationship with God...

For Evagrius, the first of the Desert Fathers to reflect systematically about prayer, the life of prayer had three stages, which he called 'prayer of the lips, the mind, and the heart'. This discipline led first to *apatheia*, the freedom from passions, before moving on to knowledge of divine reason, and finally, entry into the life of the Trinity.

Kenneth Swanson,
Uncommon Prayer, New York, Ballantine, 1987, pp. 157, 198.

But now, Lord, all these things lie in the past, and time has healed my wound. Let me listen to you who are the Truth. Let the ears of my heart move closer to your mouth, so you can tell me why tears are so sweet to those in misery. Have you, who are present everywhere, placed our troubles out of your reach? You reside within yourself, but we ricochet from one rugged experience to another; and if we weren't able to pour our troubles into your ears, what hope would be left us? How can there be such a sweet flavour in the bitter fruit we pluck from life — with all its groans, tears, sighs and wailings? Does the sweetness come from the hope that you will hear us? In the case of prayer I would say Yes, for prayer is built on a longing to get through to you... Or is it that weeping is a bitter thing that gives us pleasure only because it relieves the tension created by sorrow?

Augustine,
in Sherwood E. Wirt, *The Confessions of Augustine in Modern English*, Grand Rapids: Zondervan, 1977,
pp. 55-6.

Lord, bless your people who hope for your mercy. Grant that they may receive the things they ask for at your prompting. Grant this through Christ our Lord.

Lord, come, live in your people and strengthen them by your grace. Help them to remain close to you in prayer and give them a true love for one another. Grant this through Christ our Lord.

Daily Mass Book, Brisbane: The Liturgical Commission, 1990, pp. 37, 38.

A benediction
May God the Father give you a special gift of healing prayer. May Jesus, the Son of God, teach you how to pray. May the Holy Spirit who has been given to you to guide you in prayer, help you to pray better. May your prayer be to you as breath is to life.

May your worship be in spirit and in truth. May your confessions be sincere, and may you know your sins are forgiven. May your intercessions be answered according to his will. Through Jesus Christ our Lord. Amen.

To do: How we pray depends on who we think God is. Why not spend a few moments writing down the kind of God you generally pray to? What is God like? What do you expect to happen when you pray? How did you come to get this/these ideas about God? Is your God, to whom you pray, the same God Jesus told us about?

13
Entering the quiet

The effect of righteousness will be peace, and the result of righteousness, quietness and trust forever. My people will abide in a peaceful habitation, in secure dwellings, and in quiet resting places.

O Lord, my heart is not lifted up, my eyes are not raised too high; I do not occupy myself with things too great and too marvellous for me. But I have calmed and quieted my soul, like a weaned child with its mother; my soul is like the weaned child that is with me. O Israel, hope in the Lord from this time on and evermore.

For thus said the Lord God, the Holy One of Israel: in returning and rest you shall be saved; in quietness and in trust shall be your strength. Blessed are all those who wait for him.

The apostles gathered around Jesus, and told him all they had done and taught. He said to them, 'Come away to a deserted place all by yourselves and rest a while.' For many were coming and going, and they had no leisure even to eat. And they went away in the boat to a deserted place by themselves.

But those who wait for the Lord shall renew their strength, they shall mount up with wings like eagles, they shall run and not be weary, they shall walk and not faint.

Teach me, and I will be silent; make me understand how I have gone wrong.

He makes me lie down in green pastures; he leads me beside still waters.

I waited patiently for the Lord; he inclined to me and heard my cry.

But Jesus was silent.

I commune with my heart in the night; I meditate and search my spirit: Will the Lord spurn forever, and never again be favourable? I will meditate on all your work, and muse on your mighty deeds.

Let the arrogant be put to shame, because they have subverted me with guile; as for me, I will meditate on your precepts.

On the glorious splendour of your majesty, and on your wondrous works, I will meditate.

Beware of practising your piety before others in order to be seen by them; for then you have no reward from your Father in heaven.

Isaiah 32:17-18; Psalm 131; Isaiah 30:15, 18; Mark 6:30-32; Isaiah 40:31; Job 6:24; Psalm 23:2; Psalm 40:1; Matthew 26:63; Psalm 77:6, 7, 12; Psalm 119:78; Psalm 145:5; Matthew 6:1

The bishop of Belley, Jean Pierre Camus, wanted to know if Francis de Sales was really as holy as he seemed to be. So he drilled a hole in the wall of his bedroom in the episcopal residence to spy on him.

What did Camus discover? Only that Francis was the same in secret as he was in company. He saw the saint creep out of bed early and quietly in the mornings so as not to wake his servant. He saw him pray, write in his journal, read the office, answer some letters, then pray again. The beautiful manners, the unruffled compassion, the courtesy and humility were all on display through the peephole as they had been in the pulpit or at the dinner-table.

Francis de Sales lived a life of congruence: he was what he seemed to be. His life with God, his personal serenity, his love for others: they were all in harmony.

How does anyone get to be that way? The answer is simple, but the process is life-long: develop a wholesome spirituality!

Spirituality is mainly about how I relate to God. 'Spirit' in the Bible means breath, life. The opposite of spirit is not matter, but death. 'Spiritual' worship is the offering of all we are to God (Romans 12:1). As we noted in the last chapter, it's about my 'desire', how I pray (the very best index of who I really am).

The spiritual life cannot be nurtured without discipline. In this chapter we'll look at four disciplines — solitude, silence, study and journaling. Next chapter we'll look at four more: fasting, simplicity, confession and service.

1. *Solitude* is being alone with yourself, and with God. It is not the same as loneliness. Loneliness is inner emptiness. Solitude is inner fulfilment.

Our fear of being alone drives us to noise and crowds. But loneliness and clatter are not our only alternatives. We can enjoy solitude in cities; it is possible to be a desert hermit and never experience solitude.

In his *Life Together* Bonhoeffer wrote: 'Let (the one) who cannot be alone beware of community ... (and whoever) is not in community (should) beware of being alone'. So we need both community and solitude: each is necessary for the enrichment of the other.

If we take seriously the discipline of solitude we will at some stage pass through what John of the Cross calls 'the dark night of the soul'. It is a time of apparent desolation, but in reality God is at work in divine surgery, bringing us to a profound stillness, so that he may work an inner transformation upon the soul.

Thomas Merton observed: 'It is in deep solitude that I find the gentleness with which I can truly love my brothers. The more solitary I am the more affection I have for them'.

Solitary time with God can be in a retreat (say, for two days or eight days) but above all it ought to be daily. Daily solitude is not a luxury; it is a necessity for spiritual survival. If we do not have that within us, from beyond us, we yield too much to that around us.

Find time each day to meet with God. Make a chapel or oratory somewhere, perhaps a corner of your bedroom, away from interruptions (put the telephone answering machine on), where you do your prayer and Bible/spiritual reading and sermon preparation.

Begin your 'quiet time' with a Bible word, phrase or prayer ('Be still..', 'Maranatha', 'Lord, have mercy on me a sinner'). 'Occupy yourself in it without going further. Do like the bees, who never quit a flower so long as they can extract any honey from it' (Francis de Sales).

'*Lectio divina*' is the slow, reflective reading of the Bible. Scripture is God's personal word to me — for my 'formation' not just information. I read it reverently, ready to be 'converted' again and again, willing to be led where I may be reluctant to go, believing that God has yet more light and truth to reveal to me. I try to learn to 'meditate on the Word day and night' (Psalm 1:2).

The Daily Office is an excellent structure for daily devotions. Try the daily office in any modern Anglican prayerbook. The Daily Office, says (Baptist) Stephen Winward is absolutely scriptural, God-centred, depends on an ordered use of Scripture (including difficult and challenging passages), is corporate, educative (we're in touch with prayer traditions centuries old) and 'obligatory' (even though the discipline is sometimes hard). Of course, as the Protestant Reformers emphasised, it can be mechanical and formal, but it doesn't have to be.

2. *Silence.* St John of the Cross, the great teacher about mystical prayer, wrote: 'The Father spoke one Word, which was his Son, and this word he always speaks in silence, and in silence it must be heard by the soul'. Silence is 'the royal road to spiritual formation' (Nouwen). It is not just the absence of noise, but an opportunity to listen to the still small voice of the Spirit.

An exercise practised by all the spiritual masters is that of attending to the sounds around you. Why not stop now: what do you hear? Thank God for whatever those sounds represent.

3. *Study.* In meditation we attempt to let a word or phrase of Scripture speak to us. When we do 'Bible study' we bring our minds to bear on the text, to get into its meaning. Meditation is devotional, study is analytical. Bible study is the disciplined reading of Scripture to try to understand it. Meditation will relish a word; study will 'unpack' its meaning.

This process demands humility, as we can easily impose our own meanings on the biblical text, or organise doctrines within the narrow structure of our own biases. The central purpose of study is not doctrinal purity (though that is no doubt involved) but inner transformation. Bible study is far more likely to produce a Pharisee than meditation on Scripture. In Bible study we are 'over the Word' organising it, criticising it; in meditation and contemplation we are 'under the Word': it becomes a critic of us. The Pharisee is a 'proof-texter' — fitting biblical texts into predetermined doctrinal frameworks.

4. *Journaling* is a useful way to record the promptings of the Spirit in your life. A spiritual journal is a written response to reality: a record of one's inner and outer life (including dreams), a way to inner growth, reflection and healing. In your journal you write down, in your own way, anything of importance to you — your feelings about life, and your relationships with others and God. Through the centuries men and women have 'journaled' in times of loneliness, crisis, ecstasy, transition and conflict. Your journal will help you with one of life's great adventures — the discovery of who you really are. You can then befriend the self you discover, and later re-traverse the journey again with thankfulness.

Only you should read your journal, unless you permit extracts to be seen by others, especially your spiritual director.

These four disciplines, regularly practised, will help you 'Let go, let be, and let God'; you will experience a peace that passes understanding, not because you sought that peace directly, but in the process of discovering who you are in the quiet presence of God, you will be better able to negotiate a truce in those areas within where there was war before.

Where shall the word be found, where will the word resound?
Not here, there is not enough silence...

T. S. Eliot,
'Ash Wednesday 1930', in *Selected Poems*, London: Faber, 1944, p. 90.

Christian spirituality is a 'spirituality for combat' that goes deep
within in order to venture beyond where others dare to go. It is a
life of harmony that is caught up in a rhythm between the outer
and the inner, between solitude and compassion, between the
desert and the city. It is open to those who in the midst of
activity are able to see possibilities for ministry in response to
the 'still small voice' of God. 'To be a Christian and to pray are
one and the same thing', writes Karl Barth. 'It is a matter that
cannot be left to caprice. It is a need, a kind of breathing
necessary to life.'

James C. Fenhagen,
Ministry and Solitude, New York: Seabury Press, 1981, p. 70.

Do not give up; do not despair; do not be tempted to think it is
all a waste of time. Humanly speaking it may be a waste of time,
but then how much time have you wasted on waiting for
someone you think you love? And there is no one better to waste
time on than God. You may think you will have all eternity to
love him, and could here and now be better employed doing a
good work. But again, the simple message which God speaks is
the paradox that if you give him more time, you will have more
for other work.

Michael Hollings,
Hearts Not Garments, London: Darton, Longman and Todd, 1982, p. 16.

St Benedict said *Oratio sit brevis et pura*: 'Let the prayer be
brief and pure'. Though the time of meditation may be long,
anything we say to God arising out of it will have a quality of
simplicity. We prefer to listen to God than to make God listen to
us. Throughout the Bible, God is reproaching people for not
listening to him; he does not complain that they do not speak to
him.

Margaret Hebblethwaite,
Finding God in All Things, London: Fountain Paperbacks, 1987, pp. 94-5.

When we rest, we acknowledge that all our striving will, of itself,
do nothing. It means letting the world pass us by for a time.
Genuine rest requires acknowledgment that God, and our
brothers and sisters, can survive without us. It requires a
recognition of our own insufficiency and a handing over of
responsibility. It is a real surrender to the ways of God. It is a
moment of celebration when we acknowledge that blessing
comes only from the hand of God. This is why rest requires faith.

It is also why salvation can be pictured as rest. When we rest we accept God's grace: we do not seek to earn, we receive; we do not justify, we are justified.

Paul Marshall,
'Work and Rest', *Reformed Journal*, June 1988, p. 13.

(The attitude of the desert) is a going out of oneself to encounter the absolute and true reality of things... Authentic Christian contemplation, passing through the desert, transforms contemplatives into prophets and militants into mystics.

Segundo Galilea,
'Politics and Contemplation', in Geffre and Gutierrez (eds), *The Mystical and Political Dimensions of the Christian Faith*, New York: Herder and Herder, 1974, p. 28.

There is considerable value in corporate silence... The quantity of verbal interaction is not the only, or necessarily the best, indicator of fellowship. We know well the experience of words failing us when we try to communicate heights or depths of emotion or thought. There is a peculiar and beautiful eloquence in a person's wordless presence in community... Time and again retreatants told me that the most significant and helpful feature of their retreat was the silence. Often they wish there had been more silence...

Ross Kingham,
Surprises of the Spirit, Barnabas Communications, P.O. Box 331, Mawson ACT 2607, 1991, p. 32.

In one way or another, verbally, imaginatively, physically, intellectually, with whatever faculties are operating at the time, we say to Christ, 'I want to be with you. Let me follow you and spend this time with you, and then perhaps I will begin to understand what it is that I really want'.

The whole purpose of the (Ignatian) Spiritual Exercises can be summed up in terms of *id quod volo*: the Exercises are a way through which we find out for ourselves what it is that we want most deeply.

For everyone, ultimately, the answer is the same. We want God, because that is the way we have been made. 'You have made us for yourself, and our hearts find no peace until they rest in you'.

Margaret Hebblethwaite,
Finding God in All Things, London: Fountain Paperbacks, 1987, pp. 76-7.

A man who had been unable to pray for years began a retreat by imagining himself at Bethlehem but found he could not enter the cave. Feelings of unworthiness, and of simply not being welcome, blocked his fantasy at that point. He and his director interpreted this, not as an inability to 'make the contemplation', but as a sign that he was praying; and he continued to imagine himself barred at the entrance to the cave in his repetitions of the contemplation. After two days of this, during which the resentments and hopes of his whole past life welled up within him, he reported that he was invited to go in. The fantasy, with the block and its resolution, was so much the man himself that it became the carrier for a real encounter and meant the turning point of his spiritual life.

Robert Ochs,
God is more present than you think, New York: Paulist Press, New York, 1970, p. 62.

In contemporary society our Adversary majors in three things: noise, hurry and crowds. If he can keep us engaged in 'muchness' and 'manyness', he will rest satisfied. Psychiatrist C. G. Jung once remarked, 'Hurry is not of the Devil; it is the Devil'. If we hope to move beyond the superficialities of our culture — including our religious culture — we must be willing to go down into the recreating silences, into the inner world of contemplation. In their writings, all of the masters of meditation strive to awaken us to the fact that the universe is much larger than we know, that there are vast unexplored inner regions that are just as real as the physical world we know so well. They tell us of exciting possibilities for new life and freedom. They call us to the adventure, to be pioneers in this frontier of the Spirit.

Richard Foster,
Celebration of Discipline, London: Hodder & Stoughton, 1980, p. 13.

Some of my most profitable experiences of study have come through structuring a private retreat for myself. Usually it involves two to three days. No doubt you will object that given your schedule you could not possibly find that kind of time. I want you to know that it is no easier for me to secure that time than for anyone else. I fight and struggle for every retreat, scheduling it into my datebook many weeks in advance. I have suggested this idea to groups and found that professional people with busy schedules, labourers with rigid schedules, housewives with large families, and others can, in fact, find time for a private study retreat. I have discovered that the most difficult problem is not finding time but convincing myself that this is important enough to find the time.

Richard Foster,
Celebration of Discipline, London: Hodder & Stoughton, 1980, pp. 60-1.

The main part of the exercise: I make a note of the most important steps in my growing relationship with God (about eight is a good number). These steps, or stepping stones, may be single events, or they may be periods of growth. They may be explicitly religious, or they may be connected to the human process of maturing that I did not think of in terms of God at the time. I make a brief note of each as it occurs to me. Afterwards I can order them chronologically, so I have an idea of the overall shape of my life. There may also be steps backward, or anyway sideways.

When I have done this, I am in a position to see what in my life I want to thank God for. I take time over this, being grateful for all that now seems positive in my history.

Only after I have done that do I look at the ways in which I have fallen short. Remembering the events that I am now grateful for, how could I have given more room in my life for the things that really matter?

Margaret Hebblethwaite,
Finding God in All Things, London: Fount Paperbacks, 1990, pp. 165-6.

'In the world to come', says the Rabbi Zusya, 'I shall not be asked: "Why were you not Moses?" I shall be asked: "Why were you not Zusya?"' 'Know yourself' has long been a spiritual directive. 'Be yourself' is an additional emphasis of today...

John Garvey (ed.),
Modern Spirituality, An Anthology, London: Darton, Longman and Todd, 1985, pp. vii.

When I first started practising the spiritual disciplines I read the works of great leaders — St. Augustine, Martin Luther, John Wesley, Francis Asbury, St. Teresa — and I tried to imitate them. It was a miserable failure until I learned that God wants to work with me as an individual. Now I can read these spiritual giants and be helped by them, but I must not try to do everything the way they did.

Richard Foster,
'Doing It God's Way' in La Vonne Neff et al. (eds), *Practical Christianity*, Wheaton, Illinois: Tyndale House Publishers, 1988, p. 296.

Five ways to make spiritual disciplines a part of life:

1. Have a daily devotional time.

2. Consider having some kind of personal retreat at regular intervals. For the past year I've been taking one day a month... I get away to a retreat place and spend time praying, meditating, reflecting, and making entries in my journal.

3. Get involved in some kind of cell group.

4. Use family time to develop spiritual disciplines. The way you do this will obviously depend on your situation...

5. Join with other church members in regular corporate worship.

Howard Snyder,
'Make the Spiritual Disciplines a Part of Life' in La Vonne Neff et al. (eds), *Practical Christianity*, Wheaton, Illinois: Tyndale House Publishers, 1988, pp. 296-7.

The Christian life is lived out in the tension between self-discipline and the free gift of grace. Yet slavishly giving ourselves over to a discipline of prayer doesn't mean we will automatically experience joyous intimacy with God. A discipline of prayer may easily become a routine of life-killing legalism, all form and no substance. When piety becomes rigidly legalistic, many negative things may happen... One of the mysterious paradoxes of the Christian life is that it is in the practice of spiritual disciplines that we enter into the grace of God in Jesus Christ. Again I repeat, there is nothing mechanistic about prayer. We can't manipulate or control God with it, but it places us before him so that when he wills, he will come to us.

Kenneth Swanson,
Uncommon Prayer, New York: Ballantine, 1987, p. 54.

Lord, while I am searching for you, you have been seeking me. I pray for silence and stillness to apprehend you, for you are not to be found in noise and restlessness. Your beautiful creation — trees, flowers, grass — grow in silence. The stars, the moon, the sun move in silence. As we receive strength in silent prayer so we shall give to others in our active life. Teach me, Lord, that what I say or what I do is less important than what you say to me and what you do in me. Words and deeds which do not share the light and life of Christ increase the darkness and death.

O gracious and holy Father, give us wisdom to perceive you, intelligence to understand you, diligence to seek you, patience to wait for you, eyes to behold you, a heart to meditate on you, and a life to proclaim you through the power of the spirit of Jesus Christ our Lord.

Benedict,
cited in *Praying with the Saints*, Dublin: Veritas Publications, 1989, p. 26.

A benediction
Go into the desert and there find your God in the silence; go into the depths of your being, and find your real self; in disciplined self-examination allow God and yourself to come together. Make your confession to him and receive his forgiveness. Then go into the world in peace to love and serve the Lord. Amen.

Now: Make a serious, personal covenant with the Lord, writing down in your journal a commitment to meet with him regularly, and outlining a way of approaching that 'quiet time' that is suited to you.

Buy Kenneth Swanson, *Uncommon Prayer*, and read it through fairly quickly, then spend several months slowly reading Richard Foster's *Celebration of Discipline*.

Contact a local retreat centre, and ask for their program. Book yourself into a retreat or course each year.

Some Spiritual Exercises

In your journal, write responses to these:

1. Imagine you are the woman healed in Mark 5:21-34 or Peter at the feeding of the five thousand (Mark 6:30-52): how do you feel?
2. Make a list of the main events of your life. Why are they important?
3. Answer the question: 'What is my desire'?
4. 'The second greatest tragedy is to have never been loved. But the greatest tragedy is to be loved and never know it.' Write a love-letter to the Lord.
5. What would you do on the last day of your life?
6. Write — honestly — your own funeral oration. What will the pastor say about you, do you think?

Further Reading:
Some of the spiritual classics include *The Confessions of Saint Augustine* (there are several good modern translations), *The Imitation of Christ* by Thomas a Kempis, *Introduction to the Devout Life* by Francis de Sales and William Law's *A Serious Call to a Devout and Holy Life*.

General introductions include Richard Foster, *Celebration of Discipline*, San Francisco: Harper & Row, or London: Hodder & Stoughton, 1978; Margaret Hebblethwaite, *Finding God in All Things*, London: Fount Paperbacks, 1990; Peter Toon, *What is Spirituality? And is it for me?* London: Daybreak, 1989; Rowland Croucher, *Recent Trends Among Evangelicals, Part 3: 'Creative Spirituality'* (John Mark Ministries, 1991). Read anything by Henri Nouwen, Thomas Merton, Carlo Carretto, Anthony de Mello. Daily or weekly devotions: Rowland Croucher (ed.) *Still Waters ... Deep Waters: Meditations and Prayers for Busy People, High Mountains, Deep Valleys: Meditations and Prayers for the Down Times. Rivers in the Desert: Meditations and Prayers for Refreshment*, and *Gentle Darkness* (Albatross/ Lion, 1987, 1990, 1991, 1992).

For more serious students there are Dictionaries of Spirituality (for example by G. Wakefield, C. Cary-Elwes) and compendiums of articles about spirituality in John Garvey (ed.), *Modern Spirituality, An Anthology*, London: Darton, Longman and Todd, 1985, and *The Study of Spirituality* (edited by C. Jones, G. Wainwright and E. Yarnold).

14
Some spiritual disciplines

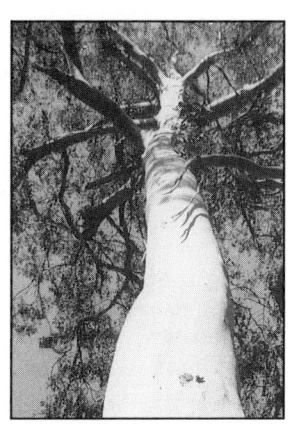

Athletes exercise self-control in all things... So I do not run aimlessly... but I punish my body and enslave it, so that after proclaiming to others I myself should not be disqualified.

If two of you agree on earth about anything you ask, it will be done for you by my Father in heaven. For where two or three are gathered in my name, I am there among them.

And whenever you fast, do not look dismal, like the hypocrites, for they disfigure their faces so as to show others that they are fasting. Truly I tell you, they have received their reward. But when you fast, put oil on your head and wash your face, so that your fasting may be seen not by others but by your Father who is in secret; and your Father who sees in secret will reward you.

There was also a prophet, Anna... She never left the temple but worshipped there with fasting and prayer night and day.

Confess your sins to one another and pray for one another, so that you may be healed.

He breathed on them and said to them, 'Receive the Holy Spirit. If you forgive the sins of any, they are forgiven them; if you retain the sins of any, they are retained.'

1 Corinthians 9:25-27; Matthew 18:19, 20; Matthew 6:16-18; Luke 2:36-37; James 5:16; John 20:23

• A young mother in a Brazilian favela had no food to give her children. So she did what she has done before, many times. She took some newspaper, rolled it into little 'cookies', soaked them in sweetened warm water, and gave them to the kids. They'll provide no nutrition, but something in their stomachs may stop them from crying from hunger in the night...

• Any who have visited churches in Korea are fascinated — and humbled — by those Christians' daily dawn prayer meetings, and their commitment to regular fasting. Thousands of Korean Christians have devoted up to forty days and nights to prayer and fasting, drinking only fresh water during that whole period! These people apparently believe that if you seek the Lord earnestly, you'll be prepared to pay a high price!

Here are two examples of food deprivation: involuntarily, it isn't good for you; as a voluntary discipline — excellent spiritual value!

Spiritual disciplines do for our spirits what regular exercise does for our bodies: they 'tone us up', help us stay in spiritual shape, strengthen us for the spiritual warfare which will inevitably come our way.

In this chapter we'll concentrate on four disciplines — fasting, simplicity, confession and service. The quotes and literature will help you explore many others. I am especially indebted to Richard Foster's *Celebration of Discipline* for many of the ideas in this chapter.

1. *Fasting.* The recent growth of interest in spirituality in all churches has focused on this particular discipline. In a world where one quarter of the people die early through malnourishment, and another quarter through over-eating (!), we are again called to re-examine our life-styles. As I type this, twenty million people in Ethiopia, Sudan and Somalia face starvation.

Fasting is abstaining from eating, or another legitimate activity, for religious purposes. Jews fasted on the Day of Atonement (Leviticus 16:29-31; 23:26-32; Numbers 29:7-11), and for other special reasons such as mourning (1 Samuel 31:13), after defeat in battle (1 Samuel 7:6), as a sign of repentance or remorse (2 Samuel 12:15-23, Joel 2:12-13), and to accompany intercession (Nehemiah 1, 4).

Jesus fasted during his wilderness preparation for ministry (Matthew 4:1-2, Luke 4:1-2), but said only two things about fasting in his teaching in the gospels: it was an act of private devotion to God, and was appropriate once he left his followers (Matthew 6:16-18, 9:14-15; see Mark 2:18-20; Luke 5:33-35). The apostolic church apparently observed fasts during times of solemn commitment (Acts 13:2-3; 14:23).

Fasting is 'praying with the body', an affirmation of one's hunger for God and his will, an act of spiritual discipline, and an assertion of the goodness of God in creation, which one appreciates better in abstention; it expresses penitence for the rejection and crucifixion of Christ by the human race; it is a following of Jesus on his way of fasting; it is one element in mortification; the acceptance of death of self in the death of Christ, and thereby an act of faith in the resurrection.[1]

Fasting has its dangers, when misused for selfish ends. The Bible notes such abuses as fasting as a means of getting things from God (manipulation or magic); it can be a substitute for genuine repentance and be formalistic; it can be masochistic — an exaggerated self-denial; psychological evidence shows fasting can sometimes lead to self-induced visions which may not be helpful.[2]

So, in summary, there are no biblical laws that command regular fasting, but, as Martin Luther said, 'It was not Christ's intention to reject or despise fasting... it was his intention to restore proper fasting'. It is clear that Christ both upheld the discipline of fasting and anticipated that his followers would do it.[3]

Fasting, as Arthur Wallis says in his book *God's Chosen Fast*, is a way of teaching our bodies to be our servants rather than our masters!

2. *Simplicity,* says Richard Foster in his best-selling *Celebration of Discipline*, is freedom. Duplicity is bondage. Simplicity brings joy and balance. Duplicity brings anxiety and fear. Because — and to the degree that — we lack a divine Centre, our need for security has led us into an insane attachment to things. Conformity to a sick society is to be sick. However, asceticism and simplicity are not the same: asceticism renounces possessions; simplicity sets possessions in proper perspective. Then there is the discipline of sharing. Martin Luther said somewhere, 'If our goods are not available to the community, they are stolen goods'.

3. *Confession.* These last two disciplines — confession and service — are 'corporate disciplines'. We cannot survive spiritually without the help of our Christian friends.

The most compelling reason for praying with others is Jesus' promise that he's there with us (Matthew 18:19, 20). Jesus took his disciples with him occasionally when he was praying in solitary places (Luke 9:18, 28). We know what Jesus prayed in Gethsemane probably because part of his prayer was overheard (Mark 14:33).

The apostolic Christians prayed together from the start. The Holy Spirit was poured out on a group at prayer (Acts 1:14). They continued to spend a lot of time in prayer together (Acts 2:42). Paul prayed constantly with his co-missioners (Colossians 1:9; 1 Thessalonians 1:2; 2 Thessalonians 1:11) and asked others to join him in disciplined prayer (Romans 15:30). James (5:16) tells us to 'confess your sins to one another and pray for one another, so that you may be healed...'

The church is glorious, not because it's perfect, but because it's being redeemed. It is a fellowship of forgiven sinners, not (yet) perfect saints. So in the company of fellow-strugglers it is okay to be imperfect!

The followers of Christ have been given the authority to receive the confession of sin and to forgive in his name (see John 20:23). Whilst most of us would have problems with the stylised form of the 'confessional', there are probably greater dangers in ignoring the biblical injunction to confess our sins to one another, praying for forgiveness and healing for each other (James 5:16).

Alphonsus Liguori writes, 'For a good confession three things are necessary: an examination of conscience, sorrow and a determination to avoid sin'.

It is important that when others are opening their griefs to us we discipline ourselves to be prayerfully quiet. Too often an embarrassed comment can destroy the sacredness of the moment.

Foster suggests that 'the ministry of retaining sins is simply the refusal to try to bring people into something for which they are not ready. Sometimes people are so anxious to get others into the kingdom that they will try to announce their forgiveness before they have sought it or even wanted it. Unfortunately, this malady is characteristic of a great deal of modern evangelism'.

Confession, says Dietrich Bonhoeffer in *Spiritual Care*, is the heart of spiritual care.

4. *Service.* 'A Christian...' said Martin Luther 'is the most free Lord of all, and subject to none; a Christian is the most dutiful servant of all, and subject to everyone.'

The discipline of submission frees us from the terrible burden of always needing to get our own way. We can be given the grace to love people unconditionally, and give up the right for them to return our love.

Jesus calls us to self-denial (which is not self-hatred or self-contempt). Self-denial is simply a way of coming to understand that we do not have to have our own way. Our happiness is not dependent upon getting what we want. So we serve to enhance the lives of others, sacrificing our time and effort for their good. 'It's damnably easy to render service, but very difficult to be a servant', said D. T. Niles.

The spiritual classics make lavish use of the language of self-denial. For example, Thomas à Kempis says 'To have no opinion of ourselves, and to think always well and highly of others, is great wisdom and perfection'. The teaching of the New Testament is revolutionary, challenging the contemporary customs of super-ordinate and sub-ordinate and calling upon everyone to 'count others better than yourselves' (Philippians 2:3).

We are to submit to God, to scripture, to our family, to our neighbours, to the believing community, to the broken and despised, and to the world. Followers of Jesus come to perceive that authority does not reside in positions or degrees or titles or tenure or any outward symbol. Rather we are given a spiritual authority, marked by both compassion and power.

Occasionally, however, revolutionary subordination to temporal authorities has its limits — when those authorities violate biblical injunctions and become destructive.

Jesus did not abolish ideas of leadership and authority, rather he radically redefined them. He did not merely reverse the 'pecking order' either. He abolished it. The symbol of his servanthood is a towel...

The 'service of hiddenness' — even for leaders — is a beautiful grace. Listen to Jeremy Taylor : 'Love to be concealed and little esteemed: be content to lack praise, never be troubled when you are overlooked or undervalued.'

Then there is the service of loving speech. We must 'speak evil of no one' (Titus 3:2) nor allow others to speak disparagingly of another. There is also the service of common courtesy, of hospitality, of listening, of bearing one another's burdens and sorrows, and sharing the word of life...

Perhaps, suggests Richard Foster, you would like to begin this beautiful journey with a prayer at the beginning of each day: 'Lord Jesus, I would so appreciate it if you would bring me someone today whom I can serve.'

Prayer cannot be divorced from daily living. Baron Friedrich von Hugel's first suggestion to Evelyn Underhill when he was invited to be her spiritual director: visit the poor in inner-city London two days a week. After all, the Spirit, says an ancient Latin hymn, is *pater pauperum*, 'father of the poor'. Bonhoeffer wrote: 'It is not some religious act which makes a Christian what he or she is, but participation in the suffering of God in the life of the world'.[4]

Reality is more internal than external. Reality is more the inner journey than being 'successful outwardly'. These and other classical disciplines of the spiritual life help us to get in touch with our frailty and finiteness and the necessity for dependence. We will explore new territories in these exercises. At times we may be discouraged. But plenty of others have gone this way before us and we can learn from them. Be daring, take a few risks, go out on a limb, find your security in God rather than in

149

your needing to conform to a weak kind of Christianity practised by so many these days. Trust your spiritual community, however. Be flexible. Be true to your spiritual tradition. And trust in the Lord, who is always with you, and will respond to your desires to please him and grow into him. 🌱

Guidelines for Fasting: A partial fast is when we restrict our diet without totally abstaining from food; a normal fast is abstention from all food but not from fluids; an absolute fast is total abstinence from food and fluids.

Enter into fasting with expectant faith. Do not wait for an emergency to drive you to fasting. Do not set too long a period of fasting to begin with. Set specific objectives in your fasting and make a written list of these. Avoid religious ostentation and boastfulness.

Before the fast: abstain from drinking coffee or tea. Take a light but wholesome meal. During the fast: drink plenty of fresh water; do not allow unpleasant physical symptoms to deter you, for example slight dizziness, nausea. These usually subside after a while. After the fast: break your fast gradually beginning with meals that are light and easy to digest. Done correctly, regular fasting is actually good for one's health. However, if you are on any medication or if you have a medical condition or are pregnant, seek your doctor's advice before attempting any fast.

Fasting enables one to have increased effectiveness in intercessory prayer, secured guidance in making decisions, increased concentration, deliverance for those in bondage, and physical well-being.

Fasting helps bring the desires of the body under control. We discipline our bodies to enhance our effectiveness for the Lord (1 Corinthians 9:27).

'Feasting or Fasting?'
World Vision of Singapore pamphlet (adapted).

One of the most astonishing exercises in Sadhana is a meditation on my own corpse (Exercise 29). This comes from a Buddhist series of reality meditations, and what is amazing is that, however horrifying it sounds in prospect, it gives a deep sense of inner peace.

There are nine stages: first you see your corpse cold and rigid, then turning blue, then cracks appear in the flesh, then decomposition sets in in some parts, then the whole body is in full decomposition, then the skeleton appears with some flesh adhering in some places, then there is the skeleton with no flesh left, then there is a heap of bones, lastly there is a heap of dust.

Margaret Hebblethwaite,
Finding God in All Things, London: Fount Paperbacks, 1987, p. 110.

One of the greatest pitfalls for people who go in for spirituality, is to waft around in a spiritual zone seeking peace, fulfilment and inner harmony, and leaving the world to rot. Centres of spirituality flourish, master's degrees are taken in prayer, meditation becomes a boom industry, and meanwhile the hungry go on being hungry, the naked go on being naked, the sick and imprisoned have no one to visit them, and the sinful structures of the world continue unchallenged.

For someone in the third world, a spirituality movement can be bad news. The theologians of liberation draw attention to the implicitly conservative nature of most of these movements when they are found in Latin America — like the Cursillo retreat movement, and the Charismatic renewal: by turning attention away from the bitter reality of the way people live, they leave everything the way it was.

Margaret Hebblethwaite,
Finding God in All Things, London: Fount Paperbacks, 1990, p. 201.

The spiritual discipline of simplicity means singleness of purpose toward God. Kierkegaard said, 'Purity of heart is to will one thing', and by that he meant it is to will the good, which is God. Simplicity is not first a lifestyle. It is an inward spiritual reality that results in an outward life-style.

I was reading a section... in *A Testament of Devotion* by Thomas Kelly called 'On the Ability to Say Yes and No', and I began crying.

That's what I want, I thought. I want to be able to say yes to people, I want to be able to say no to people, from the divine centre. I don't want my answer to be based on what people think of me, on how I can impress others, or on what kind of reputation it will build for me. I want it to be based on the call of God upon me.

When I got home I... decided to give Friday nights to my family. So I did that, and then a fellow from denominational headquarters phoned me and asked me to speak on a Friday night. I had to say no. He said, 'Are you busy?' At that time I didn't know I could say, 'Yes, I'm very busy'. I simply said, 'No'. I'm sure he thought I was shirking my responsibilities. But when I hung up, I felt a Hallelujah! inside. I don't have to be controlled by the opinions of others!

Simplicity is... related to true poverty — not the absence of money but the absence of possessiveness. I have everything but own nothing; everything is available to me, but I control none of it. The words my and mine are removed from my vocabulary...

We must learn an inner spirit of detachment. Remember that Paul said, 'I have learned the secret of being content in any and every situation, whether well fed or hungry, whether living in plenty or in want' (Philippians 4:12). The point is that we need divine grace whether or not we have money. We need grace to live in want, and we also need grace to live in plenty'.

Richard Foster,
'Simplicity' in La Vonne Neff et al., *Practical Christianity*, Wheaton, Illinois: Tyndale House Publishers
Inc., 1988, pp. 302-3.

The way most of us serve keeps us in control. We choose whom, when, where and how we will serve. We stay in charge. Jesus is calling for something else. He is calling us to be servants. When we make this choice, we give up the right to be in charge. The amazing thing is that when we make this choice we experience great freedom. We become available and vulnerable, and we lose our fear of being stepped on, or manipulated, or taken advantage of. Are not these our basic fears? We do not want to be in a position of weakness.

From *The Workbook on Spiritual Disciplines* by Maxie Dunnam. Copyright © 1984 by The Upper Room,
1908 Grand Avenue, P.O. Box 189, Nashville, TN 37202. Used by permission of the publisher.

Expression of what we find within ourselves, honest and reckless expression before the face of the Eternal, assuming responsibility for what we are, even if we are unaware of it, and asking God to help us to master the wild horses, or to revive the skeletons of horses which we dig out during the long hours of our confessions — this is the psychological method of religious self-education. It is a way of bringing to consciousness our unconscious contents, and of establishing control over our hidden powers. It is the way to mature responsibility. It is the old way of the Psalmist: 'Yet who can detect his lapses? Absolve me from my faults unknown! And hold thy servant back from wilful sins, from giving way to them' (Psalm 19:12,13, Moffatt).

Fritz Kunkel,
In Search of Maturity, pp. 253-4, quoted in Maxie Dunnam, *The Workbook on Spiritual Disciplines*,
Nashville, Tennessee: The Upper Room, 1984, pp. 82-3.

The pious fellowship permits no one to be a sinner. So everybody conceals their sins from themselves and from the fellowship. We dare not be sinners...

(Jesus) gave his followers authority to hear the confession of sin and to forgive sin in his name... When I go to (another) to confess, I am going to God... In confession we affirm and accept our cross... What happened to us in baptism is bestowed upon us anew in confession. We are delivered out of darkness into the kingdom of Jesus Christ. That is joyful news. Confession is the renewal of the joy of baptism. 'Weeping may linger for the night; but joy comes with the morning' (Psalm 30:5)...

We must ask ourselves whether we have not often been

deceiving ourselves with our confession of sin to God, whether we have not rather been confessing our sins to ourselves and also granting ourselves absolution. And is not the reason perhaps for our countless relapses and the feebleness of our Christian obedience to be found precisely in the fact that we are living on self-forgiveness and not a real forgiveness?

Luther himself was one of those for whom the Christian life was unthinkable without mutual, brotherly confession. In the Large Catechism he said: 'Therefore when I admonish you to confession I am admonishing you to be a Christian.'

Dietrich Bonhoeffer,
Life Together, San Francisco: Harper & Row, 1954, pp. 110-8.

My Lord God, I have no idea where I am going. I do not see the road ahead of me. I cannot know for certain where it will end. Nor do I really know myself. And the fact that I think I am following your will does not mean that I am actually doing so. But I believe, dear Father, that the desire to please You does in fact please You, and I hope that I have that desire in all that I am doing. I hope that I will never do anything apart from that desire. And so I believe that if I do this, You will lead me by the right road, though I may know nothing about it. Therefore, I will trust You always; though I may seen to be lost in the shadow of death, I will not fear, for You are with me and You will never leave me to face my peril alone.

Thomas Merton,
a prayer in his journal during a time of deep depression. Quoted in John Claypool, *The Light Within You*,
Waco, Texas: Word, 1983, p. 159.

Lord Jesus, speak to us more strongly than all the other voices we hear as we pray together. Help us to name and acknowledge the clamant inner demands. Save us from selfishness, from always wanting things our way. Break into our minds with your thoughts, and into our consciousness with something divine.

Examine our motives, our thoughts, our words, our actions. Judge our imagination and add inspiration to it. Shine with hope upon the dark predictions of failure we have carried with us for years. Help us question our right to resent others when you forgave us as sinners.

Cleanse our hearts, purify our ways. May we hasten to admit our sins so that we receive forgiveness and freedom from guilt.

You know our weariness in continuing struggles, our sense of failure and disappointment in what we hope for others. Grant to us a trust in your presence and mercy that will triumph over despair and give us a new vision of what you can achieve through us to your glory.

Increase our courage to share our thoughts with each other, and our sins with a pastor/confessor. Build bridges of trust and bonds of friendship to bear the burden of anxiety or the weight of responsibility. May we speak the truth in love; may we be released from possessiveness and share what we have with others; may we enter into one another's joys and sorrows. May we know that a life shared is a life received and a life enriched. Through Jesus Christ our Lord. Amen.

A benediction

Jesus died for your sins, so be forgiven! You are loved by the Father, so be healed of your self-despisings! You are accompanied everywhere by the Holy Spirit, so be helped and guided and empowered to live beyond yourself, above yourself, for the greater glory of God. Amen.

Some further spiritual exercises

1. Imagine you have just half an hour sitting or walking with Jesus in some relaxing place. Write in your journal what you might say to each other.

2. Think of your enemy, or the person you dislike or despise most. What is the person like? Any idea why he or she is like that? How does God see that person? So — what is to be your future course of action with that person? Again, write it all down in your journal.

3. Confession: write down all the things which bother you, and find a confessor to share them with.

Further reading

Richard Foster, *Celebration of Discipline*, San Francisco: Harper & Row, 1978; Arthur Wallis, *God's Chosen Fast*, CLC, 1986; Joseph F. Wemmer, *Fasting in the New Testament*, New York: Paulist Press, 1982; Dallas Willard, *The Spirit of the Disciplines*, San Francisco: Harper & Row, 1988; Maxie Dunnam, *The Workbook on Spiritual Disciplines*, Nashville, Tennessee: The Upper Room, 1984.

Notes

1. David Tripp, 'Fasting' in Gordon S. Wakefield (ed.), *A Dictionary of Christian Spirituality*, London: SCM, 1983, p. 148.
2. R. D. Linder, 'Fasting', in Walter Elwell, (ed.), *Evangelical Dictionary of Theology*, Michigan: Baker Book House, 1984, pp. 406-7.
3. Richard Foster, *Celebration of Discipline*, London: Hodder & Stoughton, 1980, chapter 4. I heard Richard Foster give a lecture at Fuller Seminary on fasting where he suggested fasting from such entities as the telephone, billboards, television and other things — any deprivation that may get our means and ends into perspective for a while.
4. Dietrich Bonhoeffer, *Prisoner for God*, London: SCM, 1953, p. 166.

Living in community

15
Do I have to join a church?

(Christ) is before all things, and in him all things hold together. He is the head of the body, the church; he is the beginning, the firstborn from the dead, so that he might come to have first place in everything. To them God chose to make known how great among the Gentiles are the riches of the glory of this mystery, which is Christ in you, the hope of glory. It is he whom we proclaim, warning everyone and teaching everyone in all wisdom, so that we may present everyone mature in Christ.

And he has put all things under his feet and has made him the head over all things for the church, which is his body, the fullness of him who fills all in all. In him the whole structure is joined together and grows into a holy temple in the Lord; in whom you also are built together spiritually into a dwelling place for God.

So then you are no longer strangers and aliens, but you are citizens with the saints and also members of the household of God, built upon the foundation of the apostles and prophets, with Christ Jesus himself as the cornerstone. In him the whole structure is joined together and grows into a holy temple in the Lord; in whom you also are built together spiritually into a dwelling place for God.

They devoted themselves to the apostles' teaching and fellowship, to the breaking of bread and the prayers. Awe came upon everyone, because many wonders and signs were being done by the apostles. All who believed were together and had all things in common; they would sell their possessions and goods and distribute the proceeds to all, as any had need. Day by day,

157

as they spent much time together in the temple, they broke bread at home and ate their food with glad and generous hearts, praising God and having the goodwill of all the people. And day by day the Lord added to their number those who were being saved.

The gifts he gave were... to equip the saints for the work of the ministry, for building up the body of Christ, until all of us come to the unity of the faith and of the knowledge of the Son of God, to maturity, to the measure of the full stature of Christ. We must no longer be children... But speaking the truth in love, we must grow up in every way into him who is the head, into Christ, from whom the whole body, joined and knit together by every ligament with which it is equipped, as each part is working properly, promotes the body's growth in building itself up in love.

You then, my child, be strong in the grace that is in Christ Jesus; and what you have heard from me through many witnesses entrust to faithful people who will be able to teach others as well. Share in suffering like a good soldier of Christ Jesus.

As God's chosen ones, holy and beloved, clothe yourselves with compassion, kindness, humility, meekness and patience. Bear with one another and, if anyone has a complaint against another, forgive each other; just as the Lord has forgiven you, so you also must forgive. Above all, clothe yourselves with love, which binds everything together in perfect harmony. And let the peace of Christ rule in your hearts, to which indeed you were called in the one body. And be thankful. Let the word of Christ dwell in you richly; teach and admonish one another in all wisdom; and with gratitude in your hearts sing psalms, hymns and spiritual songs to God. And whatever you do, in word or deed, do everything in the name of the Lord Jesus, giving thanks to God the Father through him.

Not neglecting to meet together, as is the habit of some, but encouraging one another, and all the more as you see the Day approaching.

As you sing psalms and hymns and spiritual songs among yourselves, singing and making melody to the Lord in your hearts, giving thanks to God the Father at all times and for everything in the name of our Lord Jesus Christ.

But I, through the abundance of your steadfast love, will enter your house, I will bow down toward your holy temple in awe of you.

We walked in the house of God with the throng.

Honour everyone. Love the family of believers. Fear God. Honour the emperor.

Colossians 1:17-18, 27-28; Ephesians 1:22-23; Ephesians 2:21-22; Ephesians 2:19-22; Acts 2:42-47; Ephesians 4:12-16; 2 Timothy 2:1-4; Colossians 3:12-17; Hebrews 10:25; Ephesians 5:19-20; Psalm 5:7; Psalm 55:14; 1 Peter 2:17.

Can you be a good Christian outside the church? That's like asking 'Can a nose be a nose without a face?' When asked this question, a pastor reached for a live coal from the fire, put it onto the hearth, where it blackened and lost its heat. He then restored it back to the fire and it soon burned brightly again.

According to sociologist Robert Bellah, eighty-one per cent of Americans agree that 'an individual should arrive at his or her own religious belief independent of any church or synagogue'. Many who claim to be Christians are arriving at faith on their own terms — terms that make no demands on behaviour. A woman named Sheila, interviewed for Bellah's *Habits of the Heart*, embodies this attitude. 'I believe in God', she said. 'I can't remember the last time I went to church. But my faith has carried me a long way. It's "Sheila-ism". Just my own little voice.'[1]

The church has four functions, essentially: *worship* — everything we do for the glory of God, individually or collectively; *community* — all we do to enhance the lives of one another; *formation* — the process of individuals' being formed into the image of Christ; *mission* — everything done for those outside its membership. A healthy church does all these effectively, as does every group within it, to some extent.

To enhance those four functions, we sing praises to the Lord, hear the Word of God in preaching, share a sacramental life, pray with one another, study the Scriptures together, encourage one another, and celebrate significant events in each others' lives.

Every church needs a pastor, or shepherd. The pastor — with others appropriately gifted — leads, preaches, counsels, visits the members and others, and trains the church for ministry. Typically a full-time pastor spends half the time with God, alone, and half with people; and half the people-time ought to be spent in training. Because pastors are called by God, their office should be honoured. Pastors suffer a high degree of stress these days trying to meet many conflicting expectations. Do your best to encourage your pastor/s. Allow them to have at least one day off a week, and be available to their families without having to attend lots of meetings. ('What shall it profit a pastor if he or she gathers a whole lot of people and loses health or family?').

Pastors must never forget that the 'ministry' belongs to the whole church. Pastors facilitate the ministry of others; others do not exist to 'help the pastor run the church'.

Most churches at some time have a Sunday school for children, boys' and girls' clubs during the week, a youth group, small groups for adults, women's group, and perhaps a men's group, etc. Most churches have a deacons' or elders' board, and, if larger, a finance committee, nominating committee, mission committee, etc. Your church can't do everything, particularly if it's small: why not figure out the few things your church does best and work hard at producing excellence in those areas?

Training is essential — for every ministry within the church. Leaders should be trained to lead, imparting a vision to those they lead. Church members should be trained to help their friends (counselling) and reach out to those who do not yet know the Lord (evangelism). The whole church should be a miniature theological seminary, learning about the faith. Then new Christians or those enquiring about the Christian faith ought to have a 'Christianity Explained' class. A seminar on spiritual gifts will help people discover why they are on this planet and not yet in heaven!

Classes or groups can address life-situations: young mothers with their first babies, marriage enrichment, coping with retirement, balancing the budget for young marrieds or the unemployed, how to get a job, alcoholics anonymous, GROW groups for those with emotional troubles, tutorials for high school students, etc.

One of the problems the church faces — as does any human system — is institutionalism. Every group has its traditions or structures, but when these rule the life of the group, it soon dies. Structures need renewal; but renewal needs structure, as a body needs bones. The ideal is to seek for freedom within order.

What kind of order? The New Testament churches — and churches since — seemed to make decisions three ways: first the episcopal way — leaders with almost absolute authority ruling by decree; second, the presbyterian way, with groups of elders making significant decisions for the group; third the congregational way, with the whole church meeting to decide what is God's will for them. Catholics, Anglicans and the Salvation Army are generally episcopal; Presbyterians give high authority to elders; Baptists are congregational. Most churches these days incorporate the best of all three into their 'polity'.

Institutionalism breeds legalism, with lots of rules for this and that. Certainly have a constitution — make it simple, and refer to it rarely. Who should belong to your church? Any who 'name the Name' in my view (see Romans 15:7). Churches that insist on only one form of baptism or who rebaptise those from other churches, may be guilty of Pharisaism: adding traditions to grace.

It's good to prayerfully set a few goals — just four or five a year. This keeps us future-oriented. Those who fail to plan plan to fail.

Pull your weight in the church: be available to help. Be

friendly. One person visited a church and stayed. Why? 'They're friendly. When they ask how you are, they really want to know. And if I say "Not too good" they respond with "Tell me about it". That doesn't mean we are 'addicted to affability': if we don't see eye to eye we do something about it. Two people who think and disagree are closer together than two people who don't think and agree!

And always remember, Christ is the head of the church, not any human being. Our calling is to follow him, and to follow others inasmuch as they follow him. We are not merely a social institution or a 'glee club', we are his people in the world, doing in our day what he did in his. Ours too is a ministry of reconciliation, of healing, of salvation: we exist for those outside the church, as well as for those within it.

God has ordained three institutions for the ordering of society: the family for the propagation of life, the state for the preservation of life, and the church for the proclamation of the gospel. These are not just voluntary associations that people can join or not as they see fit; they are organic sources of authority for restraining evil and humanising society.

Charles Colson,
Against the Night, London: Hodder & Stoughton, 1990, p. 69. Reproduced by permission of Hodder & Stoughton Ltd/New English Library Ltd.

Let (those) who cannot be alone beware of community. (They) will only do harm to (themselves) and to the community. Alone you stood before God when he called you; alone you had to answer that call; alone you had to struggle and pray; and alone you will die and give an account to God. You cannot escape from yourself; for God has singled you out. If you refuse to be alone you are rejecting Christ's call to you, and you can have no part in the community of those who are called...

But the reverse is also true: Let (those) who are not in community beware of being alone. Into the community you were called, the call was not meant for you alone; in the community of the called you bear your cross, you struggle, you pray. You are not alone, even in death, and on the Last Day you will be only one member of the great congregation of Jesus Christ, and thus your solitude can be only hurtful to you...

We recognize, then, that only as we are within the fellowship can we be alone, and only (those who are) alone can live in the fellowship.

Dietrich Bonhoeffer,
Life Together, New York: Harper & Row, 1954, p. 77.

We must not regard the Church purely as an institution or an organization. She is certainly visible and clearly recognizable in her teachings, her government, and her worship. These are the external lineaments through which we may see the interior radiance of her soul. This soul is not merely human, it is divine. It is the Holy Spirit itself. The Church, like Christ, lives and acts in a manner at once human and divine. Certainly there is imperfection in the human members of Christ, but their imperfection is inseparably united to his perfection, sustained by his power, and purified by his holiness, as long as they remain in living union with him by faith and love... Hence the true nature of the Church is that of a body in which all the members 'bear one another's burdens'...

Thomas Merton,
'The Mystery of the Church', in *Meditations on the Church, based on the Dogmatic Constitution on the Church, Second Vatican Council*, 1964, New York: Herder and Herder, 1967, pp. 45-6.

The one who really tries to follow Christ will know that whatever has been accomplished in the name of Christ through nineteen centuries has been accomplished not by single piccolos and flutes tooting their isolated tunes, but by the great symphony of the Church playing harmoniously under its Divine Conductor; and one will ask no higher privilege than to be a member of that symphony and play one's part, however obscure, in making the Church strong and effectual.

A. Leonard Griffith,
What is a Christian?, London: Lutterworth Press, 1962, p. 19.

It is often said that the church is full of neurotics and hypocrites, and this is perfectly true. The church should want them, when everyone else regards them as nuisances, and I wish the church had more of them.

G. A. ffrench-Beytagh,
quoted in William Barclay, *Testament of Faith*, Oxford: Mowbrays, 1977, p. 102.

The German philosopher Schopenhauer once said that people are like a pack of porcupines on a freezing winter night. The sub-zero temperature forces them together for warmth. But as soon as they press very close, they jab and hurt one another. So they separate, only to attempt, in vain, over and over again, to huddle together. Love is painful. For Jesus it meant the thorns and the agony of the nails... Today the church, as the body of Christ on earth, must also know something of this same crucifixion, together with its pain, before men and women will be drawn by the love of God to himself.

David Watson,
I Believe in the Church, London: Hodder and Stoughton, 1978, p. 367. Reproduced by permission of Hodder & Stoughton Ltd/New English Library Ltd.

The dark malaise of the Christian church in our time is that so many congregations have developed a preoccupation with their weaknesses, their problems, and their concerns. It is as if there were no open tomb or risen Lord. It is as if these congregations preferred to live locked in a closed tomb, focusing on their past and refusing to recognize the strengths God has shared with them that they might be in mission in this world...

We need more persons who are willing to be competent, compassionate, courageous, and committed missionaries, and we need fewer who are willing to be only professional ministers. That is to say, we need more persons who are willing to be active in the world in mission and fewer who are willing to be only reactive within the programs and activities of the local church.

Kennon L. Callahan,
Twelve Keys to an Effective Church: Strategic Planning for Mission, San Francisco: Harper & Row, 1983, p. xxi.

Doctors test our bodies for health, and diagnose illness. How would you test a church for its health? Try these: (1) In corporate worship, they are sometimes 'lost in wonder love and praise'; (2) For an increasing number worship 'in church' deeply affects 'worship in the world'; (3) A growing percentage of the members belong to small groups for worship, study, sharing life's concerns and prayer; (4) A growing number who 'come to church' once come back again: they sense life there; (5) People are making significant faith commitments regularly; (6) The church is increasingly involved in ministries of mercy to the disadvantaged; (7) It is also increasingly concerned about injustices in the world, and makes concerted efforts to 'stir' about some of them; (8) Helpful Christian books are regularly bought from a well-stocked bookstall; (9) Members are honest, open, forgiving each other; (10) Those for whom life has been hard find a place to belong.

Rowland Croucher,
from a seminar for clergy, 1992.

It seems rather strange that very few books on leadership have chapters on followership. As a matter of fact, followership is not even in the unabridged dictionary. There seems to be a curious assumption that while leaders need special instruction for exercising their role, followers need no such instruction.

The more I study church leadership, the more I disagree with the assumption. Many pastors who would like to, cannot lead their congregation because of a basic lack of sensitivity on the part of the people as to their role as followers...

(But, in the Bible a) sharp warning is sounded for pastors. A great deal of leadership authority is handed to them, but because they are human beings this can be, and all too often is, abused... Sociologically, churches are voluntary associations. Spiritually, churches are the family of God. Neither allows for a coercive type of leadership authority... The dangers of lordship, rather than Christian leadership, are clear.

Peter Wagner,
Leading Your Church to Growth by Peter Wagner, copyright 1984, Regal Books, Ventura CA 93003.
Used by permission.

Ask the governing body of your congregation... to list five or six significant accomplishments in ministry that occurred in or through this congregation during the past twelve months... If your congregation resembles the typical church, the respondents will include a few people who are unable to list more than one or two... perhaps one or two leaders who complete the exercise with a blank list...

This exercise illustrates one of the most important basic principles in church planning. The skill which the churches have developed to the highest level of competence is the capability of keeping secrets!

Lifting the level of self-esteem of a congregation requires breaking this conspiracy of secrecy.

Lyle Schaller,
Hey That's Our Church!, Nashville: Abingdon Press, 1975, pp. 186-7.

When sociologists study organizations they distinguish between the logic of mission and the logic of maintenance. The logic of mission considers an organization's goals and the way it functions to realize those goals. The logic of maintenance studies the way the organization seeks to perpetuate its interests. While both logics are essential for organizational survival, they often conflict. When this happens there exists a tendency, social scientists have discovered, to place more weight on the logic of maintenance than the logic of mission.

Michael H. Crosby,
The Dysfunctional Church, Notre Dame, Indiana: Ave Maria Press, 1991, p. 78.

The church with all her ministries lives continuously in history as a pilgrim people among all the communities of mankind, in obedience to Christ and in a constant solidarity with the world. This means that the Church with repentance and renewal, with the hope and joy which Jesus gives, is always ready to be reshaped in the forms of its ministry according to his call at each stage of the pilgrim life.

Max Thurian (ed.),
Ecumenical Perspectives on Baptism, Eucharist and Ministry, Geneva: World Council of Churches, 1983, p. 223.

I think the church is the only thing that is going to make the terrible world we are coming to endurable; the only thing that makes the church endurable is that it is somehow the body of Christ and that on this we are fed. It seems to be a fact that you have to suffer as much *from* the church as *for* it but if you believe in the divinity of Christ you have to cherish the world at the same time that you struggle to endure it.

Flannery O'Connor,
from a letter, quoted in John H. Westerhoff, *Building God's People in a Materialistic Society*, New York: Seabury Press, 1983, p. 145.

If the church is to be saved — if it can be saved — it will be according to the same rule that goes for all of us as individuals. That is the rule of true repentance. To turn the church's own language upon itself, it must earnestly desire to be saved. It cannot dictate its own terms of surrender. On the contrary, it must prostrate itself before its Lord in utter brokenness and humility... It must become a glad beggar again, a servant whose only joy is in serving. That way there will be no counting of cost, no worry over property or possessions, no concern about status. The load will be lightened, and the way will not seem hard. The dreams will be good again, not troubled, for they are dreams of the wholeness of humankind.

John Killinger,
The Second Coming of the Church, Nashville: Abingdon, 1974, pp. 13-14.

There was a woman in my parish who suffered more physically than anyone I've known. As a young woman she had been a haute couture model and a singer with an operatic-quality voice. A degenerative arthritis slowly destroyed her joints, wracked her with excruciating pain, and left her crippled...

Though her faith never wavered, more than once she said to me that God had abandoned her. 'Where', she asked, 'am I to see God's love for me?'

In her last years, she became the centre of attention for a group of women in the parish. Most of them were a generation younger, and had gotten to know her through a women's Bible study and other parish activities. Singly or at times together, without any planning or organization, they simply began to visit her at home and in the hospital when she was there. They would run errands, care for some household duties, but mostly just be with her, pray with her, sit with her, talk with her. Slowly in the depth of her suffering, she began to realize that she had not been abandoned by God. True, there were no moments of mystical intimacy, or interventions of dramatic healing. The love of God came to her in a quiet way, through the calm, patient affection of those women. We cannot live the Christian life in isolation. He calls us into koinonia.

Kenneth Swanson,
Uncommon Prayer, New York: Ballantine, 1987, pp. 113-14.

Most merciful God, we confess that we are in bondage to sin and cannot free ourselves. We have sinned against you in thought, word and deed, by what we have done and by what we have left undone. We have not loved you with our whole heart; we have not loved our neighbours as ourselves. For the sake of your Son, Jesus Christ, have mercy on us. Forgive us, renew us and lead us, so that we may delight in your will and walk in your ways, to the glory of your holy name. Amen.

The eucharistic liturgy of Lima, 1982, in Max Thurian (ed.), *Ecumenical Perspectives on Baptism, Eucharist and Ministry*, Geneva: World Council of Churches, 1983, p. 237.

Lord, send your light upon your family. May they continue to enjoy your favour and devote themselves to doing good. We ask this through Christ our Lord.

Daily Mass Book, Brisbane: The Liturgical Commission, 1990, p. 37.

A benediction
The Lord bless you and keep you. The Lord make his face to shine on you and be gracious to you. The Lord look upon you with favour and give you peace. Almighty God, Father, Son and Holy Spirit, bless you now and forever.

Note
1. Robert Bellah, *Habits of the Heart*, Berkeley: University of California Press, 1985, p. 228.

The Benediction was taken from the eucharistic liturgy of Lima, 1982, in Max Thurian (ed), *Ecumenical Perspectives on Baptism, Eucharist and Ministry*, Geneva: World Council of Churches, 1983, p. 246.

16

Why are there so many Christian denominations?

Holy Father, protect them in your name that you have given me, so that they may be one, as we are one... I ask not only on behalf of these, but also on behalf of those who will believe in me through their word, that they may all be one. As you, Father, are in me and I am in you, may they also be in us, so that the world may believe that you have sent me.

The kingdom of heaven may be compared to someone who sowed good seed in his field; but while everybody was asleep, an enemy came and sowed weeds among the wheat, and then went away. So when the plants came up and bore grain, then the weeds appeared as well.

Beware of false prophets, who come to you in sheep's clothing but inwardly are ravenous wolves. You will know them by their fruits... A good tree cannot bear bad fruit, nor can a bad tree bear good fruit. I am afraid that as the serpent deceived Eve by its cunning, your thoughts will be led astray from a sincere and pure devotion to Christ. For if someone comes and proclaims another Jesus than the one we proclaimed... or a different gospel from the one you accepted, you submit to it readily enough... for such are false apostles, deceitful workers, disguising themselves as apostles of Christ. And no wonder! Even Satan disguises himself as an angel of light. Some people have deviated... and turned to meaningless talk, desiring to be teachers of the law, without understanding either what they are saying or the things about which they make assertions. Brothers and sisters, do not be weary in doing what is right. Take note of those who do not obey what we say in this letter; have nothing to do with them, so that they may be ashamed. Do not regard them as enemies, but warn them as believers.

Making every effort to maintain the unity of the Spirit in the bond of peace... There is one body and one Spirit, just as you were called to the one hope of your calling, one Lord, one faith, one baptism, one God and Father of all, who is above all and through all and in all. That Christ may dwell in your hearts through faith, as you are being rooted and grounded in love. I pray that you may have the power to comprehend, with all the saints, what is the breadth and length and height and depth, and to know the love of Christ that surpasses knowledge. ...The head, from whom the whole body, nourished and held together by its ligaments and sinews, grows with a growth that is from God.

But speaking the truth in love, we must grow up in every way into him who is the head, into Christ, from whom the whole body, joined and knit together by every ligament with which it is equipped, as each part is working properly, promotes the body's growth in building itself up in love. Pray in the Spirit at all times in every prayer and supplication. To that end keep alert and always persevere in supplication for all the saints. And this is my prayer, that your love may overflow more and more with knowledge and full insight.

John 17:11, 20-21; Matthew 13:24-26; Matthew 7:15, 18; 2 Corinthians 11:3-4, 13-14; 1 Timothy 1:6; 2 Thessalonians 3:13-15; Ephesians 4:3-6; Ephesians 3:17-19; Colossians 2:19; Ephesians 4:15-16; Ephesians 6:18; Philippians 1:9.

• In March 1982, when the Archbishop of Canterbury went to Liverpool, he was met by about a hundred noisy protesters, waving banners and jeering him, because of his well-known views about the need for Christian unity. His address was constantly interrupted by people yelling 'Judas', 'Hang him', 'Traitor', etc. The interjections occurred even when he was praying. The protesters believed that the Roman Catholic Church was unreformed, the 'harlot' of Revelation 13...

• Archbishop Oscar Romero was a small man — about five feet high — who urged his priests in El Salvador to 'put feet on the gospel' and challenge the idea that God ordained a few to be rich and the majority to be poor. At Easter 1980 he was celebrating Mass in a hospital near his cathedral. As he raised the chalice, a shot rang out, and Oscar Romero's blood mingled with the spilt wine...

• For many years, when Americans were asked 'Which living persons do you admire most?', two Christians always appeared near the top of the lists: Billy Graham and Mother Teresa. Billy Graham has probably spoken to more people face to face than anyone else in history. Mother Teresa is probably the best-known Catholic Christian in the world, after the Pope. Billy Graham is a Baptist evangelist. Mother Teresa is an Albanian-born Catholic nun. Billy Graham lives in a beautiful home in one of the world's wealthiest countries — the U.S.A. Mother Teresa ministers to the poorest of the poor, in Calcutta and other places. What do they both have in common? Simply, a sincere commitment to follow Jesus Christ...

A well-known Japanese Christian, speaking about the many Christian churches, would, in halting English, call them 'damnations'. Was he wrong? 'I believe in one holy catholic and apostolic church', Archbishop William Temple once remarked, 'but regret that it doesn't exist'.

The great American Methodist missionary, Stanley Jones, once asked how another missionary group had got such a lovely property. The reply: 'The man who owned it built such high and expensive walls around it that he went bankrupt... and had to sell the property'. Imagine that — bankrupt building walls! Jones wondered (as I do) whether that is not dangerously near the history of Christian churches today?

There are many varieties of religious experience. We tend to gravitate towards those who have some affinity with our own beliefs, experience, or social and educational background. Or else we have a particular kind of personality, and we enjoy being with those like us. Latin American Pentecostals will not be comfortable worshipping like German Lutherans, and vice-versa. The human species is greatly varied, so are their religions.

But that's not the problem. The difficulty begins when Latins and Germans tell each other, 'You've gotta be like me!' Or the Brethren say to the Pentecostals, 'Your gift of tongues is worthless'. Or the fundamentalist says of the Uniting Church 'They're too liberal, and therefore not as Christian as I am, a conservative'. Or the Catholics (in pre-Vatican II thinking) tell others they're at best 'separated brethren'.

Yes, the Roman Catholic Church believed it was the one true church. Vatican II's *Decree on Ecumenism* helped to change all that. Theologian Oscar Cullmann says of this decree: 'This is more than the opening of a door: new ground has been broken. No Catholic document has ever spoken of non-Catholic Christians in this way'.[1]

Traditionalists (for example Anglo-Catholics) believe worship patterns are fixed: in worship we re-present to God our lives in liturgies which go back into the history of the church. Renewalists (for example Pentecostalists) believe worship patterns are flexible: in worship we spontaneously offer to God our praise 'as the Spirit moves', in forms which may change from week to week.

169

The pattern throughout the history of the Western church has been: out of a perception of 'deadness', renewal. Eventually the renewal movement settles down and becomes institutionalised — so another renewal is needed.

But the order versus freedom question is only one of many which has divided churches from one another. 'How should the church be governed?' is another: Anglicans are episcopal — ruled by bishops; Presbyterians believe in rule by elders; Baptists and Congregationalists allow the congregation to decide major matters. Then there are different views about ministry: Anglicans appoint bishops, priests or presbyters, and deacons; Presbyterians have ruling elders and teaching elders, and deacons; Baptists have pastors and deacons (with a growing number now appointing elders).

Another issue is baptism: Baptists baptise adolescents or adults only, and exclusively by immersion; although Anglicans allow and affirm baptism of adults by immersion, most of their baptisms are of children by sprinkling or pouring. (As we will see in chapter 20, the main issue is not the age of the recipient of this sacrament, nor the amount of water used, but its being done once, in the name of the Father, Son and Holy Spirit. This is an example of churches majoring on matters of lesser importance.)

The earliest baptismal confession — 'Jesus is Lord' — and the Christian credo of the catacombs — 'Jesus Christ, God's Son, Saviour' — were all that were needed for the earliest Christians to identify one another.

Each Christian denomination has its strengths and weaknesses. This is a personal opinion, but I believe (with Robert Webber) that the Anglican tradition (Episcopalian in the U.S.) has six strengths: an appreciation of mystery, worship tied to theologically respectable liturgical forms, a well-developed sacramental theology, a historical identity, an ecumenical affiliation, and a holistic spirituality. On the other hand, the Pentecostalists, Brethren, Baptists and Churches of Christ insist on a greater lay participation in worship, Bible study and evangelism, and tend to produce more 'hands-on, out-going' Christians. The Uniting Church in Australia (combining former Methodist, Presbyterian and Congregational Churches) combines some of the best elements in several traditions. The Salvation Army majors (pardon the pun) on ministries of compassion.

The great weakness of all the mainline churches is their tendency towards institutionalism and spiritual inertia. On the other hand, there are sectarian tendencies in other denominations. The Brethren have to be careful about their exclusiveness (sometimes claiming to possess a monopoly on biblical truth).

The Pentecostalists have to watch the tendency to produce first and second-class Christians not on the basis of character, but on the possession of certain spiritual gifts (especially tongues, healing, word of knowledge). The Churches of Christ and Baptists make a particular form of baptism a ticket to membership and debar people of good Christian character who have not had sufficient water applied to them. The Salvation Army ought to be careful not to give music too great a prominence: many in their bands and songster groups do not attend Christian growth groups.

In summary: the Holy Spirit is at work in every denomination, and every local church (and in every Christian). The devil is also at work. This 'spiritual warfare' shouldn't surprise us: Jesus said an enemy would be sowing weeds among the grain, and it will all be sorted out at the great judgment (Matthew 13:24-30).

A comment about the ecumenical movement, which Archbishop William Temple, in 1942, called 'the great new fact of our time'. The further to the right the denomination (that is the more conservative theologically), the more suspicious it is likely to be about joining together with other churches. The far right has developed conspiracy theories about all this (a one-world church ruled by the Pope, etc.).

My own response to the ecumenical movement is mixed. I've noticed that those who expend great energy working for the organic union of denominations ('ecclesiastical joinery'), good as that may be, sometimes lose touch with the evangelistic nature of the church. On the other hand, Jesus did pray that his followers would be one, and that this would be noted by 'the world'. At present conservatives are working hard to perpetuate the divisiveness which is scandalous in the eyes of 'the world'. If other Christians are my brothers and sisters in the Lord, perhaps there is a reason why I should not have full fellowship with them, but at present I can't think of it! I have so much to learn from them, to add to the knowledge of God derived from my own limited background.

What doctrines should Christians agree about? Try these: there is only one God — Father, Son, and Holy Spirit; Jesus Christ is Lord and Saviour and will come again as judge; we are united with Christ through repentance and faith, and belong to his church through baptism; our faith is divinely revealed in the Scriptures; Christianity is essentially living out a life of justice and love, in the power of the Spirit.

Let me urge you to affirm the distinctives of your own tradition, but also recognise its weaknesses and the strengths in others'. Thomas Aquinas, the great 13th century Catholic theologian wrote, *Ubi amor, ibi oculus* ('Where there is love there is vision'): knowing and loving are linked. D. L. Moody, the

171

19th century American evangelist used to say, 'If you go through the world with love in your heart, you will make the world love you, and love is the badge that Christ gave his disciples'. What unites us is more important — much, much, more important — than what divides us. Let us accept one another, then, for the glory of God, as Christ has accepted us (Romans 15:7).

When I was in the Royal Air Force doing my national service, the Christian fellowship I attended used to have an open Bible study and discussion group. It came as quite a jolt to us all one evening, as we shared our experience of the fatherhood of God, to realize that we represented eight different denominations, including Roman Catholicism. Yet, somehow, our church allegiance, important though it was, did not matter. What was of greater importance was our common starting point in having a relationship with God. We belonged to one another through him.

George Carey,
A Tale of Two Churches: Can Protestants & Catholics Get Together? Downers Grove, Illinois: Intervarsity Press, 1985, p. 59.

Christians have more that unites them than what divides them. We have begun to move toward one another. The signs include: • theological dialogue no longer based on polemics but on a desire to understand and heal the past, characterized by a number of interfaith conversations that are still going on, • worship as Christians from different traditions worship and pray together, • charismatic experience as mainstream denominations have been penetrated by the renewal movement, leading to fresh insight from the Spirit and vital Christian experience, • the personal challenge individual Christians have experienced to consider the contributions each of us can make to the cause of Christian unity.

George Carey,
A Tale of Two Churches: Can Protestants & Catholics Get Together? Downers Grove, Illinois: Intervarsity Press, 1985, pp. 154-5.

I spent all of my childhood and most of my adult life dreading going to church. It was the place where I was supposed to get my spiritual batteries charged and it ended up being the spiritual drain of the week. I thought the problem was me. Since I've become an Episcopalian, I've discovered that what I needed was an experience of God-centred worship. I now love to be at church.

James Stambaugh,
Curator, Billy Graham Museum, Wheaton College, quoted in Robert Webber, *Evangelicals on the Canterbury Trail: Why Evangelicals are Attracted to the Liturgical Church*, Waco, Texas: Word Books, 1985, p. 31.

(The spiritual tradition of the liturgical church is) sane, wise, ancient, modern, sound and simple; with roots in the New Testament and the Fathers... its golden periods and its full quota of saints and doctors.

Martin Thornton,
English Spirituality, quoted in Robert Webber, *Evangelicals on the Canterbury Trail: Why Evangelicals are Attracted to the Liturgical Church,* Waco, Texas: Word Books, 1985, p. 143.

Evangelicals bring to the liturgical tradition these strengths — the sense of personal conversion, a deep concern to be orthodox, an attachment and love for the Scripture, and a sense of mission.

Robert Webber,
Evangelicals on the Canterbury Trail: Why Evangelicals are Attracted to the Liturgical Church, Waco, Texas: Word Books, 1985, p. 170.

(The social ideas of church leaders have been) derived from the surrounding intellectual and political culture and not, as churchmen themselves always tend to assume, from theological learning... Each generation of Christians offers up in each age what they judge most to convey the presence of Christ. A lot of what is transient gets caught up in the process.

E. R. Norman,
Church and Society in England 1770-1970, quoted in Gavin White, *How the Churches Got to be That Way,* London: SCM Press, 1990, p. 63.

I was in a mainline church and did nothing. It didn't seem to matter what kind of faith I had. For years I participated in the life of the church, and served on its committees, but didn't grow spiritually one little bit. Then, after a spiritual experience they sometimes call 'baptism in the Holy Spirit' I joined the Pentecostals. They had me participating in an evangelistic crusade in Indonesia within a few months. I had to declare my commitment. Now, a year later, I've grown more in the spiritual life than in the previous twenty years in that dead church.

A Christian man in Victoria, Australia, to the author, 1989.

'Now abides faith, hope and love, and the greatest of these is baptism.'

Churches of Christ pastor. Sardonic comment heard in a Churches of Christ pastors' conference.

You know, I think in another hundred years or so people are going to look back on the period between the Reformation and the twentieth century as the second Dark Ages of the church... I believe that the divisions which have haunted the church over the last four centuries have begun in our time to be healed. The walls that have separated us are being broken down. A great new convergence of the traditions are occurring which will change the face of the church...

Robert Schuller,
quoted in Robert Webber, *Evangelicals on the Canterbury Trail: Why Evangelicals are Attracted to the Liturgical Church,* Waco, Texas: Word Books, 1985, p. 171.

173

Divisions in the church have always existed, and there have always been occasions when it has been necessary for somebody, somewhere, to leave and to set up a rival body. Yet in time the reasons for the divisions become less pressing, or are overcome by new developments, and it is possible to put back together the fragments of an earlier age.

Gavin White,
How the Churches Got to be That Way, London: SCM Press, 1990, p. 105.

Eli Halevy was a distinguished French historian who wrote of the history of England. He noted, as any Frenchman would, that England had no French Revolution. This remarkable fact had to be explained. What did England have in the eighteenth century which France did not? The answer was obvious. Methodism. The Methodists had given English workers and peasants an ideology which led them to work and not to agitate, and their religious hopes had made them indifferent to social and economic complaints... Today the Halevy thesis is out of fashion, but it still reappears in modern forms.

Gavin White,
How the Churches Got to be That Way, London: SCM Press, 1990, p. 33.

It has been argued that missionaries went to Africa and Asia with cultural baggage; undoubtedly they did. Nobody goes anywhere without cultural baggage, and Christianity can no more live without a culture than bacteria in a laboratory can live without a culture.

Gavin White,
How the Churches Got to be That Way, London: SCM Press, 1990, p. 74.

The gift of tongues is not given to every Pentecostalist, and the desperate attempts to keep it alive suggest that it may be declining. It is something most world religions seem to produce for periods in their history... The spread of Pentecostalism has been erratic. Nobody knows why it has been successful in South Africa but scarcely elsewhere in Africa. Nobody knows why it flourishes in parts of Latin America but not in Asia.

Gavin White,
How the Churches Got to be That Way, London: SCM Press, 1990, pp. 86-7.

The members of the Eternal Church of the Believer were all part of a very special group inside society at large. The Church told you never to donate money to (other) causes. You tithed your ten per cent... and when there was some great new need, the Church would ask for a second tithe... As a Church member you had to live up to certain codes of dress and behaviour. You did not seek medical help because it was a proven fact that faith kept the members healthier than all those people who had not found the true religion... Sometimes you could not understand why certain rules were imposed on you. But in the end you realized every rule was there for a good reason...

Part of the reason for the success of the Eternal Church of the Believer... (was because) it was a way out of a life of dreariness and despair. It made them part of some great shiny thing that overshadowed their workday, and gave them a source of both pride and a kind of humble arrogance. I am forever saved and you are forever damned. Hooray for me.

John D. Macdonald,

One More Sunday, London: Hodder & Stoughton, 1984, pp. 114, 187. Reproduced by permission of Hodder & Stoughton Ltd/New English Library Ltd.

A church in whom the Bible will have the last word will never be able to forget that it is not the kingdom of God and that it lives under the constant judgment of God.

William A. Visser 't Hooft,

The Renewal of the Church, London: SCM Press, 1956, p. 93.

Lord, we come to worship,
Lord, we come to praise,
Lord, we come to worship you
in oh so many ways.
Some of us shout,
Some of us sing,
Some of us whisper
the praise we bring,
But, Lord, we are all gathering
To bring to you our praise.

Ishmael

(English Christian singer) quoted in George Carey, *A Tale of Two Churches: Can Protestants & Catholics Get Together?* Downers Grove, Illinois: Intervarsity Press, 1985, p. 158.

Who are we whom God has called? Few of us are wise, few are powerful. Yet to shame the wise God has chosen what the world counts folly; to shame the strong God has chosen what the world counts weakness.

In union with Christ Jesus, we are all children of God. Baptised into union with Christ, we have put on Christ like a garment. There is no such thing as Jew or Greek, slave or free, male or female; we are all one in Jesus Christ.

175

A New Zealand Prayer Book, Auckland: Collins, 1989, p. 115.

A benediction

Because God's wisdom is so vast, his truth sometimes beyond our knowing, his family so diverse, his love so all-encompassing, go now into his world, enjoying your status as his son or daughter. Go in his love and share his peace with all you meet, whatever their race, religion, sex, age or gifting. In the name of the Father, Son and Holy Spirit — a diverse Trinity but one God. Amen.

Further Reading

George Carey, *A Tale of Two Churches: Can Protestants & Catholics Get Together?* Downers Grove, Illinois: Intervarsity Press, 1985; Robert Webber, *Evangelicals on the Canterbury Trail: Why Evangelicals are Attracted to the Liturgical Church*, Waco, Texas: Word Books, 1985; Gavin White, *How the Churches Got to be That Way*, London: SCM Press, 1990.

Note

1. Quoted by Walter M. Abbott, S.J., (ed.), *The Documents of Vatican II*, London: Geoffrey Chapman, 1966, p. 338.

Capsule 1

An overview of church history

The early churches experienced diversity: the church in Corinth was not the same as that which produced the fourth Gospel, or another in Thessalonica. But there was unity-in-diversity; they were being persecuted, first by Jews, then by Romans, and many Christians in the first three centuries paid for their faith with their lives.

Why were they persecuted? Christians declared 'Jesus is Lord'; for loyal Romans, Caesar was lord. Other religions lost devotees, and their temple priests and traders lost business. Christians opposed the cruel Roman sports, and so all kinds of accusations were levelled against them including cannibalism (because of their doctrine of the Lord's Supper) and subversion (the Roman authorities had a horror of 'secret societies').

But people began to admire Christians' courage and strong faith, and their numbers grew.

Enter Constantine. Dramatically converted at the Battle of Milvian Bridge (AD 312) he was the first Roman emperor to give Christianity protection by law. Temples were converted into churches; many harsh laws were 'christianised'. The Christian church became the State church. Grants were made for new church buildings; church leaders accepted high government positions.

However, though peace ruled, spiritual decay set in. Promotion within the church often became a matter of selfish ambition and bribery. Policy became increasingly determined by State officials and not by prayerful believers. Masses of half-converted people were added to the church.

Meanwhile, church leaders and conferences had to deal with various heresies, like *gnosticism* — a mix of Christianity, eastern mythologies and pagan philosophy. God, they said, was unknowable and remote, with many 'emanations' between him and human beings; *montanism* — fanatics and ascetics who majored on 'enthusiasm', the gifts of the Spirit, and the imminent end of the world; and *Arianism*, which taught that the Son was inferior to the Father.

After 'barbarians' invaded the Roman Empire at the end of the fourth century, popes became more powerful, and some of them were very evil. Priests and monks were often wealthy, living in luxury. Indulgences — the purchase of God's blessings with money — were commonly sold throughout Europe. Outward acts like Masses for the dead, pilgrimages, and the veneration of sacred objects and places tended to replace inward faith.

About AD 1000, the Orthodox Churches broke away, and have continued as separate entities (like the Greek Orthodox and Russian Orthodox Churches) ever since.

Yet some of the greatest Christians ever — like Francis of Assisi — lived in these 'Dark Ages'. The Protestant Reformation grew out of a disenchantment with the evils and errors of the medieval church. Martin Luther nailed his 95 theses to the Wittenburg church door in 1517. Out of this Reformation grew the Lutheran churches (mainly in northern Europe), the Church of England, the Calvinistic (Presbyterian) family of churches, and the Anabaptists (forerunners of the Baptists and Mennonites).

Later there were to be movements which grew out of these, for example the Methodists and later the Plymouth Brethren out of the Church of England.

According to one authority (David Barrett, *World Christian Encyclopaedia*, reported verbally at the Lausanne II Congress in Manila, 1989), there are 20,800 different Christian 'denominations' in the world today.

A bishop once wrote a pamphlet asking where the church stood. Someone responded that the church did not stand at all, but 'moves and pushes and slides and staggers and falls and gets up again, and stumbles on and presses forward and falls into the right position after all'. That's what church history is all about.

Capsule 2

Sects and Christian deviations

In every church or denomination, there are good and not-so-good features. No church can legitimately point the finger of accusation at others. We are all in need of redemption.

However, the New Testament warns about false teachers, and they have always been with us. These are people who get a major doctrine (like the full deity and manhood of Jesus) wrong. They often have other wonderful qualities: they are very committed to the Lord, they may know their Bibles very well, and are sometimes very 'holy' people. But some key Christian tenets have always been non-negotiable.

Here we will not elaborate on particular 'sects' or 'cults' but look at the general picture. Someone comes to your door with a Special Message for you. They have mapped history from the Old Testament prophets and the Book of Revelation, and Armageddon is just around the corner. If you join their group, you'll be saved. If not...

What drives these people? Cults and sects are strongest where the church is weakest. But everyone has a basic need for spiritual answers to life's great dilemmas. In modern society more people feel alienated and lonely. So these groups appeal to their converts' needs for acceptance and meaning, providing instant community. 'You can be someone special', they say. 'The world — or your church — has hurt you. Join us for healing'. Even at Jonestown, where more than 900 died in a mass suicide, the people thought they had discovered a better way of life.

These new religions tend to form around a self-proclaimed prophet. These charismatic leaders insist on rigorous codes of conduct and behaviour for their followers, complete sometimes with new names, new clothes, new hairstyles, even new birthdays. They tell their members the rest of the world is evil, and forbid contact with other groups which might contaminate the purity of their 'truth'.

When someone comes along and says 'I have the key to the cosmos, I know the answer', it can be liberating at first for a confused person. They feel they've 'come home'. They belong. Everything now is so certain. They are offered free gifts, meals, or a free 'no obligation' lecture. Sometimes you'll be asked 'Are you afraid to hear another point of view?' Some sects have perfected the use of subliminal messages, conveyed through key words which are stressed in ordinary conversation.

Then the group will reinforce motivation by making the novice behave in a certain way. The new recruit will then be more likely to trust the leaders. 'Just trust me', they will be told, 'you can ask questions later'. Sometimes disorientation due to lack of sleep, a heavy work schedule, deprivation of certain vitamins, etc. heighten suggestibility. Privacy is taken away, and loyalty demanded.

But eventually most will drop out. The leader has feet of clay. The group promises more than it delivers. The prophet's forecasts (about the return of Christ in a certain year, etc.) are proved false. They find better-put-together people in another group.

Advice from those who specialise in understanding these cults includes: record all names, addresses and phone numbers of people known to be associated with the cult; don't criticise your child's involvement, keep 'cool', avoid threats, and remain open for all communication. Don't send money or hand over original documents, and don't give up trying to get your children back.

If the cult is associated with the occult, and has seances, etc., don't get involved! If you once did, seek a pastoral counsellor to get help.

The main lesson: many people will use their brand of religion to harm people. There are enough young people who have been harmed by cults to warrant a warning. Although your church may not be as exciting, stick with it, prayerfully asking the Lord how you can enhance its worship and witness.

17

Is Ghandi in heaven? Christianity and other religions

In the beginning was the Word, and the Word was with God, and the Word was God. All things came into being through him, and without him not one thing came into being. What has come into being in him was life, and the life was the light of all people. And the Word became flesh and lived among us, and we have seen his glory, the glory as of a father's only son, full of grace and truth.

You shall have no other gods before me. You shall not make cast idols. You shall not bow down to their gods, or worship them, or follow their practices. Take care that you are not snared into imitating them, after they have been destroyed before you: do not inquire concerning their gods, saying, 'How did these nations worship their gods? I also want to do the same'. And when you look up to the heavens and see the sun, the moon, and the stars, all the host of heaven, do not be led astray and bow down to them and serve them, things that the Lord your God has allotted to all the peoples everywhere under heaven.

For the customs of the peoples are false: a tree from the forest is cut down, and worked with an axe by the hands of an artisan...

If you turn aside from following me, you or your children, and do not keep my commandments and my statutes that I have set before you, but go and serve other gods and worship them, then they will say, 'Because they have forsaken the Lord their God, who brought their ancestors out of the land of Egypt, and embraced other gods, worshipping them and serving them; therefore the Lord has brought this disaster upon them'.

The Lord said: Because these people draw near with their mouths and honour me with their lips, while their hearts are far from me, and their worship of me is a human commandment learned by rote...

For all the peoples walk, each in the name of its god, but we will walk in the name of the Lord our God forever and ever.

Do not oppress the alien, the orphan, and the widow, or shed innocent blood... do not go after other gods to your own hurt. They exchanged the glory of the immortal God for images resembling a mortal human being or birds or four-footed animals or reptiles... they exchanged the truth about God for a lie and worshipped and served the creature rather than the Creator, who is blessed forever!

'And you know the way to the place where I am going.' Thomas said to him, 'Lord, we do not know where you are going. How can we know the way?' Jesus said to him, 'I am the way, and the truth, and the life. No one comes to the Father except through me'.

Timothy, guard what has been entrusted to you. Avoid the profane chatter and contradictions of what is falsely called knowledge; by professing it some have missed the mark as regards the faith. I am saying this so that no one may deceive you with plausible arguments, holding to the outward form of godliness but denying its power. Avoid them!

If anyone says to you, 'Look! Here is the Messiah!' or 'There he is!' do not believe it. For false messiahs and false prophets will appear and produce great signs and omens, to lead astray, if possible, even the elect. He opposes and exalts himself above every so-called god or object of worship, so that he takes his seat in the temple of God, declaring himself to be God.

Peter, filled with the Holy Spirit, said to them, 'Rulers of the people and elders... Let it be known to all of you, and to all the people of Israel, that this man is standing before you in good health by the name of Jesus Christ of Nazareth, whom you crucified, whom God raised from the dead... There is salvation in no one else, for there is no other name under heaven given among mortals by which we must be saved.

John 1:1, 3, 14; Exodus 20:3; Exodus 34:17; Exodus 23:24; Deuteronomy 12:30; Deuteronomy 4:19; Jeremiah 10:3; 1 Kings 9:6,9; Isaiah 29:13; Micah 4:5; Jeremiah 7:6; Romans 1:23, 25; John 14:4-7; 1 Timothy 6:20-21; Colossians 2:4; 2 Timothy 3:5; Matthew 24:23,24; 1 Thessalonians 2:4; Acts 4:8, 10, 12.

'God is dead, Marx is dead, and I don't feel too good myself!' In a pluralistic culture we are more aware of others' beliefs.

A missionary in Nigeria visited a young man in a back street of Lagos. On his bedside table were the *Bible*, the *Book of*

Common Prayer, the *Koran*, three copies of *Watchtower* (magazine of the Jehovah's Witnesses), a biography of Karl Marx, a book of Yoga exercises, and *How to Stop Worrying and Start Living* by Dale Carnegie.

These days we travel more, TV shows documentaries of foreign cultures, students study abroad, multiculturalism in the West is here to stay...

Intolerance is increasing too. Militant Hindus have a motto 'Save India from Christian imperialism!' Many Moslem countries make it a punishable offence to proselytise. Then there's Lebanon, and Northern Ireland... Religion and politics can be volatile subjects, particularly when they mix.

Something else has happened that has never happened before. People (to paraphrase T. S. Eliot) have left God not for other gods, they say, but for no gods; and this has never happened before. It is possible both to deny gods and worship gods — gods like rationality, money, power, sport, etc. And it will all lead to an age advancing progressively backwards...

Of all the world's religions, Christianity has the greatest number of followers (33%), followed by Islam (18%), Hinduism (13%), and Buddhism (6%).

What is religion? Definitions are legion: 'what we do with our solitariness'; 'how we relate to others'; 'our answer to fear'; 'an ultimate attempt to enlarge and complete one's personality by finding the supreme context in which we rightly belong'. Everyone is religious, in some sense.

Although Freud termed religion 'mass neurosis' — religious believers were infantile, unable to break outgrown ties with their parents — Carl Jung said of his patients over thirty-five, 'all have been people whose problem in the last resort was that of finding a religious outlook on life'.

There is an increasing hunger for religious reality. 'Baby-boomers' under forty-five are not in church as often as their elders, but they claim to be as religious. They read Shirley Maclaine and play around with the New Age movement. In a noisy world people searching for 'God who is Sound and Silence' as the Maitri Upanishad puts it are going in larger numbers to Buddhist monasteries and Hindu ashrams — places of quiet serenity, simple life-style, meditation, brief talks and questions. More young people are reading the Hindu *Bhagavad Gita*, the Chinese *I Ching*, or do Yoga, transcendental meditation or Zen courses.

Let's ask the hard questions in order: Was Ghandi a Christian? No, as we saw in the movie, *Ghandi*, although he admired Jesus, he lived and died a Hindu. But E. Stanley Jones said of him: 'He taught me more of the spirit of Christ than anyone in East or West'.

A harder question: Is Ghandi in heaven? Christians offer three broad answers:

1. Conservative Christians have their doubts. The principle of Karma (cause and effect — paying off your own guilt) is poles apart from grace (God's free forgiveness, which you don't deserve). Augustine's theology inspired western Christians to believe that those outside the church are damned. A more refined view might be Karl Barth's 'Religion is unbelief', or Hendrik Kraemer's conviction that non-Christian religions were not means of salvation in any sense.

However, others would argue, what kind of God would organise for most of his human creatures to burn in hell forever — many of them because, by accident of birth, or the disobedience of the Christian minority to evangelise, they had never heard the gospel? Is he not the Father of Jesus, who prayed for those who crucified him? Does he not want all to be saved and come to know the truth (1 Timothy 2:3, 4)?

2. More liberal Christians would answer: 'Be tolerant. There's value in all religions. They all lead ultimately to God. Of course Ghandi is with him!' The problem with this view is its failure to take seriously the question of truth. If the original Christians were 'liberal' there would have been no mission, no universal church.

3. Is there a way between these two extremes? Yes, the more cautious say, 'Only God knows: our eternal destiny is in his hands alone'. With evangelicals like Howard Guinness (*The Seekers*) or J. N. D. Anderson (*Christianity and Comparative Religion*) they ask: Does God 'accept' only people within the 'covenant community' — whether Jewish (in the Old Testament) or Christian (in the New Testament)? No: what about Melchisedek, Rahab, and Cornelius? Certainly Jesus Christ is unique, and divine: he alone was God in human form. We are not to take everyone's views, mix them up, and get an identikit picture of God. Jesus is the only way to God. But that may not mean that only Christians are saved (see Romans 2:11-16).

Roman Catholics, at the Second Vatican Council, moved from *extra ecclesiam nulla salus* (outside the Church, no salvation) to 'The Catholic Church rejects nothing of what is true and holy in other religions'. Devotees of non-Christian religions may be 'implicit believers' or, in Karl Rahner's phrase, 'anonymous Christians'. Hans Kung says these religions may provide ordinary, whereas the Christian Gospel provides extraordinary means of salvation.

Don Richardson (*Eternity in Their Hearts*) says God has revealed himself to more people than we might imagine. The one invisible God is resident in many folk religions. Christianity doesn't replace this revelation, he says, but completes it. Pachacuti, King of the Incas, led a religious reform in the 1400s encouraging his people to worship Viracocha, the Creator, rather than Inti, the sun god. His hymns to Viracocha sound like the Hebrew Psalms. When missionaries came to the Santals in India in the 1800s, they found a tradition about Thakur Jiu, 'the Genuine God'. Many became Christians. The Chinese had Shang Ti, the Lord of heaven. The Karens of Burma believed in Y'wa, the true God.

Non-Christian religions are a testimony to people's search for God. They may be far from the God of Jesus, but God is not far from any one of them. God cares for all his human creatures with a love we who are biassed in favour of those who are like us can't imagine. His rain falls on the just and the unjust...

All religions have good and evil elements. As novelist Mary McCarthy observed: religion makes good people good and bad people bad. Christians have burnt heretics, Jews robbed Palestinians of lands and homes, some Hindus still burn widows (sati), tribal witchdoctors put curses on people, Moslems wage religious wars. (An eminent Egyptian scholar said privately to Hendrik Kraemer: 'I no longer believe in Islam but, if anyone were to attack the prophet publicly, I would kill him!'). Never forget that Jesus was rejected and sent to his death by people who belonged to a highly moral and spiritual religion. But, you say, well, Christianity has sanctioned evil, but in essence it is good. True: people from other religions say the same of their faiths too.

Christianity, said Karl Barth, stands as much under the judgment of the gospel as other religions. Roman Catholicism will be judged for the Inquisition; and the Protestant John Calvin for standing by as Geneva burned the 'heretic' Servetus...

Will everyone be saved? George Macdonald says all answers to such a question are deceptive. Two things are certain: all who are saved are saved through Jesus Christ. And a merciful God can handle the judgment of his loved creatures without our help! Jesus said everyone's going to be surprised at the last judgment. We should aim to be secure in our own faith, and be open-minded about matters that are God's prerogative.

So why evangelise? To get them into heaven? Yes, but there are better motives: the glory of God, obedience to Christ, and sincere love for others. Although Christ is not known everywhere, he is everywhere. We are called to make him known, not to make him present.

Some don'ts and do's in evangelism: Don't major on the faults in other religions: the faults in your own are bad enough. Don't argue: you may win the argument but lose the person: today the world is a conference table not a lecture hall, so learn to listen as well as you talk. Above all, be compassionate: Jesus preached judgment on Jerusalem when it rejected him, but he also wept for the city. Share your faith, as a beggar sharing bread with another beggar. Ask 'what are my friend's felt needs?', and start there. (An African proverb says 'Hungry people have no ears!'). Invite overseas students home: perhaps your family could 'adopt' one. (Most in the Book of Acts were converted while away from home.) Teach English to someone. Encourage your church to translate the service into another language, or host an ethnic church.

And, beyond all that, remember Jesus' approach to Nicodemas. This cultured man wanted to talk about the contrasts between Jesus' teaching and that of Judaism. The conversation started courteously enough, but very soon Jesus said to him, 'You must be born again!'

That is still the essence of the good news — even for the very religious.

Good teaching is found everywhere. In every religion there is something good, but good teaching alone cannot give life. Life is only to be had through the giver of life, not through the pages of books.

Sadhu Sundar Singh,
in Alys Goodwin, *Sadhu Sundar Singh in Switzerland*, Madras: Christian Literature Society, 1989, p. 49.

Where is the truth in other faiths? There are three bad ways to solve this problem. One is to lump all religions together and dismiss them all. As G. K. Chesterton once observed, to stop believing in God does not mean that people will believe in nothing. They may substitute a nationalistic for a religious faith, and be more fanatical than before. Another is to affirm that each religion is part of a whole. 'There is only one religion, though there are a hundred versions of it.' (George Bernard Shaw). The third is to be absolutist: only people like me have the truth! Amos (9:7-9) thundered against the exclusivism that believed God only cares for people 'like us'. 'People of Israel, I think as much of the people of Sudan as I do of you...'

Rowland Croucher,
from an unpublished sermon, 'Do Other Religions Also Lead to God?'

God comes to us in Jesus who is the way. We are like people who have fallen into a pit and in that fall have been injured. Our legs and our arms are broken. For anyone to lower a ladder into the pit and say, 'This is the only way out, climb it', only adds to our desperation. But if the ladder is lowered not for us to climb out, but for one to climb down and lift our broken body into his arms, carrying us upwards and to safety — that is good news indeed!

Henk Booy,
quoted by A. M. Watts, 'Christian Claims in a Pluralist Society', *Christian Century*, 1 March 1989, p. 223.

The neutral observer... looks at the plurality of religions from the outside: for him or her the existence of more than one true religion is self-evident... The committed believer looks... from the inside...: what is the true religion for me? ...I confess openly that my standpoint is that of a Christian. I am convinced that Christianity is the true religion. I cannot prove it — faith can never be demonstrated — but I can offer good reasons, which convince me... We come to a third and ultimate perspective...: there is a vertical dimension, that of the Absolute. As Christians we do not believe in Christianity but in God. Christianity, as a complex of dogmatic teachings, liturgical rites and codes of behaviour, does not escape the ambivalence of our human, historical condition. As Karl Barth used to say, religion is always a shaky and relative thing: not religion as such, but the absolute Being to which it is directed is the true absolute. This is the primordial and ultimate reality which we call God, which the Arabs call Allah, which Jews and Indians decline to name, but worship none the less. In relation to this ultimate and absolute reality of God, even the true religion is relative... Even Christianity is in via: ours is a Church on pilgrimage, on the way, which has not yet arrived at the goal of seeing God face to face. To admit this is neither liberalism nor relativism nor syncretism; it is faith, pure and simple.

Hans Kung,
'Ecumenism and truth: the wider dialogue', *The Tablet*, 28 January 1989, pp. 92-3.

In the past we have sometimes been guilty of adopting towards adherents of other faiths attitudes of ignorance, arrogance, disrespect and even hostility. We repent of this. We nevertheless are determined to bear a positive and uncompromising witness to the uniqueness of our Lord, in his life, death and resurrection, in all aspects of our evangelistic work including interfaith dialogue.

The Manila Manifesto, Lausanne II Conference of Evangelicals in Manila, 1989.

Krister Stendahl is fond of saying that no interfaith conversation is genuinely ecumenical unless the quality of mutual sharing and receptivity is such that each party makes him or herself vulnerable to conversion to the other's truth.

Leonard Swidler,
'Interreligious and Interideological Dialogue' in L. Swidler (ed.), *Towards a Universal Theology of Religion*, Maryknoll, New York: Orbis Books, 1988, p. 38.

The other religions are not to be understood and measured by their proximity to or remoteness from Christianity. They are not beginnings which are completed in the Gospel... To fit them into this model is to lose any possibility of understanding them. Moreover, what do the concepts of 'near' and 'far' mean in relation to the crucified and risen Jesus? Is the devout Pharisee nearer or further than the semi-pagan prostitute? Is the passionate Marxist nearer or further than the Hindu mystic? ...Is the Gospel the culmination of religion or is it the end of religion?

Lesslie Newbigin,
The Finality of Christ, London: SCM, 1969, pp. 43f.

It has become customary to classify views on the relation of Christianity to the world religions as either pluralist, exclusivist, or inclusivist... (My) position is exclusivist in the sense that it affirms the unique truth of the revelation in Jesus Christ, but it is not exclusivist in the sense of denying the possibility of the salvation of the non-Christian. It is inclusivist in the sense that it refuses to limit the saving grace of God to the members of the Christian church, but it rejects the inclusivism which regards the non-Christian religions as vehicles of salvation. It is pluralist in the sense of acknowledging the gracious work of God in the lives of all human beings, but it rejects a pluralism which denies the uniqueness and decisiveness of what God has done in Jesus Christ.

Lesslie Newbigin,
The Gospel in a Pluralist Society, Grand Rapids, Michigan: William B. Eerdmans, 1989, pp. 182-3.

People are saved by faith even though the informational level varies... Paul had a great deal more insight into the way of salvation than Abraham did... but Abraham was not less saved than Paul was... This does not make the pagan who responds to God, as Jethro did, a Christian. We should not call him even an 'anonymous' Christian. It would be reasonable to consider him a pre-Christian perhaps. The main thing is that such a person, though for the moment lacking Christ through no fault of his own, and thus I suppose 'lost', is not going to be damned, because he cried out to the merciful God in the only way he could and was heard.

Clark Pinnock,
'Can the Unevangelized be saved?', *The Canadian Baptist*, November 1981, p. 9.

A man who was merely a man and said the sort of things Jesus said would not be a great moral teacher. He would either be a lunatic — on a level with the man who says he is a poached egg — or else he would be the devil of hell. You must make your choice. Either this man was, and is, the Son of God: or else a madman or something worse. You can shut him up for a fool, you can spit at him and kill him as a demon; or you can fall at his feet and call him Lord and God. But let us not come with any patronising nonsense about his being a great human teacher. He has not left that open to us. He did not intend to.

C. S. Lewis,
Mere Christianity, New York: Macmillan, 1960/1978, p. 56.

A world of nice people, content in their own niceness, looking no further, turned away from God, would be just as desperately in need of salvation as a miserable world — and might even be more difficult to save.

C. S. Lewis,
in Charles Colson, *Against the Night*, London: Hodder & Stoughton, 1990, p. 139.

Lord God, Creator of the universe, who has revealed your loving nature and purposes for our lives in Jesus, help us to love you, to obey you, to honour you, to adore you. We have not loved you as we ought, and we are sorry. We have not obeyed Jesus' command to take the good news to everyone, and we are sorry. We have not honoured you by honouring others; rather we have felt superior to them, and we are sorry. We have not adored you, but rather our mental caricature of who you are — a god created in our image — and we are sorry.

Help us to abandon any religion that is immature, destructive or unloving. Help us to see you as the Father of all, to whom all are dear, and whose patience and long-suffering are everlasting. May we regard the truth we have received in Jesus as a precious resource to be given away, not hoarded. Remind us constantly that there is much, much more that we do not yet know, and to be very humble when in dialogue with others whose lives have followed the beat of a different drummer.

In the name of Christ, your Son, Amen.

A benediction

And now may the Spirit of Jesus, the One who hugged the demoniac, touched the leper, accepted the worship of a prostitute, and who honoured Samaritans, infect our thoughts and attitudes, so that the God who is not far from any one of us, will touch the lives of others we meet this day, for the honour of his name. Amen.

Further reading

Ajith Fernando, *The Christian's Attitude toward World Religions*, Wheaton, Illinois: Tyndale, 1987; Ian Gillman, *Many Faiths One Nation: A Guide to the Major Faiths and Denominations in Australia*, Sydney: Collins, 1988; David Johnson, *A Reasoned Look at Asian Religions*, Minneapolis: Bethany House Publishers, 1985; Josh McDowell & Don Stewart, *Concise Guide to Today's Religions*, Amersham-on-the-Hill, Bucks: Scripture Press, 1983; McGinlay Hugh, *Sharing Dreams and Visions in Australia*, Melbourne: JBCE, 1988; Vinay Samuel & Chris Sugden (eds), *Sharing Jesus in the Two Thirds World*, Grand Rapids, Michigan: Eerdmans, 1983.

18
Worship: the highest privilege humans have

How I love your temple, Almighty Lord! How I want to be there...
With my whole being I sing for joy to the living God.

Glory and majesty surround him, power and joy fill his temple.

Praise the Lord, all people on earth, praise his glory and might. Praise the Lord's glorious name; bring an offering and come into his temple: worship the Lord in the beauty of holiness.

The Lord is in his holy temple; let all the earth keep silence before him!

Happy are the people who know the festal shout, who walk, O Lord, in the light of your countenance; O come, let us worship and bow down, let us kneel before the Lord, our Maker! Worship the Lord with gladness; come into his presence with singing. Glory in his holy name; let the hearts of those who seek the Lord rejoice. Seek the Lord and his strength; seek his presence continually. Let those who fear the Lord say, 'His steadfast love endures forever'. 'Let us go to his dwelling place; let us worship at his footstool.'

But the hour is coming, and is now here, when the true worshippers will worship the Father in spirit and truth, for the Father seeks such as these to worship him. God is spirit, and those who worship him must worship in spirit and in truth.

To the church of God that is in Corinth, to those who are sanctified in Christ Jesus, called to be saints, together with all those who in every place call on the name of our Lord Jesus Christ, both their Lord and ours: after the secrets of the unbeliever's heart are disclosed, that person will bow down before God and worship him, declaring, 'God is really among you'.

Therefore, since we are receiving a kingdom that cannot be shaken, let us give thanks, by which we offer to God an acceptable worship with reverence and awe.

The twenty-four elders fall before the one who is seated on the throne and worship the one who lives forever and ever; they cast their crowns before the throne, singing. He said in a loud voice, 'Fear God and give him glory, for the hour of his judgment has come; and worship him who made heaven and earth, the sea and the springs of water'.

Christ's message in all its richness must live in your hearts. Teach and instruct each other with all wisdom. Sing psalms, hymns and sacred songs; sing to God with thanksgiving in your hearts.

Worship the Lord your God and serve only him. Whatever you do... do it all for God's glory. Everything you do or say should be done in the name of the Lord Jesus, as you give thanks through him to God the Father. Offer yourselves as a living sacrifice to God, dedicated to his service and pleasing to him. This is the true worship that you should offer.

Psalm 84:1,2 GNB; 1 Chronicles 16:27-29 GNB, KJV; Habakkuk 2:20; Psalm 89:15, 95:6, 100:2, 105:3-4, 118:4, 132:7; John 4:23; 1 Corinthians 1:2, 14:25; Hebrews 12:28; Revelation 4:10, 14:7; Colossians 3:16 GNB; Matthew 4:10 GNB; 1 Corinthians 10:31 GNB; Colossians 3:17 GNB; Romans 12:1 GNB;

Praise God from whom all blessings flow
Praise him for one hour here below;
Praise him with nickel and with dime,
Praise God we're getting out on time.

'It's dead, a mechanical routine. I don't get anything out of it.' 'My friends have voted with their feet and stay away.' 'Our church services are so cold, they're like mournful funerals: everyone is so sombre and distant.' 'Ours are like a fowl-yard: so much chattering and giggling and irreverence.' 'We'll have to rescue ours from show business!' 'Why not cut the preliminaries and have a better sermon? ' 'Let's liven it up with happier singing.' 'Let's be more experimental.' 'Our vicar has the liturgical fidgets; you don't know what to expect.' 'Let's give people what they want or we'll lose them.' 'It's people's duty to attend worship, no matter how dull and boring it may be.'

Something is happening to people's expectations of worship in this television age. They want the stale water of liturgies-as-usual turned into the wine of celebration. Worship services for many are a morose experience. As the Devil says in *The Brothers Karamazov*, 'Everything would be transformed into a religious service: it would be holy, but a little dull'.

Worship is the sublime and awesome key to everything the church does. The mission of the early church was the fruit of worship. We too cannot meet the world until we have met God. According to the often-quoted words of William Temple, to worship is to quicken the conscience by the holiness of God, to feed the mind with the truth of God, to purge the imagination by the beauty of God, to open the heart to the love of God, to devote the will to the purpose of God.

Worship is a contraction of the old English word 'worth-ship'. It's recognising that which is worth most, in the ultimate sense. In the old marriage service a man and a woman promised to 'worship' each other; to accord value and worth to each other. Divine worship is a love affair too! *The Westminster Shorter Catechism* asks 'What is our chief end?' It's 'to glorify God and enjoy him forever'. So the worshipper's key question is 'What can I offer the Lord for all his goodness to me?' (Psalm 116:12).

Worship is the appropriate response to the God who gives everything life, to the Holy One, who inhabits eternity, to the King of kings and Lord of lords, who is God our Saviour. Worship is meeting — God with us, to which we respond with wonder, amazement and awe.

Saint Benedict founded an order with the motto '*laborare est orare*', 'to work is to pray'. Worship is service (it's the same word in the New Testament): serving the Lord in our praises, praising the Lord in our ministry to others, ministering to the Lord in prayerful solitude — it's all worship. Worship is both individual and corporate, done both in 'the secret place' and in the redeemed community. For a devout Christian, worship is all of life, and is life-long.

So worship isn't quite something 'observed' or 'attended', it is something we are and do. As 'we are what we eat' so 'we are what we worship' and we become like the God we worship. So we step back from the rush of life and ponder its realities at an ultimate level at a special time each week. But for true worshippers every time and every place is special.

The inward imperative as we 'come to worship' is to 'take the shoes from (our) feet, for the place on which (we) stand is holy ground' (Exodus 3:5). Remember the solemn warning in Ecclesiastes: 'Guard your steps when you go to the house of God' (Ecclesiastes 5:1). 'Let us offer to God acceptable worship, with reverence and awe, for our God is a consuming fire' (Hebrews 12:28,29). We had better be careful, then: the way we worship could be hazardous!

Worship in Old Testament times was sometimes liturgical,

sometimes free. There we seem to have two worship traditions. One was priestly, cultic, authoritarian and dynastic, the other more congregational, democratic, prophetic and ethical. Worship was both ritual and hearty service (Deuteronomy 11:13, Psalm 40:6-8, 50:12-15, Micah 6:6-8). Christian church history has similarly seen worship move from one extreme to the other.

The New Testament nowhere prescribes a detailed order of worship. The worship of the early church comprised teaching, fellowship, breaking of bread and prayers: God meets his people in the Word, in each other, in holy communion, and in prayer (Acts 2:42), and also in the more formal Jewish worship in the Temple (Acts 2:46, 3:1, 5:12). Paul chose a close fraternity with the synagogue. The synagogue service consisted of an invitation to prayer, the prayer itself, the reading of scriptures, a homily based on the scripture reading and concluded with the benediction. At the end of the first century there was a move toward a more structured and formal service of worship (most churches move in this direction over time).

Building on the legacy of the New Testament, the Protestant Reformation's emphasis was on the Word and inner reality rather than the sacraments and formality. So churches in the Reformation tradition devote about half — or more — of their time to the sermon. The Age of Reason ensured a highly rational content in worship, with eloquent sermons of high literary and intellectual merit. For Calvin's followers, the Sunday service became primarily a preaching service, with communion observed infrequently.

Biblical worship was sometimes active. So we should involve the whole congregation in worship: not just singing hymns, but with responsive readings, litanies, united prayers, times of community sharing, bringing the offerings forward, moving to greet one another, etc.

Biblical worship was also sensual: appealing to eye, ear — and nose! Do a checklist of your worship-service: what is there for the eyes (form, light, colour, architecture, dress, etc.), the ear (besides voices of leader, congregation, musical instruments — see Psalm 150 — and choir, recorded music, voices, special effects), taste and smell in the holy communion: what else? Touch is important: we all have 'contact need' since separation from the womb. In the gospels, physical contact was important for Jesus as he ministered to people: so, when it is appropriate, we may hold hands to sing or pray, or clasp arms, or share an embrace as an expression of genuine Christian love.

However worship is not just a subjective, ecstatic, 'feeling' experience. It is more than 'self-expression'. Corporate worship ought not to be an emotional tool for producing 'conversions'.

The Bible does not use the word 'worship' as simply a description of experience. Worship is something you do, it is a response to God's Word and God's ways and God's will, however you feel about it (although this does not mean there is no place for feelings and sensory experience).

Rudolf Otto explored the importance of the non-rational in religion and attempted to analyse the feeling which remains where the concept falls short. Otto coined the word *numinous* to describe 'the holy' after words have failed. The numinous cannot be taught; it can only be felt. It is 'thanking God for his unspeakable gift' (1 Corinthians 9:15). The numinous, says Otto, encompasses both boundless awe and boundless wonder, both fear and fascination. This deep, awesome aspect of all sincere religious emotion he called the *mysterium tremendum* (from *tremo*, tremble; also *tremor*, dread). So we must resist the temptation to 'domesticate the holy', whereby our solemn assemblies become informal social gatherings, our deep communion with God little more than friendship with one another.[1]

A lot of our worship is intellectual, moving too exclusively in the realm of thoughts and words and ideas. It is addressed to the ears rather than the eyes. Our world is 'word-weary'. We are slaves to the printed word. Perhaps we need printed guidance for worship — the middle-classes are comfortable reading — but let us not forget the less well-educated persons who may not be. For them particularly we should encourage 'folk arts' which open new avenues to express worship and praise, provide new methods of teaching and instruction, and draw people more into an atmosphere of enjoyment and festivity. In charismatic/ pentecostal churches where the Holy Spirit is invited to take over the worshipper, we have moved sometimes from the rational to the mystical. Worship needs to be both rational (Romans 12:1-3) and spiritual (John 4:23).

We worship as whole beings: our 'self' is psychological, cultural, biological. We worship with mind and heart and will. We involve the emotions, genuine feelings of joy and desolation, exaltation and bereavement. Worship ought to be a living event, to which we bring our human, frail, brokenness. The Spirit helps us in our infirmities... so we can come to God with our fears, joys, guilt, anger, affirmations, tensions and loneliness. In his presence we renew our lives which are mixed up in work, conflict, love and creation. We worship with 'all that is within us' and 'all that is around us' (the wonders of creation too are an incentive to praise the Creator: see Psalm 19).

Above all, authentic worship is always Christ-centred.

The early church remained in the apostles' teaching because Christ taught his disciples; they had fellowship because they all

193

belonged to the church, Christ's body; they celebrated communion because Christ ordained it; they prayed because Christ taught them how to pray.[2]

Name him, (Christian), name him
with love as strong as death,
but with awe and wonder
and with bated breath:
he is God the Saviour,
he is Christ the Lord,
ever to be worshipped,
trusted and adored.

Caroline Maria Noel,
'At the Name of Jesus', *The Australian Hymn Book*, Sydney: Collins, 1977, no. 170.

We worship not because worship benefits us (although it does), not because we need to (although we do), nor because it is relevant to our daily lives (although it is), but because God is.

Richard John Neuhaus,
Freedom for Ministry, San Francisco: Harper & Row, 1956, p. 120.

Where it is emptied of this unearthly element, this awe-struck and creaturely sense of the Holy and Immortal, worship loses its most distinctive characteristic. The seraphic hymn gives its very essence: 'Holy! holy! holy! Lord God of Hosts, heaven and earth are full of thy glory. Glory be to thee, O Lord Most High'. That is worship.

Evelyn Underhill,
quoted in Stuart A. Frayne, *What is Worship?*, n.d., p. 20.

The biblical passage which says of Abraham and the three visiting angels: 'And he stood over them under the tree and they did eat' is interpreted by Rabbi Zusya to the effect that we stand above the angels, because we know something unknown to them, namely, that eating may be hallowed by the eater's intention. Through Abraham the angels, who were unaccustomed to eating, participated in the intention by which he used to dedicate it to God. Any natural act, if hallowed, leads to God, and nature needs us for what no angel can perform on it, namely, its hallowing.

Martin Buber,
'Heart Searching and the Particular Way', in John Garvey (ed.), *Modern Spirituality: An Anthology*,
London: Darton, Longman and Todd, 1985, p. 7.

Religion, as von Hugel loved to say, is adoration; our humble acknowledgment of the Transcendent, the Fact of God — the awestruck realism of the seraphs in Isaiah's vision — the meek

and loving sense of mystery which enlarges the soul's horizon
and puts us in our place...

Adoration, as it more deeply possesses us, inevitably leads on
to self-offering: for every advance in prayer is really an advance
in love. 'I ask not for thy gifts but for thyself' says the Divine
Voice to Thomas à Kempis.

Evelyn Underhill,
'Spiritual Life' in John Garvey (ed.), *Modern Spirituality: An Anthology*, London: Darton, Longman and
Todd, 1985, pp. 21, 22.

Vladimir (pagan prince of Russia) wanted to unite the people
under one religion, so around 988 he sent envoys to examine the
major religions... The story of Vladimir's choosing Orthodox
Christianity is part legend, part fact... what impressed the grand
prince was the dazzling worship his ambassadors described
seeing in the great Cathedral of Hagia Sophia in Constantinople;
'We knew not whether we were in heaven or on earth, for surely
there is no such splendour or beauty anywhere upon earth. We
cannot describe it to you. Only we know that God dwells there...
and that their service surpasses the worship of all other places.
We cannot forget that beauty'.

'The 100 Most Important Events in Church History', *Christian History*, (Mary Ann Jeffreys, editorial
coordinator, Christian History, 465 Gunderson Drive, Carol Stream, IL 60188), Issue 28 (Vol. IX, No. 4),
p. 19.

It happened one high holy day when the king was in attendance
at the Temple and grew impatient with the way the priests were
handling the incense. If it were today, we might surmise he was
in the habit of eating in a cafeteria after church and anxious to
get in line ahead of the Methodists. However, for some reason on
this particular day the monarch became annoyed with the
handling of the service, so he got up out of the royal pew and
went straight into the altar area itself and with his own
unconsecrated hands placed the incense on the altar as if to say,
'Let's get this over with so we can get on to something more
interesting'. Even in that day of carelessness, such an act had a
ring of shocking presumption... By his actions the king implied
there was nothing going on here except a human process and he
could do the 'hocus-pocus' as well as a priest. But he was soon to
learn differently! While he was still in the altar area, a gasp went
up from the whole congregation, for there on Uzziah's forehead
and hands the dread white splotches of leprosy suddenly
appeared... Uzziah fled from the temple never to return — or
even to his palace. He who had occupied David's throne was
relegated to a leper's cottage and there he died a few weeks
later.

John Claypool,
'Worship as Involvement', unpublished sermon preached at Broadway Baptist Church, Fort Worth, Texas,
23 September 1973.

Most Protestant church attenders act as if the church was a theatre, where they are the critical audience and where the minister is the actor whose art they are expected to enjoy and criticise. The situation in the church where the attenders have found their real relationship is a very different one. The stage is still there, but the attenders are now upon it. They are the actors. The audience is there too — God is the audience. The pastor is there also, but he is inconspicuous in the scene. He is only the prompter. He is behind the wings whispering the text that they, the actors are speaking aloud before God. Here is a new attitude towards worship. It has become an occasion for coming more consciously into the presence of God and of reviewing our lives under his loving scrutiny.

Soren Kierkegaard,
from an essay 'Purity of Heart', quoted by Principal-Emeritus B. G. Wright, 'Some Thoughts on Worship',
Australian Baptist, 24 June 1981.

A striking feature of worship in the Bible is that people gathered in what we could call only a 'holy expectancy'. They believed they would actually hear the *Kol Yahweh*, the voice of God. When Moses went into the Tabernacle he knew he was entering the Presence of God. The same was true of the early church. It was not surprising to them that the building in which they met shook with the power of God. It had happened before (Acts 2:2, 4:31). When some dropped dead and others were raised from the dead by the word of the Lord the people knew that God was in their midst (Acts 5:1-11, 9:36-43; 20:7-10). As those early believers gathered they were keenly aware that the veil had been ripped in two and like Moses and Aaron they were entering the Holy of Holies. No intermediaries were needed. They were coming into the awful, glorious, gracious Presence of the living God. They gathered with anticipation, knowing that Christ was present among them and would teach them and touch them with his living power...

Your pastor and the services of worship need to be bathed in prayer. Paul prayed for his people; he asked his people to pray for him. C. H. Spurgeon attributed his success to the prayers of his church. Frank Laubach told his audiences, 'I am very sensitive and know whether you are praying for me. If one of you lets me down, I feel it. When you are praying for me, I feel a strange power. When every person in a congregation prays intensely while the pastor is preaching, a miracle happens'. Saturate the services of worship with your prayers. Visualise the Lord high and lifted up filling the sanctuary with his presence.

Richard Foster,
Celebration of Discipline, Sevenoaks: Hodder & Stoughton, 1980, pp. 38, 140-141.

When we worship as a congregation, we are really united with all of God's people everywhere and at all times. Indeed, we may not realize our affinity with the strict Calvinist when we sing 'Rock of Ages, cleft for me', or with a Unitarian ('Nearer my God to thee'), with a Roman Catholic ('Lead, Kindly Light'), with a Quaker ('Dear Lord and Father of mankind'), as well as with ancient psalmists and modern poets.

Ken Manley,
'Baptist Worship Past... Present', *The Australian Baptist*, 3 March 1971.

This is the shining principle embedded in the Benediction: all the grace of the Lord Jesus Christ — all of it — is for each of us. And all the love of God — all of it — is for each. And all the helpfulness and instruction and consolation of the Holy Spirit — all of it — is for each. All the sea for every fish; all the air for every bird. It is not that each of ten million believers has one ten-millionth share of the grace of Christ, and of the love of God, and of the fellowship of the Spirit; but the whole, in its indivisible and perfect entirety, is for each individual among them. Let us make the most of it.

F. W. Boreham,
The Tide Comes In, London: Epworth Press, 1958, p. 53.

Leader: The Lord be with you.
*Response: **And also with you***

For the greed which exploits others and wastes the good earth,
Lord, forgive us.

For wanting more and more while so many have less and less,
Lord, forgive us.

*For our indifference to the suffering of the poor: the hungry, the homeless, the tortured and the oppressed, **Lord, forgive us.***

For the lust which misuses others for our own selfish desires,
Lord, forgive us.

*For the pride which leads us to trust too much in ourselves and not in you, **Lord, forgive us.***

*We confess that we have sinned — in thought, in word, in deed; and in what we have not said or done. **Father, forgive us.***

If we confess our sins to God, he will keep his promise and will forgive us our sins and purify us from all wrongdoing. God has forgiven us... Thank you, Lord... We can now make a fresh start. Renew us Lord. Create in us a clean heart. Fill us with your Holy Spirit. Re-engage us in your service. We commit ourselves to forgive others as you have forgiven us. We're yours, Lord: we're all yours.

Our Father in heaven, hallowed be your name. Your kingdom come, your will be done on earth as in heaven. Give us today our daily bread, Forgive us our sins as we forgive those who sin against us. Lead us not into temptation, but deliver us from evil. For the kingdom, the power, and the glory are yours, now and forever. Amen.

Holy One, holy and eternal, awesome, exciting and delightful in your holiness; make us pure in heart to see you; make us merciful to receive your kindness and to share our love with all your human family; then will your name be hallowed on earth as in heaven.

Support us, Lord, all the day long, until the shadows lengthen, and the evening comes, the busy world is hushed, the fever of life is over, and our work done; then, Lord, in your mercy, give us safe lodging, a holy rest and peace at the last.

God our judge and our companion, we thank you for the good we did this day and for all that has given us joy. Everything we offer as our humble service. Bless those with whom we have worked, and those who are our concern. Amen.

We have come to the holy mountain and to the city of the living God, the heavenly Jerusalem; before myriads of angels, before the full assembly of the first-born citizens of heaven.

We have come to God who is the judge of all, and the spirits of the good, made perfect; we have come to Jesus, mediator of the new covenant.

Let us give thanks, and worship God with reverence and awe, for our God is a consuming fire...

God, you are our beginning and you will be our end; we are made in your image and likeness. We praise and thank you for this day. This is the day on which you created light and saw that it was good. This is the day in whose early morning light we discovered the tomb was empty, and encountered Christ, the world's true light. For us your acts are gracious and your love endures for ever...

A *New Zealand Prayer Book*, Auckland: Collins, 1989, pp. 113, 112, 108.

Charge and benediction
You have worshipped the Lord in the community of faith. Now go and worship him in your work in your homes and in the world. And as you go, remember: the Lord, in his great mercy, will enrich you with his grace and strengthen you with his word and his Spirit. Through Christ our Lord. Amen.

Capsule 3

The components of authentic worship

John Claypool, in a sermon entitled 'Worship as Involvement' tells of a woman in Kentucky who came to him one Monday morning. She wanted to talk about her experience the day before when her four-year-old son had come to 'big church' for the first time. She described how excited he had been and all of the questions he had asked. He wanted to know about everything. Why were the people up front dressed in robes? Where was the organist? Why did some people put money in the plates and some did not? What was behind the curtain behind the choir? She reported that the experience was like having cold water thrown in her face, for it made her aware of how routine worship had become for her. 'Seeing his excitement really made me ashamed, for to be honest it has been years since I have paid much attention to the details of the church building or the parts of the service. I have gotten in the habit of coming to church and going through the motions and not giving the whole thing much thought. But yesterday made me want to turn over a new leaf. I want you to give me a refresher course. Show me what each part of the service is supposed to mean so that I can not only answer my child's questions, but learn how to worship vitally myself.'

Here's how I would explain a worship service:

1. Encounter and adoration
Christian worship services begin with a 'Call to Worship and Invocation'. Here nothing excels the 'Sursum Corda' for feeling and dignity. The leader says: 'Lift up your hearts'. Our response: 'We lift them up unto the Lord'. In corporate worship we come to 'adore him'. Worship is the expression of a love affair between us and our wonderful God.

2. Confession and celebration: sorrow and joy
'Tremble with fear and stop sinning' (Psalm 4:4). Gathered worship is a positive way of dealing with guilt. Self-examination, confession, and the biblical word of 'assurance' are a fundamental part of worship. Every worship service should provide opportunity for a realistic experience of confession and renewing an awareness of God's acceptance and forgiveness. 'Your sins are forgiven you' — it's the best news sinners can ever hear. How amazing that a holy God can have this sort of grace. The rest of the service moves into acts of celebration for that forgiveness. God and his people are reconciled. Alleluia!

3. Exhilaration and silence: praise and awe
When you were a kid, and started making a noise, your parents said 'Shh! You're in church. This is God's house. You must be

quiet!' But the characteristic note of the biblical worship is exhilaration.

'Sing and shout for joy, people of Israel! Rejoice with all your heart' (Zephaniah 3:14).

We yell ourselves hoarse when our team wins the grand final. Our worship is not a solemn memorial service for a dead hero, but the joyful celebration of the victory of a living Lord. In the primitive church 'Jesus is Lord!' was at first a shout of triumphant praise to Christ the King. Only later did it become the church's first creed to be affirmed by those about to be baptised.

Just this morning I read the litany towards the end of the Church of England's Morning Prayer in their 1980 *Alternative Service Book*:

Minister: Let your priests be clothed with righteousness
People: and let your servants shout for joy!

and wondered what would happen in an Anglican church if the people actually did that!

However, authentic worship has an element of mystery too. Jacob at Bethel in the story of Jacob's Ladder exclaimed: 'What an awesome place this is! It must be the house of God; it must be the gate that opens into heaven!' (Genesis 28:17). The appropriate response to awe is silence and wonder. And there is healing power in quietness and rest. There should be silence after the reading of Scripture, and maybe at other times.

4. Solitude and community: fasting and feasting

God meets us, personally, alone, in solitary places: Jacob at Bethel, Moses before a burning bush, Isaiah in the temple, Jesus in the wilderness, Paul in a 'third heaven', John on an island. Corporate worship is the coming together of those who have met God in private during the week.

Fellowship is caring for one another, as we are cared for by Christ. It is the sharing of joys and sorrows. It is in true Christian community that we experience and demonstrate the fellowship of Christ. So in the early church absenteeism was considered to be spiritually disastrous (Hebrews 10:25). A church — however large — must not resemble an assembly of strangers. Put ten to fifteen minutes — sometimes more or less — into your worship-time for people to share their lives with one another. This time begins with 'passing the peace', or greeting one another, in an appropriate way. Then we share our joys and sorrows, learnings and aspirations. Psalm 66:16 invites us to 'Come and listen, all who honour God, and I will tell you what he has done for me...' If there's a celebration or a bereavement or a tragedy, let people verbalise their feelings. Encourage them to tell brief faith-stories about the theme of the service. If God is saying something to someone for the benefit of the whole church now is the time for them to share it. (Usually, such a 'word from the Lord' ought to be 'checked out' by the pastor/s first especially if it's highly charged, and will affect the community of faith in a significant way.) Then there's a 'hey kids' time. Then someone who can do it sensitively in the spirit of this worship-segment will mention the 'notices', but they'll be disguised as 'opportunities for ministry and prayer'! 'Announcements' are often given as a sort of 'commercial break'; surely we can do better than that! One or two may (briefly) seek recruits for visiting a gaol, or developing a Spanish ministry, or to join a social justice group, or visit homes for a community-survey or whatever.

Covenant is an important ingredient in building community. A covenant is more than a contract. Covenants bind us together by voluntary intent, and the 'penalties' for breaking the covenant are relational. A covenant is also more than a creed. Creeds tend to be exclusive, emphasising the 'truth' thus excluding 'heretics' who might see reality differently. Covenants on the other hand are relational rather than propositional.

Here's a modern covenant statement, adapted from one produced by the United Church of Canada several years ago: We humans are not alone, we live in God's world. We believe in God: who created and is creating, who has come in the true man, Jesus, to reconcile and renew, who works within us and among us by his Spirit. We trust him. He calls us to be his church: to celebrate his presence, to love and serve others, to seek justice and resist evil. We proclaim his reign over us and the whole world. In life, in death, in life beyond death he is with us. We are not alone: thanks be to God![3]

Pastoral prayer. If preachers prepare what they say to us for God, pray-ers should also prepare what they say to God for us. Our public praying should include contemporary concerns. And let's all say 'Amen': it means 'that's right!' (or 'right on!'), 'I agree with that!', 'may it be so!', 'that's my prayer too!'.

Worship and the Sacraments. A sacrament is 'an outward and visible sign of an inward and spiritual grace.' The two key sacraments are baptism and the eucharist, the Lord's Supper. We will look at these in chapter 20.

5. Recital and proclamation: Scripture and sermon

When we hear the Scripture read, we are listening to the voice of the living God. We don't listen to the Bible reading simply to learn something interesting. Our silent prayer is always 'Beyond the sacred page I seek you, Lord. My Spirit yearns for you, O Living Word'. The Bible readings should be somewhere near the preaching, to make clear the connection. I like the discipline of the lectionary; it ensures our readings and preaching range over the whole Bible. But don't follow it slavishly: in biblically literate congregations there is merit in preaching consecutively through various books of the Bible, with rotating themes from Old Testament, Gospel and Epistle.

Worship and preaching. 'Going to worship' is more than 'going to preaching'. Preaching is not done well in many churches. Homilies in some liturgical churches are polite sermonic essays which won't offend — or change — anybody. Well-educated preachers in some mainline churches fill their sermons with theological abstractions. Pentecostal preaching is often a loud reiteration of exhortations lacking theological substance. And other churches which may have better preaching often don't know how to be 'lost in wonder, love and praise' in their worship.

The preacher stands between heaven and earth, speaking for God to us, and strengthening our faith, hope and love. Good preaching is inspired and inspiring, bringing the Bible to life, and life to the Bible: it is rooted in the biblical text but relevant to our needs. Good preaching is pastoral (comforting the afflicted) and prophetic (afflicting the comfortable). It is interesting, warm, 'confessional' (the preacher is a sinner needing grace too), dialogical and interactive. Good preaching has both heat and light: heat without light leaves us scorched and brittle; light may help us 'see' — there can be no preaching worth the name if there is no thinking — but knowledge without faith won't save anybody. Good preaching touches mind and heart and will: we learn, we love and we change.

6. Call and response: the Word and the world

In true worship God speaks, we answer, God speaks again, we respond. 'The Lord said to (Jeremiah)'... 'I answered...' 'But the Lord said to me...' (Jeremiah 1:4-7). 'I heard the Lord say, "Whom shall I send? Who will be our messenger?" I answered, "I will go! Send me!" So he told me to go...' (Isaiah 6:8-9). Conversation is two-way dialogue. So is worship.

When God speaks, we respond. Over and over in the Bible God tells us he is not pleased with worship that's just words or formulas, and does not lead to a changed life. Indeed if worship does not change us it is not true worship. As Jesus, God's Word, was totally obedient to the will of his Father, so we must respond with our total selves (Romans 12:1, 2).

As we 'praise the Lord's glorious name' we will 'bring an offering' (Psalm 96:8, 1 Chronicles 16:29). The offering — whether of money, or baskets of first fruits, or commitment to serve ('those who want to pursue the idea of ministry to the deaf go to the far corner'), or signing a petition — happens best towards the end of the worship-service, as a response to all that before. And yet a case can be made for the offering to happen near the community-time: it is also a 'collection' for the needs of others. Perhaps once a month have a special offering for the poor.

Worship and mission. A seminary teacher shocked our class with this statement: 'You learn nothing in church. You learn by doing!' When Benedict founded his order of monks their motto was *'laborare est orare',* 'to work is to pray.' These two aspects of daily existence must go together. If the Word remains words, it does not come to its full potency. The Word must become flesh again. Indeed, if mission involves justice, mercy and faithfulness (Micah 6:8, Matthew 23:23, Luke 11:42), then worship without these mission-components is not worship.

Worship is like what happens to jumbo jets when those planes are taken out of duty for a while to be overhauled. The check-up is not an end in itself: it is to make sure the jet is capable of serving people better. So worship and mission go together.

Worship and evangelism. If our worship does not issue in evangelism it is, again, not true worship. The average western church-attender has listened to eight thousand sermons and fifteen thousand prayers and after all that most have not led another to faith in Christ!

The climax of worship. What is the high point of the drama of worship? The preaching of the Word, as Luther thought, or the offering of prayer (Calvin), or the 'altar call' (Finney)? In the sacraments, it is receiving bread and wine, or when water is applied to our bodies in baptism. If the Lord's Supper is the high point, perhaps it should follow the preaching.

The 'altar call' happens occasionally in mainline churches, and regularly in fundamentalist and pentecostal churches. This practice is fairly recent, arising out of American revivalism: the church got on quite well without it for many centuries! However, that said, I like the idea of people being invited to be prayed with for any need they may have, at any service.

The charge and benediction link worship in the house of God with worship in the world. The 'charge' challenges the congregation with a series of commands or imperatives to carry out in the world whatever the Word has brought to us that day. The benediction follows in the same breath, with the promise of God's presence, grace and power to enable us to fulfil such a charge. The charge and benediction are two sides to one coin; they are not a prayer, but an offering from God to the people through God's spokesperson. This can be a great empowering moment — a powerful, verbal, blessing on the people of God as they go to do battle with the world, the flesh and the devil.

203

7. *Tradition and spontaneity: order and freedom*

Our Christian worship comes to us out of the past. The story of worship has three ancient strands: Jewish, Pentecostal and Sacramental. Most of the debates about worship from the second century onwards have centred on one or more of these legacies. 'The Jewish legacy, particularly through the synagogue centred on the word of God in the scriptures. The sacramental legacy, of the Upper Room and the Lord's Supper, focuses our attention on the Cross of Christ and the heart of the gospel. The legacy of Pentecost (puts its) stress upon freedom and power through the presence of the Holy Spirit. When any one of these elements is exalted at the expense of the others, worship becomes distorted and impoverished. If any one of them is left out, the result is disastrous. Each of them has to be present in the overall experience of worship.'[4]

Two major trends are emerging: so-called 'free' churches are incorporating more liturgical components into their worship, and the more liturgical churches are moving towards greater freedom of worship form and content. In worship, our flexible and changeable experiences encounter the currents of the church's institutional traditions. These traditions remind us of an unchangeable God. Jesus is the same yesterday, today and forever. So it is not necessary to polarise between structured and unstructured forms of worship. Add some spontaneity to your traditional services, and some traditional liturgies to your free celebrations. In addition, if your church moves to two morning worship services, make one more (but not exclusively) traditional, the other more (but not exclusively) free.

'Now the Lord is the Spirit, and where the Spirit of the Lord is, there is freedom' (2 Corinthians 3:17). Whatever one's temperament, as a condition of genuine worship we must be in awe before the amazing mystery and splendour of the Lord, Jesus Christ, before we can worship. Such worship is the response of grateful hearts before the transcendent majesty of God whose glory we see 'in the face of Jesus Christ'.

Notes

1. Rudolf Otto, *The Idea of the Holy*, trans. John W. Harvey, Oxford: Oxford University Press, 1950.
2. Bernard Schalm, 'Biblical Directives for Worship', *Christianity Today*, 14 September 1973, p. 17.
3. See an amplified form in Robert D. Dale, *To Dream Again*, Nashville: Broadman Press, 1981, pp. 131-32.
4. Stuart Frayne, 'Worthy of the Name', *The Australian Baptist*, 3 August 1988, p. 16.

19

Spiritual direction: an idea whose time has come (again)

He was praying in a certain place, and after he had finished, one of his disciples said to him, 'Lord, teach us to pray, as John taught his disciples'. He went up the mountain and called to him those whom he wanted, and they came to him. And he appointed twelve, whom he also named apostles, to be with him, and to be sent out to proclaim the message. Jesus said to them again, 'Peace be with you. As the Father has sent me, so I send you'. Come to me, all you that are weary and are carrying heavy burdens, and I will give you rest. Take my yoke upon you, and learn from me; for I am gentle and humble in heart, and you will find rest for your souls. For my yoke is easy, and my burden is light.

When you pass through the waters, I will be with you; and through the rivers, they shall not overwhelm you; when you walk through the fire you shall not be burned, and the flame shall not consume you. For I am the Lord your God, the Holy One of Israel, your Saviour... You are precious in my sight, and honoured, and I love you.

There are varieties of gifts, but the same Spirit... To one is given through the Spirit the utterance of wisdom, and to another the utterance of knowledge through the same Spirit, to another faith by the same Spirit... to another discernment of spirits... All these are activated by one and the same Spirit, who allots to each one individually just as the Spirit chooses.

He answered, 'I have been very zealous for the Lord, the God of hosts; for the Israelites have forsaken your covenant, thrown down your altars, and killed your prophets with the sword. I alone am left, and they are seeking my life, to take it away'. Then the Lord said to him, 'Go, return on your way to the wilderness of Damascus; when you arrive, you shall anoint Hazael as king over Aram'. So he set out from there, and found Elisha son of Shaphat, who was ploughing... Elijah passed by him and threw his mantle over him.

Therefore, friends, select from among yourselves seven men of good standing, full of the Spirit and of wisdom... they chose Stephen, a man full of faith and the Holy Spirit, together with Philip, Prochorus, Nicanor, Timon, Parmenas, and Nicolaus, a proselyte of Antioch. The word of God continued to spread; the number of the disciples increased greatly in Jerusalem, and a great many of the priests became obedient to the faith. Barnabas took Mark with him and sailed away to Cyprus. But Paul chose Silas and set out, the believers commending him to the grace of the Lord. Paul wanted Timothy to accompany him; and he took him...

Remember your leaders, those who spoke the word of God to you; consider the outcome of their way of life, and imitate their faith. You then, my child, be strong in the grace that is in Christ Jesus; and what you have heard from me through many witnesses entrust to faithful people who will be able to teach others as well. And these are the ones sown on the good soil: they hear the word and accept it and bear fruit, thirty and sixty and a hundredfold.

Do not say, 'I am only a boy'; for you shall go to all to whom I send you, and you shall speak whatever I command you.

Love one another as I have loved you.

Luke 11:1; Mark 3:13-14; John 20:21; Matthew 11:28-30; Isaiah 43:2-4; 1 Corinthians 12:4-11; 1 Kings 19:14-15, 19; Acts 6:3, 5, 7; Acts 15:39, 40; Acts 16:2-3; Hebrews 13:7; 2 Timothy 2:1-2; Mark 4:20; Jeremiah 1:7; John 15:12.

Mark Link sent a letter to a number of students in the high school where he taught. He invited them to • attend the eucharistic liturgy once a week (in addition to Sunday) • give 10 minutes of each day to meditation; and • meet with a spiritual director every week (or 2 weeks) to help them with their spiritual growth, particularly with their prayer.

The response, he says, exceeded expectation. The book on prayer he wrote for those students is still one of the best around (*YOU: Prayer for Beginners and Those Who Have Forgotten How*, Argus, 1976).

I met a pastor-friend in a shop. Asked what his goal was for the coming year, his response was immediate: 'To find a spiritual director'.

In the words of William Barry, spiritual direction is 'that form of pastoral care which offers direct help to another person to enable that person to relate personally to him or her, to respond to God personally, and to live the consequences of that relationship'.[1]

John the Baptist, Jesus and Paul seemed to have this sort of relationship with their disciples. Luther said every priest ought to have a 'father in God'. No one is an island. In our spiritual journey two are better than one.

The role of the spiritual director. The spiritual director helps another Christian become himself or herself in faith. He or she helps the other to recognise God's working in all the events of life. The seventeenth-century Benedictine mystic, Dom Augustine Baker, wrote, 'In a word, (the spiritual director) is only God's usher, and must lead souls in God's way, and not (his or her) own'. Spiritual direction is simply and clearly to lead us to our real Director. The director shares my vision of the Lord, and the Lord's vision of me, and is the one to whom I say regularly, 'Keep me true to this vision; help me to be faithful'. The director helps me to discover which 'rumours' are of God in my life and which are not.

The best spiritual directors are highly skilled at 'noticing', listening and attending to the key interior movements in a person's prayer. However this is not just a mystical thing. Because prayer covers all the major areas of one's life, so does spiritual direction. Thomas Merton told of a Russian spiritual director who was criticised for spending so much time earnestly advising an old peasant woman about the care of her turkeys. 'Not at all', he replied. 'Her whole life is in those turkeys.'[2]

How does spiritual direction happen? As spiritual direction involves two people listening together to the Lord in the events and relationships of life, it is essential to be honest about the directee's 'desire'. What does he or she really want with the Lord? What are the presenting — and the real — motivations and problems? What are the 'inner movements' within the directee's life? Where is the 'good spirit' — God's Holy Spirit — at work and where might there be another spirit operating?

If a spiritual director is to help with these complex issues, he or she will need some special spiritual gifts. First, we must say that friendship is not a prerequisite for spiritual direction, though love and trust are. 'We come to God', declared St Augustine, 'by love, not by navigation'. The director doesn't usually give advice, but rather discernment and encouragement. And experienced directors will be alert to the dangers of dependency and transference. (The latter, put simply, involves the sense of someone relating to us as if we're someone else. Lots of emotion is dumped on us which doesn't belong to us.)

Essentially the spiritual director discerns what Ignatius called the 'movement of spirits', whether good or evil, in the other. 'Consolation' is a life-giving movement towards God, though it won't always be pain- or struggle-free. 'Desolation', on the other hand, might even be pleasurable, but leads away from God, into chaos, confusion and turmoil.

So the key gift a spiritual director will possess is that of 'discernment of spirits'. He or she, as Kenneth Leech suggests, will be one who can 'read the signs of the times and the writing on the walls of souls'. The spiritual director will be a person of above-average faith, hope and love; of experience (spiritual, theological, psychological, and in the life of prayer), and of learning (steeped in Scripture and the wisdom of the spiritual masters).

How can I find a spiritual director? First, do some reading in the area (see list below). Ask yourself: do I know someone who fits the characteristics outlined by these authors? Ask God for guidance, of course. Sometimes, if a more mature person can't be found, you can try mutual direction with a caring Christian friend. Attend courses and retreats. Ask your local Anglican or Catholic priest for contacts: their traditions have not excluded this discipline, as most have.

Richard Foster suggests that while spiritual direction can become formalised, it need not be. 'If we have the humility to believe that we can learn from our brothers and sisters and the understanding that some have gone further into the divine Centre than others, we can see the necessity of spiritual direction. As Virgil Vogt has said "If you cannot listen to your brother, you cannot listen to the Holy Spirit".[3]

Spiritual direction is quite different from distant advice-giving... Spiritual direction is a ministry of sweat and tears, not without agony and even moments of despair... (It) always leads to a fellowship of the weak...

Spiritual direction does not mean that one spiritual person tells another less spiritual person what to think, say or do in order to become a more spiritual person. It is not the knower speaking to the ignorant. Spiritual direction means that two or more sinful, broken, struggling people come together to listen to the direction of the Spirit.

Henri J. M. Nouwen,
in the Foreword to Francis W. Vanderwall, *Spiritual Direction: An Invitation to Abundant Life*, New York: Paulist Press, 1981, p. x.

Competent directors (are) needed (because of) the bewilderment so often expressed about how to pray. The question raised by the anonymous pilgrim in *The Way of a Pilgrim* remains as searching as when he raised it. Everyone told him he ought to pray, but no-one told him how to pray, and the book is the story of his search for an answer to that question. There are countless books around these days on how to pray; indeed, far too many. But it is significant that the Pilgrim found his answer not in widely addressed sermons or teaching, but in one-to-one discussion with others... He needed individual spiritual direction.

Gordon Jeff,
Spiritual Direction — for Every Christian, London: SPCK, 1987, pp. 10-11.

There are many similarities between spiritual direction and psychotherapy, but they are fundamentally different undertakings... (But) to attempt too strict a separation, to try to divorce mind from spirit, would be artificial and not at all helpful. We are human souls, with body, mind and spirit all reflecting facets of our unified being. To look at the spirit without also addressing the mind is as absurd as caring for the mind without attending to physical health...

The most obvious difference in content between psychotherapy and spiritual direction is that the former focuses more on mental and emotional dimensions (thoughts, feelings, moods and so on) while the latter focuses more precisely on spiritual issues such as prayer life, religious experiences, and sense of relationship to God.

Gerald May,
Care of Mind/Care of Spirit: Psychiatric Dimensions of Spiritual Direction, San Francisco: Harper & Row, 1982, pp. 12-13.

The spiritual director is concerned with the whole person, for the spiritual life is not just for the life of the mind, or of the affections, or of the 'summit of the soul' — it is the life of the whole person. For the spiritual (person) (*pneumatikos*) is the one whose whole life, in all its aspects and all its activities, has been spiritualized by the action of the Holy Spirit, whether through the sacraments, or by personal and interior inspirations. Moreover, spiritual direction is concerned with the whole person not simply as an individual human being, but as a son of God, another Christ, seeking to recover the perfect likeness to God in Christ, and by the Spirit of Christ.

Thomas Merton,
Spiritual Direction and Meditation, pp. 6-7, quoted in Kevin Culligan, *Spiritual Direction: Contemporary Readings*, New York: Living Flame Press, 1983, pp. 219-20.

Theodora, one of the great female ascetics of the desert, gave a good summary (of the qualities of a spiritual director) when she said,

'(Spiritual directors) ought to be strangers to the desire for domination, vain-glory, and pride; one should not be able to fool them by flattery, nor blind them by gifts, nor conquer them by the stomach, nor dominate them by anger; but they should be patient, gentle and humble as far as possible; they must be tested and without partisanship, full of concern, and a lover of souls...'

If we agree to work together (in spiritual direction), I will ask him or her to do an inventory of oblation before we meet again in two weeks. Oblation means offering. In the liturgy, the oblation takes place when the offering of money and bread and wine is raised before the altar. In personal prayer, oblation is the offering of self to God. An inventory of oblation takes place in six parts. I ask people to prayerfully hold before God six different aspects of their being: their emotions, will, intellect, imagination, relationships and work. A time of prayer is set aside for each of these six aspects...

Kenneth Swanson,
Uncommon Prayer, New York: Ballantine, 1986, pp. 138-9, 151.

In the Middle Ages not even the greatest saints attempted the depths of the inward journey without the help of a spiritual director... Spiritual direction is a beautiful expression of divine guidance through the help of our brothers and sisters...

The relationship is of an adviser to a friend. Though the director has obviously advanced further into the inner depths, the two are together learning and growing in the realm of the Spirit.

Richard Foster,
Celebration of Discipline, Sevenoaks: Hodder & Stoughton, 1980, pp. 159-60.

Three gifts in particular distinguish the spiritual father. The first is insight and discernment, the ability to perceive intuitively the secrets of another's heart, to understand the hidden depths of which the other is unaware...

(He) uses few words or by his silence, he is able to alter the whole direction of (another's) life...

The second gift of the spiritual father is the ability to love others and to make others' sufferings his own. Of Abba Poemen... it is briefly and simply recorded: 'He possessed love, and many came to him'. He possessed love — this is indispensable in all spiritual fatherhood...

'As God himself knows', Varsanuphius insists to his spiritual children, 'there is not a second or an hour when I do not have you in my mind and in my prayers... I care for you more than you care for yourself... I would gladly lay down my life for you...'

A third gift of the spiritual father is the power to transform the human environment, both the material and the non-material. The gift of healing, possessed by so many of (them), is one aspect of this power. More generally, the starets (spiritual guide) helps his disciples to perceive the world as God created it and as God desires it once more to be. 'Can you take too much joy in your Father's works?' asks Thomas Traherne. 'He is himself in everything.' The true starets is one who discerns this universal presence of the Creator throughout creation, and assists others to discern it...

In the Eastern Orthodox tradition at its best, the spiritual father has always sought to avoid any kind of constraint and spiritual violence in his relations with his disciple. If, under the guidance of the Spirit, he speaks and acts with authority, it is with the authority of humble love...

Many people imagine that they cannot find a spiritual father, because they expect him to be of a particular type: they want a St Seraphim, and so they close their eyes to the guides whom God is actually sending to them. Often their supposed problems are not so very complicated, and in reality they already know in their heart what the answer is. But they do not like the answer, because it involves patient and sustained effort on their part: and so they look for a *deus ex machina* who, by a single miraculous word, will suddenly make everything easy.

Kallistos Ware,

'The Spiritual Father in Orthodox Christianity', in John Garvey (ed.), *Modern Spirituality: An Anthology*, London: Darton, Longman and Todd, 1985, pp. 45-52, 55.

Tom MacGreggor (a pastor) sought honestly to find a way to fulfil the role of spiritual guide. What would be his agenda in offering spiritual guidance? In his journal he made the following list of priorities:

1. Recognise that Christ is the true director of souls.
2. Offer myself to be his agent with each person.
3. Listen deeply to the life that is being shared with me.
4. Look for signs of the presence of God in the story I hear.
5. Ask questions that will help the person seeking guidance to confront his or her life.
6. Share my own life with the person.
7. Suggest different ways issues may be confronted.
8. Respect the freedom and integrity of the person seeking guidance.
9. Pray with and for the person.
10. In all things seek the will of God.

Ben Campbell Johnson,

'The Pastor as Spiritual Guide' in *Pastoral Ministry: A Focus for Ministry*, Philadelphia: Westminster Press, 1988, pp. 112-13.

A woman in a London flat was told of her husband's death in a street accident. The shock of grief stunned her like a blow, she sank into a corner of the sofa and sat there rigid and unhearing.

For a long time her terrible tranced look continued to embarrass the family... Then the school teacher of one of her children... called... and sat down beside her. Without a word she threw an arm around the tight shoulders, clasping them with her full strength. (One cheek touched the other.) Then as the unrelenting pain seeped through to her, the newcomer's tears began to flow, falling on their two hands... For a long time that is all that was happening. And then at last the (widow) began to sob. Still not a word was spoken and after a little while the visitor got up and went...

That is the embrace of God, the kiss of life. That is the embrace of his mission, and of our intercession. And the Holy Spirit is the force in the straining muscles of an arm, the film of sweat between pressed cheeks, the mingled wetness of the backs of clasped hands. He is as close and as unobtrusive as that, and as irresistibly strong.

John V. Taylor,
The Go-Between God: The Holy Spirit & the Christian Mission, London: SCM Press, 1972, p. 243.

O Christ, my Lord, again and again I have said with Mary Magdalene, 'They have taken away my Lord and I know not where they have laid him.'

I have been desolate and alone.

And you have found me again, and I know that what has died is not you, my Lord, but only my idea of you, the image which I have made to preserve what I have found, and to be my security.

I shall make another image, O Lord, better than the last. That, too, must go, and all successive images, until I come to the blessed vision of yourself, O Christ, my Lord.

Archbishop George Appleton,
quoted in Gordon Jeff, Spiritual Direction — for Every Christian, London: SPCK, 1987, pp. 39-40.

For your prayer, why not write a personal letter to the Lord expressing your response to the above. It might go something like this:

Dear Lord,

I envy those disciples of yours, watching you, listening to you, learning from you, day and night for three years. I echo their request: 'Lord, teach me to pray!'

Teach me how to relate to you in deep honesty. Teach me how to understand and accept my real self. Give me courage to explore the inner recesses of my being and not be afraid of what I find there. Walk with me gently through the paths of my memories; minister to me with your healing touch where I am bruised; help me to understand that in the dark night you may seem to be silent but you are not absent.

Lord, lead me to someone who can be Christ to me. Give me trust when I open my life to that person. Give me faithfulness and honesty when I relate the areas of my life I am ashamed about. Give me confidence that if I confess my sins to you and that one, I am cleansed and forgiven. Prepare the person of your choice to receive me, welcome me, love me: but I will not expect miracles — just the companionship of another along my spiritual journey.

Lord Jesus, you welcome sinners, you love those who haven't yet 'arrived', you are gentle and humble and will help me carry my burden if I am willing to share it with you. You are the conqueror of the spirit world: guard me from evil spirits, help me to open my life to the good spirit, the Holy Spirit.

I am weak: help me to become stronger; I am tired: give me more spiritual energy; I am a child in the faith: help me grow to maturity. For your glory, Lord. Amen.

A benediction

May Jesus of Nazareth, who is still looking for disciples, find you and claim you; and may you respond to his call, and follow him all the days of your life. To him be glory for ever and ever. Amen.

Notes
1. William A. Barry, "Spiritual Direction and Pastoral Counselling", *Pastoral Psychology*, 26 (1), 1977, p. 6.
2. Thomas Merton, *Spiritual Direction and Meditation*, quoted in Richard Foster, *Celebration of Discipline*, Hodder & Stoughton, 1980, p. 160.
3. Ibid., p. 161.

Capsule 4

Contemplation and conversion

Spiritual directors try to encourage a contemplative attitude in those who seek direction. True contemplation causes us to forget our surroundings, and the passage of time. It is an experience of transcendence, of self-forgetfulness, of absorption in the contemplated object. It involves us in wonder, gratitude and joy. Because the Lord is invisible, he is sometimes hard to 'apprehend'; because of his 'otherness' he is hard to listen to. So

213

true contemplation goes beyond words, into the realm of the imagination. Much verbal prayer can be self-absorbing. True contemplation is 'lost in wonder, love and praise' with something or someone other than the self as the object. Reflection rather than analysis is the primary mode of contemplation.

Agnes Sanford says (in *The Healing Gifts of the Spirit*) to people who say 'I can't find God' that they should do some simple things they like to do, that will put them in the way of God 'so that he can find you'. Above all, scripture and nature can be means for this to happen. One of the richest experiences of my life resulted from my director's suggesting I imagine I am Peter in the story of the feeding of the five thousand. Try it!

An important corollary of spiritual direction is an attitude open to 'conversions'. Whereas most of us believe we are truly converted to the Lord only once, there is a sense in which we are experiencing transitions, movements, conversions, all our lives if we are growing people. Henri Nouwen (*Reaching Out*) writes for example about moving from loneliness to solitude, hostility to hospitality, illusion to prayer. Connolly (*The Practice of Spiritual Direction*) talks about moving from disappointment to receptivity. And there is a constant movement in a Christian from sinfulness to forgiveness.

John of the Cross teaches us how to cope with the 'dark night', when we feel we have nothing to hang on to. How can we know this experience is from God? He says there are three signs: an inability to pray the way I used to; a sense of going backwards; but also a genuine desire for God. Although such an experience is painful, God is there, he says. (That is why we need a discerning spiritual director in times like these: otherwise we might be tempted to wallow in despair.)

Further Reading
Start with one or two of the following: Mark Link's *You* and/or *Breakaway* (Allen, Texas: Argus, 1976/1980) or Francis W. Vanderwall's *Spiritual Direction: An Invitation to Abundant Life*, New York: Paulist Press, 1981, Alan Jones, *Exploring Spiritual Direction: An Essay on Christian Friendship*, Minneapolis: Seabury Press, 1982, Gordon Jeff, *Spiritual Direction for Every Christian*, London: SPCK, 1987. Then read one or two of these more advanced books: William A. Barry & William J. Connolly, *The Practice of Spiritual Direction*, New York: Seabury, 1983, Kenneth Leech, *Soul Friend: A Study of Spirituality*, London: Sheldon Press, 1977, Morton Kelsey, *Companions on the Inner Way: The Art of Spiritual Guidance*, New York: Crossroad, 1983. A more technical book is Gerald May, *Care of Mind, Care of Spirit: Psychiatric Dimensions of Spiritual Direction*, San Francisco: Harper & Row, 1982.

20
Living sacramentally

I am the living bread that came down from heaven. Whoever eats of this bread will live forever; and the bread that I will give for the life of the world is my flesh. One Lord, one faith, one baptism.

He went into all the region around the Jordan, proclaiming a baptism of repentance for the forgiveness of sins. I have baptised you with water; but he will baptise you with the Holy Spirit. This is the one who came by water and blood, Jesus Christ, not with the water only but with the water and the blood. And the Spirit is the one that testifies, for the Spirit is the truth. And when Jesus had been baptised, just as he came up from the water, suddenly the heavens were opened to him and he saw the Spirit of God descending like a dove and alighting on him.

Go therefore and make disciples of all nations, baptising them in the name of the Father and of the Son and of the Holy Spirit. The one who believes and is baptised will be saved; but the one who does not believe will be condemned.

Peter said to them, 'Repent, and be baptised every one of you in the name of Jesus Christ so that your sins may be forgiven; and you will receive the gift of the Holy Spirit. But when they believed Philip, who was proclaiming the good news about the kingdom of God and the name of Jesus Christ, they were baptised, both men and women. As they were going along the road, they came to some water; and the eunuch said, 'Look, here is water! What is to prevent me from being baptised?' Crispus, the official of the synagogue, became a believer in the Lord, together with all his household; and many of the Corinthians who heard Paul became believers and were baptised.

When you were buried with him in baptism, you were also raised with him through faith in the power of God, who raised him from the dead. Do you not know that all of us who have been baptised into Christ Jesus were baptised into his death? Therefore we have been buried with him by baptism into death, so that, just as Christ was raised from the dead by the glory of the Father, so we too might walk in newness of life. As many of you as were baptised into Christ have clothed yourselves with Christ. And baptism which this prefigured, now saves you — not as a removal of dirt from the body, but as an appeal to God for a good conscience through the resurrection of Jesus Christ.

He took a loaf of bread, and when he had given thanks, he broke it and gave it to them, saying, 'This is my body, which is given for you. Do this in remembrance of me'. Then he took a cup, and after giving thanks he said, 'Take this and divide it among yourselves'. And he did the same with the cup after supper, saying, 'This cup that is poured out for you is the new covenant in my blood'.

When he was at the table with them, he took bread, blessed it and broke it, and gave it to them.

For I received from the Lord what I also handed on to you, that the Lord Jesus on the night when he was betrayed took a loaf of bread, and when he had given thanks, he broke it and said, 'This is my body that is for you. Do this in remembrance of me'. In the same way he took the cup also, after supper, saying, 'This cup is the new covenant in my blood. Do this, as often as you drink it, in remembrance of me'. For as often as you eat this bread and drink the cup, you proclaim the Lord's death until he comes. Whoever, therefore, eats the bread or drinks the cup of the Lord in an unworthy manner will be answerable for the body and blood of the Lord. For all who eat and drink without discerning the body, eat and drink judgment against themselves.

The cup of blessing that we bless, is it not a sharing in the blood of Christ? The bread that we break, is it not a sharing in the body of Christ?

John 6:51; Ephesians 4:5; Luke 3:3; Mark 1:8; 1 John 5:6; Matthew 3:16; Matthew 28:19; Mark 16:16; Acts 2:38; 8:12; 8:36; 18:8; Colossians 1:12; Romans 6:3-4; Galatians 3:27; 1 Peter 3:21; Luke 22:19,17,20; Luke 24:30; 1 Corinthians 11:23-29; 1 Corinthians 10:16.

A sacrament is 'an outward and visible sign of an inward and spiritual grace'. The word comes from the Latin *sacramentum*, the term used for the coin given to a soldier to signify his oath of loyalty when recruited to serve the Emperor. His allegiance was to Caesar as lord. In the Christian sacraments, we pledge our loyalty to Christ: 'Jesus is Lord' (Romans 10:9).

For people in tune with the Infinite God everything is sacramental. Teilhard de Chardin has said, 'Because of creation and even more because of incarnation there is nothing profane for those who know how to see'. God's grace gifts are many and varied — our very life, the world of nature and of other people, prayer, the Scriptures, the Christian community, corporate worship. These are all 'means of grace'.

But the Lord serves us especially in 'the sacraments' of water, bread and wine. They are special reminders of God's grace to us, unworthy as we are. He pledges in them his loyalty to us. His steadfast love is with us forever.

Baptism. Water, of course, is the common element for cleansing. When 'pagans' wanted to join the Jewish faith they were baptised, cleansed, with water. John the Baptist told religious Jews they, too, needed to be baptised as a sign of their repentance. This they naturally found hard to take.

Jesus was baptised by John, then Jesus' disciples baptised converts during his ministry. At the end of his life he commissioned his disciples to make disciples everywhere, baptising them in the name of the Father, the Son, and the Holy Spirit (Matthew 28:18-20).

Baptism is associated in the New Testament with a rich variety of meanings: the washing away of our sins (Acts 22:16); putting off the old life like soiled clothes, and putting on Christ, like a new, clean garment (Galatians 3:27, Ephesians 4:22-24); being buried and raised with Christ (Colossians 2:12). Baptism, like the waters in Noah's time, is linked with our salvation (1 Peter 3:21), so we, like him, should be godly in a corrupt and sinful world. Baptism is the sign of the new covenant God makes with us, our children, and all that 'far away' (Acts 2:39, Colossians 2:11-12). It is an act of faith (often of real courage, too) before witnesses. It's a proclamation, a dramatisation of Christ's work for sinful humanity (Romans 6). Baptism means we are now owned by Christ (the words 'in the name' signify ownership) (Acts 2:38, 8:16, 10:48, etc.). Baptism is associated, too, with 'baptism in the Holy Spirit': two aspects of what Paul calls 'one baptism' (Ephesians 4:5; see also Titus 3:5, John 3:5, Luke 3:22, Acts 2:38, 1 Corinthians 12:13). Finally, baptism is the door into the church.

Baptism is not really an individual event. You don't baptise yourself. You are asking to belong. You are coming into a new community. Paul says we are 'baptised into Christ' (Romans 6:3) and baptised into the Body of Christ, the Church (1 Corinthians 12:13).

So baptism is an 'acted creed'. 'I saw Satan fall like lightning from heaven' ought to be our response at every baptism. Baptism is the rite of entry into the church. It is ordination for ministry. It ought to be the time when a person receives the fullness of the Spirit, and before the congregation is assured of his or her 'spiritual giftedness'. The baptismal service should have some sort of creed or covenantal statement to express the body of beliefs and commitments of the church into which the candidates are being baptised. The Apostles' Creed was originally called the Baptismal Creed.

The mode of baptism, the amount of water used and the age of the baptised may vary from church to church. The more important factor is that one is baptised in the name of Father, Son and Holy Spirit. The time is coming, hopefully, when more churches will recognise each other's baptism in this way.

If you have not been baptised, why should you? Not to save you — we are saved by God's grace and our response in faith, not by anything we do (John 3:35, Ephesians 2:8,9). The best reason for being baptised is that Jesus, your Master, commands it (Matthew 28:19). He himself was baptised to 'do all that God requires' (Matthew 3:15). Every step of obedience you take (and this is certainly a major one) strengthens and encourages you to follow Christ still further.

The Lord's Supper, or 'eucharist', is really high drama, and refers to the memorial feast instituted by Jesus just before he died. As he celebrated the passover with his friends, he gave them bread and wine, saying 'this is my body', 'this is my blood'. Paul's words in 1 Corinthians 11:23-26 suggest that the Lord's Supper had become a focal point of worship in the early churches. Justin Martyr in the early second century in his *First Apology* states that Christians met on the first day of the week to worship and 'break bread' together. With very few exceptions this sacred meal has been practised in all Christian denominations to the present day.

'Eucharist' means 'thankfulness': this service is a thankful remembrance of our Lord's death for us. Roman Catholics use the term 'Mass', from the Latin *missa*, a 'service' or perhaps 'feast'. The early Christians thought of Christ in terms of the past ('remember me'), present ('you proclaim the Lord's death'), and future ('till he come') (1 Corinthians 13:13, Hebrews 13:8).

The Communion is not just a private affair between an individual and Jesus, but a public act of the entire assembly, a public sign of our intention to be united with each other (1 Corinthians 10:17).

Anglican article 28 offers three aspects of the Lord's Supper: # it is a sign of Christian love; # it is a symbol of Calvary, and the provision, through Christ's death, of forgiveness of sins and a new life; and # it is a means of grace. By faith we believe that when we receive this sacrament our lives are strengthened and our faith renewed. As the bread and wine are assimilated into our bodies, so, by faith, the person of Christ enters again spiritually into the life of the communicant.

You ask, 'But what if I don't feel I'm good enough?' That's a serious question, and you are invited to confess your sins and accept again the forgiveness of Christ before you partake of the sacred elements. But if we have to wait until we are sinless to participate, none of us would qualify!

There is great value in a weekly celebration of the eucharist: in Acts 20:7 coming together for this purpose on the Lord's Day is mentioned as though it were a matter of course. There may also be other occasions where Christians can meet around the table of the Lord. At the time of the Communion we might make another opportunity to get right with one another. Sometimes let us move around and say something meaningful to another: a word of encouragement, confession, maybe a plea for forgiveness.

Do it differently sometimes, and think about what you are doing. For example, for churches where people come to the front to receive the bread, why not take it to them, symbolising the good news that grace meets you not after you become worthy, but in order to help you become worthy? Perhaps servers of the wine could position themselves around the meeting-place, and people go to them. That is, as grace is given to us freely, we have to be willing to receive it: I will get up and go and claim the gift Christ offers. If the elements are normally served to the congregation, let them come to the front to receive them sometimes. Or serve each other. Or sing some meaningful worship-songs during communion.

A sacrament is when something holy happens. It is transparent time, time which you can see through to something deep inside time.

Generally speaking, Protestants have two official sacraments (the Lord's Supper, Baptism) and Roman Catholics these two plus five others (Confirmation, Penance, Extreme Unction, Ordination, and Matrimony). In other words, at such milestone moments as seeing a baby baptised or being baptised yourself, confessing your sins, getting married, dying, you are apt to catch a glimpse of the almost unbearable preciousness and mystery of life.

Needless to say, church isn't the only place where the holy happens. Sacramental moments can occur at any moment, any place, and to anybody. Watching something get born. Making love. A high-school graduation. Somebody coming to see you when you're sick. A meal with people you love. Looking into a stranger's eyes and finding out he's not a stranger.

If we weren't blind as bats, we might see that life itself is sacramental.

Frederick Buechner,
Wishful Thinking, London: Collins, 1973, pp. 82-3.

Ignatius says, When eating, think of Jesus. Zen says, When eating, think of eating. Are these two approaches so different? Is not Jesus our food? Is not every food symbol of the Eucharist? Is not God present in all we eat? Is not every action of ours an act of faith? Do what you do, and eat when you eat. Jesus is with you.

Anthony de Mello,
in Carlos G. Valles, *Mastering Sadhana*, New York: Doubleday, 1988, p. 99.

Through these visible re-enactments, God's grace is awakening and empowering our participation in the life of Christ. We are born in Christ in baptism, and through Holy Communion we are nurtured, sustained and, it is hoped, eventually sanctified (made mature in holy living) in Christ...

The sacraments presuppose that God has met us in history and that this meeting calls us to regular recollection and re-enactment in order to experience God's real presence in our midst. The grace of God is offered to us in and through these sacraments in a way that we cannot grasp by our own moral efforts. Protestants revolted against what they perceived to be superstitions of medieval penance and sacramentalism. Yet never do the Protestant confessions lose sight of the basic idea that grace is being offered, and, by faith, communicated to the believer in baptism and Holy Communion by Christ's own ordinance. They are means of grace.

Thomas Oden,
Pastoral Theology: Essentials of Ministry, San Francisco: Harper & Row, 1983, pp. 106-7.

(The early church fathers Tertullian, Irenaeus, and Cyprian, Augustine, Ambrose, Athanasius, St John Chrysostom, etc.) thought in terms of one sacrament — one visible, tangible means by which we are brought to God. That means is Jesus Christ. He is the sacrament par excellence. The fathers never argued for salvation by the sacraments. Rather, the sacraments of water and bread and wine, they said, are the visible, tangible signs of Christ's saving action.

Robert E. Webber,
Evangelicals on the Canterbury Trail: Why Evangelicals are Attracted to the Liturgical Church, Waco, Texas: Word Books, 1985, p. 48.

Baptism consists of getting dunked or sprinkled. Which technique is used matters about as much as whether you pray kneeling or standing on your head. Dunking is a better symbol, however. Going under symbolises the end of everything about your life that is less than human. Coming up again symbolises the beginning in you of something strange and new and hopeful. You can breathe again.

Question: How about infant baptism? Shouldn't you wait until the child grows up enough to know what's going on?

Answer: If you don't think there is as much of the less-than-human in an infant as there is in anybody else, you have lost touch with reality.

When it comes to the forgiving and transforming love of God, one wonders if the six-week-old screecher knows all that much less than the Archbishop of Canterbury.

Frederick Buechner,
Wishful Thinking, London: Collins, 1973, pp. 5-6.

The differences between infant and believers' baptism become less sharp when it is recognised that both forms of baptism embody God's own initiative in Christ and express a response of faith made within the believing community... The practice of infant baptism emphasises the corporate faith and the faith which the child shares with its parents... The practice of believer's baptism emphasises the explicit confession of the person who responds to the grace of God in and through the community of faith and who seeks baptism... In some churches which unite both infant-baptist and believer-baptist traditions, it has been possible to regard as equivalent alternatives for entry into the Church both a pattern whereby baptism in infancy is followed by a later profession of faith and a pattern whereby believer baptism follows upon a presentation and blessing in infancy. This example invites other churches to decide whether they, too, could not recognise equivalent alternatives...

Commentary (12) on Baptism, Eucharist and Ministry, Faith and Order Paper No. 111, World Council of Churches, Geneva, 1982, p. 5.

What the Church of England does not do, but any of the Baptist Churches do, is to administer an adult rite to those already previously baptised, and it is that principle which distinguishes between the two denominational traditions and not the principle as to whether adults should be baptised or not. All Christians are agreed that adults who come to faith in Christ and have not been baptised should then be baptised.

Submersion or dipping is the Church of England's first and preferred option. Every candidate ought to be shown that this option is not only open to him or her, but is the Church of England's preferred option... It is an 'option' — not a necessity — and its usefulness and desirability must be worked out between minister and candidates on each occasion, and it is not absurd to have one font or baptismal tank with some candidates undergoing dipping and others receiving pouring (just as adult and infant candidates may also be mixed together, though that is not necessarily to imply that only adults should be submerged, or only infants have water poured on them).

Colin Buchanan,
Adult Baptisms, Bramcote, Notts: Grove Books, 1985, pp. 4, 20.

The presence of Christ in the ordinary events of our lives and his presence in the sacraments are not in opposition to each other. In the sacraments we celebrate in a special ritual way the love of Christ we experience in our lives. In turn, these celebrations help us become more aware of the presence of Christ in all our human experiences...

The sacraments are external realities that first touch our senses. Through the messages that reach and get through our senses, Christ 'speaks' and 'touches' the depths of our being... (But) if we have not had happy, enriching experiences of breaking and sharing authentic bread around a table of love, then how can that sign speak to us at eucharist? If the celebration of the eucharist obscures as much as possible the sign of a shared meal (an altar instead of a table, people scattered in a large building rather than gathered in an intimate community, tasteless wafers instead of loaves of wholemeal bread) is not the experience of Christ in the meal sacrifice diminished accordingly?

William P. Roberts,
'New Riches in Old Signs' in *Praying*, Kansas, No. 12, 1985, pp. 11, 12.

The road from the Last Supper in the Upper Room on the night when Jesus was betrayed to modern eucharistic faith and practice in the Christian church has been long, tortuous and diverse. Along it, Christians have been persecuted by the State and by each other. Sometimes they have worshipped in joyful assurance of their Lord's presence and in confident expectation of his triumphant return. Sometimes Christ's presence in the sacrament has been hidden and distorted by magic and superstition. Sometimes, great Christians have struggled with lofty words to explain and lay hold of the sublime truths conveyed in the celebration of the Lord's Supper. Often Christian understanding has been partial and shallow. After centuries of neglect many Protestant Christians are rediscovering the importance and centrality of the eucharist in worship. After centuries of suspicion many Catholics and Protestants are feeling the urge to break bread together again, and to heal the rifts which have divided them for so long.

Donald Bridge and David Phypers,
The Meal That Unites?, London: Hodder & Stoughton, 1981, p. 166. Reproduced by permission of Hodder & Stoughton Ltd/New English Library Ltd.

An increasing number of Christians feel that a united communion service is the most expressive demonstration of true Christian unity, since it means... we welcome to the Lord's Table those whom we believe Christ has received even though we may have differing views on such matters as church order.

To practise 'open communion' is not to deny real and meaningful denominational differences, but it is to recognise that churches other than one's own are also part of the body of Christ. The invitation to partake should surely be extended to all true believers and the onus thereafter is upon the individuals concerned.

Gilbert W. Kirby,
Too Hot to Handle, London: Marshall, Morgan & Scott, 1978, p. 36.

To eat this particular meal together is to meet at the level of our most basic humanness, which involves our need not just for food but for each other. I need you to help fill my emptiness just as you need me to help fill yours. As for the emptiness that's still left over, well we're in it together, or it in us. Maybe it's most of what makes us human and makes us brothers and sisters.

The next time you walk down the street, take a good look at every face you pass and in your mind say, Christ died for you. That girl. That slob. That phoney. That crook. That saint. That damned fool. Christ died for you. Take and eat this in remembrance that Christ died for you.

Frederick Buechner,
Wishful Thinking, London: Collins, 1973, p. 53.

Breaking one bread, which is the medicine of immortality, the antidote against death which gives eternal life in Jesus Christ.

Irenaeus,
quoted in Margaret Pepper (ed.), *The Pan Dictionary of Religious Quotations*, London: Pan Books, 1989, p. 166.

O sacred feast in which we partake of Christ: his sufferings are remembered, our minds are filled with his grace and we receive a pledge of the glory that is to be ours.

Antiphon from the Vespers of Corpus Christi in Tony Kelly, *Touching the Infinite*, Melbourne: Collins Dove, 1991, p. 129.

Father, accept us, as we offer and present ourselves, our souls and bodies, to be a holy and living sacrifice; through Jesus Christ our Lord, to whom with you and the Holy Spirit be all honour and glory, now and for ever. Amen.

223

Alternative Great Prayer of Thanksgiving B, *Uniting in Worship*, Melbourne: Uniting Church Press, 1988, p. 108.

O God, by your word and Spirit, bless and sanctify (the) bread and (the) wine, that they may be for us the communion of the body and blood of Christ, and that he may ever live in us and we in him.

Jesus, you are the bread of life; those who come to you will never be hungry; those who believe in you will never thirst. You are the living bread from heaven; the bread you give us is your own flesh, and you give it for the life of the world.

All who eat your flesh and drink your blood live in you and you in them; for your flesh is the food we need, your blood is our salvation; all who eat your flesh and drink your blood have eternal life.

Look to Jesus in the wilderness, breaking bread and feeding the multitude.

A New Zealand Prayer Book, Auckland: Collins, 1989, p. 124.

Thou art thyself both he who offers and he who is offered, he who receives and he who is distributed.

Liturgy of St John Chrysostom,
quoted in Margaret Pepper (ed.), *The Pan Dictionary of Religious Quotations*, London: Pan Books, 1989, p. 166.

Lord, grant that your faithful people may continually desire to relive the mystery of the eucharist and so be born to lead a new life. We ask this through Christ our Lord.

Daily Mass Book, Brisbane: The Liturgical Commission, 1990, p. 38.

Grant, O Lord that I may receive your precious body and blood to make me holy, to enlighten and strengthen me, to ease the burden of my many sins, to protect me from the traps of the devil, to overcome my sinful and evil habits, to subdue my wayward urges, to help me to live your commandments, to increase in me your divine life, to bring me into your kingdom.

John Chrysostom,
quoted in *Praying with the Saints*, Dublin: Veritas Publications, 1989, pp. 49-50.

A benediction
May God Almighty bless you, the Father, the Son and the Holy Spirit. Go in peace to love and serve the Lord: In the name of Christ. Amen.

21
Only one thing is important — to be a saint

I have no greater joy than this, to hear that my children are walking in the truth... If you continue in my word, you are truly my disciples.

Like obedient children, do not be conformed to the desires that you formerly had in ignorance. Instead, as he who called you is holy, be holy yourselves in all your conduct; for it is written, 'You shall be holy, for I am holy'.

Do you not know that a little yeast leavens the whole batch of dough? Clean out the old yeast so that you may be a new batch, as you really are unleavened. For our paschal lamb, Christ, has been sacrificed. Therefore, let us celebrate the festival, not with the old yeast, the yeast of malice and evil, but with the unleavened bread of sincerity and truth.

I appeal to you therefore, brothers and sisters, by the mercies of God, to present your bodies as a living sacrifice, holy and acceptable to God, which is your spiritual worship... to present you holy and blameless and irreproachable before him.

So if you have been raised with Christ, seek the things that are above, where Christ is, seated at the right hand of God.

God's temple is holy, and you are that temple. What sort of persons ought you to be in leading lives of holiness and godliness...?

3 John 4; John 8:31; 1 Peter 1:14-16; 1 Corinthians 5:6-8; Romans 12:1; Colossians 1:22; Colossians 3:1; 1 Corinthians 3:17; 2 Peter 3:11-14.

Saints are many people but they have this in common: they remind you of Jesus. They love everyone. They know who they are. Saints inhabit every Christian denomination or group. They're people you feel good around: they radiate goodness. They're sinners — indeed more aware of their sins than anyone — but they have had a personal experience of God's grace and forgiveness. Because of that they can't be negative about the personhood (as distinct from the behaviour) of anyone else: they are very accepting people.

Saints not only remind you of Jesus, but they tend to see Jesus in others. Teilhard de Chardin once prayed, 'Grant me to recognise in others, Lord God, the radiance of your own face'.

They are simple people — not naive, or simplistic, but simple. They inhabit 'simplicity the other side of complexity' rather than 'simplicity this side of complexity' (or 'complexity the other side of simplicity'). They are simple as much because they're smart as holy!

And they are joyful people — partly because their lives aren't cluttered with material possessions and unspiritual entanglements. They enjoy God forever. God is all they need. They believe that if you have God and everything else you have no more than if you had God only; and if you have everything else and not God you have nothing.

In 1975, *Time* magazine listed the following as living saints: Mother Teresa of Calcutta, Schwester Selma Mayer in Jerusalem, Archbishop Dom Helder Camara in Brazil, Coptic monk Matta El Meskin in Egypt, Annie Skau in Hong Kong, and John Lewis in San Antonio.[1]

Here we'll explore just one characteristic of all the saints: they have been cured of pharisaism. Cured? Yes, pharisaism is a spiritual and social disease.

The pharisees of Jesus' day were 'separatists'. They distanced themselves from evil, segregating themselves from anyone unclean. 'Away' was their directional signal when it came to dealing with evil. The evils they were concerned about were mainly of two kinds: heresy and sexual sin.

Now Jesus upset these people because his judgments were more against 'sins of the spirit' rather than sins of heterodoxy or sins of the flesh. Not that he made light of these. The truth sets us free, he said. After his pastoral word to the woman caught in adultery — 'neither do I condemn you' — he then adds, 'Go and sin no more'. (The pharisees — ask them! — always remember the latter but not the former statement by Jesus to this woman.)

The pharisees' mind-set was to demand repentance before

they practised acceptance. With Jesus these were reversed. 'I accept you,' he says to sinners, 'so let's work on change together'.

For the pharisee, the law is the means of telling the good guys from the bad guys. But, underneath, many pharisees are jealous of the bad guys who are enjoying their sins, but the pharisee isn't enjoying righteousness half as much. Immorality, Mencken said, is the morality of those who are having a better time. A pharisee is a good person in the worst sense of the word. Kenneth Bailey talks about 'law-breaking sinners' and 'law-keeping sinners' and each being worse than the other! For the saint, whose life is characterised by thankfulness, gratefulness, the law is a reminder, codifying a thankful response to the law-giver.

Every Christian is on a journey from sainthood to pharisaism or back the other way...

❦

In his holy flirtation with the world, God occasionally drops a handkerchief. These handkerchiefs are called saints.

Frederick Buechner,
Wishful Thinking, London: Collins, 1973, p. 83.

One of the most noticeable things about the saints is that they channelled their thirst for God into caring for the necessities close to hand — healing the sick and the lepers; feeding the poor and the needy; preaching the word of God to as many people as possible; providing education for the unlettered. Because they were totally absorbed with God, they were also totally absorbed with his creatures. The saints were joyous realists. Much is written today about self-acceptance and feeling good about oneself. The saints, as seen in their prayers, accepted themselves as sinners and knew that they were accepted by God for what they were. They stood in complete sincerity before God and believed deeply that growth and success were from him who was behind and beneath all their strivings. Their lives were thus filled with great joy. St Teresa wrote that she believed joy to be as essential to holiness as good works.

Praying with the Saints, Dublin: Veritas, 1989, p. 6.

'The simplicity that is in Christ.' — 2 Corinthians 11:3 'The simplicity that is toward Christ.' — *Revised Version.*

The word 'simple' itself is a word which has come down in the world... When it first appeared, centuries ago, in English literature, it stood for a noble, shining, virtue; but no one likes to be called 'simple' today. As originally used, it meant single-hearted, crystal-clear, straightforward. But today the word smacks of its own unfortunate derivative 'simpleton', and so is under a cloud...

The world's greatest people have invariably been characterised by a deep simplicity of life and character. Tennyson's lines in his 'Ode on the Death of Wellington' are familiar:

> Foremost captain of his time,
> Rich in saving common-sense,
> And, as the greatest only are,
> In his simplicity sublime.

'As the greatest only are', says Tennyson; and the poet is right. The really great — the Isaiahs, the Pauls, the Bunyans, the Wilberforces — have been at heart as simple as a child. And that is true also of those who, although their names never appear on any roll of fame, are nevertheless great in God's sight — utterly obscure and unknown to us, yet great in character. A person may be a saint without many of the qualities which this complex world ranks high: no one can be a saint without a deep simplicity of soul...

When St Anthony of Egypt, sickened by the worldliness and vice of the great pagan cities around him, cut the cables, he sacrificed all his wealth and standing, and made his home in the desert. So it was again when St Francis of Assisi led his little band of friars out from the moral and social entanglements of mediaeval Italy into something like the joy and freedom of first-century Galilee. So it was most dramatically when Martin Luther, leading on the Reformation, cut at one stroke through the complex casuistry of papal doctrine, and gave back to the individual soul the directness and immediacy of true religion...

'The common people', we are told, 'heard him gladly'. They did not hear their own Rabbis gladly. Their own Rabbis only fogged their minds, and blurred the issues, and spoke above their heads. But when Jesus spoke it was all so practical that they could connect it up at once with their own experience; it was so straight that none could miss its meaning; it was so concrete that it came on them as a glorious discovery after the weary abstractions to which their Rabbis had persistently treated them. Remember that simplicity of speech is a very different thing from superficiality of thought. The simplest language is often the profoundest...

J. S. Stewart,
The Gates of New Life, Edinburgh: T. & T. Clark, 1956, pp. 211-17.

There's a well-known phrase of Ignatius: 'an intimate knowledge of our Lord, who has become very human for me, that I may love him more and follow him more closely'. We may remember the song from Godspell:

Day by day, day by day,
oh dear Lord, three things I pray:
to see thee more clearly,
love thee more dearly,
follow thee more nearly, day by day.

It is based on a prayer of Saint Richard, that goes like this:

Thanks be to thee, Lord Jesus Christ,
for all the benefits and blessings
which thou hast borne for me.
O most merciful Friend, Brother and Redeemer,
may I know thee more clearly,
love thee more dearly,
and follow thee more nearly.

Margaret Hebblethwaite,
Finding God in All Things, London: Fountain Paperbacks, 1987, p. 77.

'I judge no one... but if I judge...' The gentle and gracious souls who would never dream of criticising us are the very people whose silent and unconscious condemnation is the most devastating. A straight stick, lying beside a crooked one, does not judge its twisted neighbour, yet its very straightness is the crooked stick's most terrible exposure... It seems to vindicate the contention of Francis of Assisi, who held that those who live a beautiful Christian life have no need to resort to words in order to rebuke the iniquities that disfigure the Church and world around them.

F. W. Boreham,
The Tide Comes In, London: Epworth Press, 1958, pp. 21-2.

The villains of Jesus' parables were seldom people who did the things they ought not to have done; they were usually those who left undone the things that they ought to have done. The priest who passed by on the other side; the rich man who let Lazarus lie unhelped at his gate; the servant who made no use of his talent — these were the objects of his severest condemnation.

F. W. Boreham,
The Tide Comes In, London: Epworth, 1958, p. 62.

Stand still, and look deep into the motivations of life. Are they such that true foundations of sanctity can be built on them? For truly we have been born to be saints — lovers of Love who died for us! There is but one tragedy: not to be a saint.

Catherine de Hueck Doherty,
Poustinia, Notre Dame, Indiana: Ave Maria Press, 1979, pp. 23-4.

Paul the Simple, an Egyptian saint, once heard Anthony the Great read the first verse of the first Psalm: 'Blessed is the one that does not walk in the counsel of the ungodly', and immediately, Paul departed into the wilderness. Only after some thirty years, when Anthony met him again, Paul said to him with great humility: 'I have spent all this time trying to become the man that does not walk in the counsel of the ungodly'. We do not need understanding on many points to reach perfection; what we need is thirty years of work to try to understand and to become that new person.

Metropolitan Anthony of Sourozh,
'Meditation and Worship' in John Garvey (ed.), *Modern Spirituality: An Anthology*, London: Darton, Longman and Todd, 1985, p. 28.

It is all too easy for us to treat the Pharisees as embodying all that is worst in humankind. But in fact they were probably the best men of their time, the most religious, the most devoted to the will of God, the most eager to express their loyalty to him in obedience to his every word, the most determined never to compromise with the world around them. But, as St Paul came to see it in retrospect, they were exposed to a fatal flaw: the trouble with their outstanding righteousness was that, all too easily, it could be viewed precisely as their righteousness. It was a righteousness that could be measured, so that, at a certain point, you could say that you had now achieved it. This meant that it could all too easily come adrift from its original inspiration in devotion to God and become self sufficient, an end in itself...

The basic form of complacency, after all, is that one is pleased with oneself.

Simon Tugwell,
'The Beatitudes' in John Garvey (ed.), *Modern Spirituality: An Anthology*, London: Darton, Longman and Todd, 1985, pp. 60.

Lord, have mercy on me,
A pharisee.
Not when I pray,
But surely, surely, thrice a day.
I say,
'See her, see him. How foolish they...'
Each one at whom I laugh
Diminishes by half.
So I grow tall
By proving others small.
Lord, pity me
A pharisee.

Margaret Beidler,
'Pity me' (Luke 18:10-13) in *Faith at Work*, October 1977.

As St Paul came to see it in retrospect, (pharisees) were exposed to a fatal flaw: the trouble with their outstanding righteousness was that, all too easily, it could be viewed precisely as their righteousness. It was a righteousness that could be measured, so that, at a certain point, you could say that you had now achieved it. This meant that it could all too easily come adrift from its original inspiration in devotion to God and become self-sufficient, an end in itself... The basic form of complacency, after all, is that a person is pleased with himself.

Simon Tugwell,
'The Beatitudes' in John Garvey (ed.), *Modern Spirituality: An Anthology*, London: Darton, Longman and Todd, 1985, p. 61.

It is, of course, true, whatever denomination you may happen to belong to, that the majority of your good churchgoers will be living under law and not under grace. The human heart is incurably legalistic... We prefer the limited demands of an ecclesiastical system, heavy though they may be, to the unlimited demands of genuine surrender to Jesus Christ. Within its own limits, legalism may produce admirable types of character. The pharisees were by no means contemptible people; they had a zeal for the law of God, and a devotion to it that would put many Christians to shame. The trouble is that what law can achieve is always limited, since the most that it can effect is modification of character from without, and not transformation from within. That inner transformation can really begin only when we pass from the sphere of law to that of grace, from the status of a servant to that of a son or daughter.

Stephen Neill,
On the Ministry, London: SCM, 1952, p. 101.

Elmer had, even in Zenith, to meet plenty of solemn and whiskery persons whose only pleasure aside from not doing agreeable things was keeping others from doing them.

Sinclair Lewis,
Elmer Gantry, London: Panther Books, 1927, 1961, p. 319

It is significant that the One born that night was called 'Emmanuel', not 'Pharisee'. The word Emmanuel means 'God with us', while 'pharisee' means 'the separate one', and when it comes to doing something redemptively about the power of destruction in the world, the difference between 'with' and 'away' is absolutely crucial... The approach of Jesus was the utter antithesis to phariseeism. He moved about, not as the Separate One or as a self-righteous Purist, but as 'the friend of sinners.'

231

John Claypool,
'The First Christmas: Jesus', sermon preached in Northminster Baptist Church, Jackson, Mississippi, 23 December 1979.

... This demonic process has affected every religious order which has ever existed. The escape into canon law has always been an escape from the aweful challenge of religion and intimacy combined.

Andrew Greeley,
Confessions of a Parish Priest, New York: Pocket Books, 1986, p. 341.

A pharisee is a righteous man whose righteousness is nourished by the blood of sinners.

Thomas Merton,
Conjectures of Guilty Bystander, quoted in T. P. McDonnell (ed.), *Through the Year with Thomas Merton*, New York: Image Books, 1985, p. 8.

I have long regarded the year AD 383 as one of the most disastrous turning points in history, since in that year for the first time, in the condemnation of the Spanish heretic Priscillian, the blood of Christians was shed by Christians...

...In the 16th century we find Francis Xavier, purest and most devoted of Roman Catholic missionaries, writing to the king of Portugal to urge that the Inquisition should be introduced into India, as an indispensable aid to the work of evangelisation, and unfortunately securing a favourable answer to his request.

Stephen Neill,
On the Ministry, London: SCM, 1952, p. 120.

When 'righteous' persons determine to do God's will, but are not first born again and awakened to a higher life, they cannot discern what is God's will... They believe their own desires and wishes are the will of God. For example, they refrain from human arrogance, imagining they are humble; but they retain their pride under the guise of the lofty demands of divine truth... They refrain from all lust for power and revenge, but they have by no means abandoned the lust for power and revenge. Nor do they in reality become less desirous of power and revenge, but rather more so. For now they can do so completely without regard for others in the name of God. They imagine that when they now seek to force through something, they do so for the sake of the kingdom of God. When they persecute or crush another, they do it thinking that the welfare of the church or of the Gospel or of Christianity demands it. The purely human desire for revenge and domination is thus represented under the guise of zeal for morality and the kingdom of God, for what is good and true. This is satanic. This is hypocrisy. However, hypocrites will never be conscious of it so long as they remain in their unregenerate state.

Hugo Odeberg,
Pharisaism and Christianity, St Louis, Missouri: Concordia, 1962, pp. 100-1.

232

Many of the insights of saints stem from their experiences as sinners.

Eric Hoffer,
The Passionate State of Mind, New York: Harper & Row, 1954, p. 9.

It is easier to make a saint out of a libertine than out of a prig.

George Santayana,
The Life of Reason, 1905, p. 11.

The servants were permitted to hold evening prayer in the kitchen, under Mrs Fairley's indifferent eye and briskly wooden voice. Upstairs, Mrs Poulteney had to be read to alone; and it was in these more intimate ceremonies that Sarah's voice, was heard at its best and most effective. Once or twice she had done the incredible, by drawing from those pouched, invincible eyes a tear. Such an effect was in no way intended, but sprang from a profound difference between the two women. Mrs Poulteney believed in a God that had never existed; and Sarah knew a God that did.

John Fowles,
The French Lieutenant's Woman, London: Pan Books, 1987, p. 54.

All (the publican) knows, from being himself an extortioner, a moneylender, a thief, and so forth, is that there are moments when for no reason, because it is not part of the world's outlook, he will forgive a debt, because suddenly his heart has become mild and vulnerable; that on another occasion he may not get someone put into prison because a face will have reminded him of something or a voice has gone straight to his heart. There is no logic in this. It is not part of the world's outlook nor is it a way in which he normally behaves. It is something that breaks through, which is completely nonsensical, which he cannot resist; and he knows also, probably, how often he himself was saved from final catastrophe by this intrusion of the unexpected and the impossible, mercy, compassion, forgiveness. So he stands at the rear of the church, knowing that all the realm inside the church is a realm of righteousness and divine love to which he does not belong and into which he cannot enter. But he knows from experience also that the impossible does occur and that is why he says 'Have mercy, break the laws of righteousness, break the laws of religion, come down in mercy to us who have no right to be either forgiven or allowed in'. And I think this is where we should start continuously all over again.

Archbishop Anthony Bloom,
School for Prayer, London: Darton, Longman and Todd, 1970, pp. 8-9.

I identify joyfully and painfully with the founder of my contemplative prayer fellowship. Whenever he has written to me, he has always ended his letters: 'With as much love as I have so far received'. He and I know that we have hardly scratched the surface — hardly begun to be filled with all the fullness of God's love.

Peter Dodson,
Contemplating the Word, London: SPCK, 1987, pp. 55-6.

Lord, grant your people your protection and grace. Give them health of mind and body, perfect love for one another and make them always faithful to you. Grant this through Christ our Lord.

Daily Mass Book

Please look at me, dear Lord. In your merciful and loving kindness is my hope, for you see me just as a good doctor, anxious only to heal and correct. This I ask you, kind Lord, trusting in your powerful mercy and your merciful power. Forgive my sins; rouse me from my half-heartedness; forget my ingratitude. I acknowledge in myself those voices and evil passions which still fight within me, whether due to long-standing evil habits or carelessness repeated every day or deep-seated flaws of my weak nature or hardly recognised temptings of evil spirits. Against all these enemies may your gentle grace give me strength and courage.

Aelred

As an adolescent I had prayed a pitiful prayer for a clean life, saying, 'Give me chastity and give me control over myself, but not yet.' I was afraid you might answer me too quickly and straighten me out before I was ready; for what I really wanted was not to be cured but to be fulfilled.

Augustine

The saints, Lord, are profound and simple people, who pray profoundly simple prayers. Like 'Lord, have mercy on me, a sinner.' Their perspective derives from a comparison between themselves and the holiness of God.

The pharisees, Lord, are profoundly complex people, who pray, 'Lord, I thank you I'm not as bad as so-and-so.' Their perspective derives from a comparison between the best in themselves and the worst in others, and any hypocrite can do that.

So, Lord, my simple prayer is this: help me to be more like Jesus, and less like the pharisees, day by day. Amen.

A benediction

May your sins be forgiven by Jesus, who loved sinners. May your pride be healed by Jesus, who was meek and lowly. May your self-esteem respond to his gentle acceptance, and may you live all the days of your life in the love of God the Father, the grace of Jesus the Son, and the communion of the Holy Spirit. Amen.

Note
1.   *Time* cover story, 'Saints Among Us', 29 December 1975, pp. 47-56.

22
How to be a child of God: peace and peace-making

Let me hear what God the Lord will speak, for he will speak peace to his people, to his faithful, to those who turn to him in their hearts

To all God's beloved... Grace to you and peace from God our Father and the Lord Jesus Christ. Since we are justified by faith, we have peace with God through our Lord Jesus Christ.

In days to come, the mountain of the Lord's house shall be established as the highest of the mountains, and shall be raised up above the hills. Peoples shall stream to it, and many nations shall come and say: 'Come, let us go up to the mountain of the Lord, to the house of the God of Jacob; that he may teach us his ways and that we may walk in his paths.' For out of Zion shall go forth instruction, and the word of the Lord from Jerusalem. He shall judge between many peoples, and shall arbitrate between strong nations far away; they shall beat their swords into ploughshares, and their spears into pruning hooks; nation shall not lift up sword against nation, neither shall they learn war any more; but they shall all sit under their own vines and under their own fig trees, and no one shall make them afraid; for the mouth of the Lord of hosts has spoken.

You know the message he sent to the people of Israel, preaching peace by Jesus Christ — he is Lord of all... For he is our peace; in his flesh he has made both groups into one and has broken down the dividing wall, that is the hostility between us. He has abolished the law with its commandments and ordinances, that he might create in himself one new humanity in place of the two, thus making peace, and might reconcile both

235

groups to God in one body through the cross, thus putting to death that hostility through it. So he came and proclaimed peace to you who were far off and peace to those who were near; for through him both of us have access in one Spirit to the Father.

Through him (Christ) God was pleased to reconcile to himself all things, whether on earth or in heaven, by making peace through the blood of his cross. It is to peace that God has called you. And let the peace of Christ rule in your hearts, to which indeed you were called in the one body. And be thankful. May the God of peace himself sanctify you entirely; and may your spirit and soul and body be kept sound and blameless at the coming of our Lord Jesus Christ.

Peace I leave with you; my peace I give to you. I have said this to you, so that in me you may have peace. In the world you face persecution. But take courage; I have conquered the world! And the peace of God, which surpasses all understanding, will guard your hearts and your minds in Christ Jesus.

Blessed are the peacemakers, for they will be called children of God. If it is possible, so far as it depends on you, live peaceably with all. (Make) every effort to maintain the unity of the Spirit in the bond of peace. Speak evil of no one, avoid quarrelling, be gentle, and show every courtesy to everyone. And a harvest of righteousness is sown in peace for those who make peace.

May the Lord give strength to his people! May the Lord bless his people with peace!

Those of steadfast mind you keep in peace — in peace because they trust in you.

Psalm 85:8; Romans 1:7; Romans 5:1; Micah 4:1-3; Acts 10:36; Ephesians 2:14-18; Colossians 1:20; 1 Corinthians 7:15; Colossians 3:15; 1 Thessalonians 5:23; John 14:27a; John 16:33; Philippians 4:7; Matthew 5:9; Romans 12:18; Ephesians 4:3; Titus 3:2; James 3:18; Psalm 29:11; Isaiah 26:3.

There once were two cats of Kilkenny,
Each thought there was one cat too many;
So they fought and they spit,
And they scratched and they bit,
Till, excepting their nails,
And the tips of their tails,
Instead of two cats there weren't any.

• The world spends more on arms than it spends on anything else.

• Six times as much public money goes for research on weapons as for research on health.

• The Third World spends 66% more on the military than on education.

• It's only a matter of time before weapons of mass destruction will be in the hands of petty tyrants.

• In World War I an estimated 54 million died, 90 million were wounded, leaving 28 million maimed. The toll in World War 2 was 38.5 million (20 million of them Soviet citizens).

• The Gallipoli campaign (historian John North called it a 'singularly brainless and suicidal type of warfare') which left an estimated 120,000 dead and 250,000 wounded on both sides has been glorified in Australian war folk-history. It was the first time Australians went into battle as Australians.

• In the 1980s, only 18% of those who started wars won them.

• The proportion of civilian deaths in wars is increasing dramatically, due to the increased destructiveness of the arms used. In one year recently, 1988, more than 4.5 million people died in wars.

• New York and Washington — cities where the school system is falling apart, the homeless and hungry crowd the streets — almost overnight found millions of dollars to celebrate a military victory in the Gulf War...

Wars are as old as history. Only saints and simpletons believe wars in this kind of world will cease. Wars are the ultimate tragedy. Unlike natural disasters they are preventable. Wars mean horrifying injuries: burns, spinal injuries, blindness, loss of limbs. Families lose loved ones. People are wasted in the prime of life.

Views by Christians about war range across a wide spectrum, from fundamentalist preachers in America who bless military weapons, to conscientious pacifists who would not resist an aggressor to protect their own children. It's horrifying to hear sometimes of Christians who find war — or war movies — entertaining.

The early churches encouraged their members not to join the army (though converts already serving in the army could stay). Some Christians became martyrs for peace. When called for military service, Maximilius said: 'I cannot serve as a soldier. I cannot do evil. I am a Christian'. He was executed in AD 295 on the orders of a Roman proconsul. This all changed after Christianity became the state religion under Constantine.

Christians have taken one of three stances on war and peace: pacifism (which probably originated with them), the 'just war', and the Crusade (inherited from the Roman world and the Old Testament).

Augustine, who thought 'the purpose of all war is peace' may have been the first to suggest the idea of a 'just war'. The conditions for a just war are (1) it must be waged by a lawful authority; (2) the cause must be just (that is to restore peace and bring about justice); (3) war is the only way to solve the problem and secure justice; (4) the war must be waged by justifiable means (no torture, massacres or atrocities, respect for neutrals); (5) there must be a reasonable hope of victory ('unwinnable' wars can never be just); (6) the probable good should outweigh the likely evil. The whole idea of a just war is that it must be fought when nothing else will deter a tyrant; not to do so is judged a moral failure.

The fourth condition raises problems for Christians in modern warfare. Current 'hi-tech' weapons — indiscriminate bombing by thousands of 'sorties', 'carpet bombing' by B-52 bombers, smart warheads that go through windows, laser-guided bombs that crack reinforced bunkers leaving nearby nursery schools undamaged — all these de-personalise the enemy. In long-range killing soldiers don't see the limbless torsos of the victims, or smell the scorched flesh, or hear the screams of the disembowelled.

Modern journalism and film-makers have brought the horrors of war into our living-rooms. The Vietnam war was the first war to be fought on two fronts: in the jungles of Asia and on our TVs, which is why the anti-war movement is largely a post-TV phenomenon.

The Crusades or 'holy wars' waged against Islam from the 11th century onwards were thought of as a 'special case'. The enemy were 'infidels', so the 'just war' theory did not apply: it was okay to use swords, racks and burning oil to butcher Turks and Palestinians. While some Crusaders were mercenaries, others sincerely believed they were fighting for the cause of Christ.

The Reformers generally adopted the 'just war' theory, and this led Luther to condemn the peasants' revolt and support the State in ruthlessly crushing it. Another Reformer, Zwingli, actively engaged in war and in fact died in battle. Calvin and Cromwell were also militaristic. However, Anabaptists, Mennonites and, later, Quakers generally adopted pacifist positions.

Pacifism flourished in the 1930s but largely collapsed with the outbreak of World War 2. English-speaking Christians generally felt that war was 'just'.

Was the 1991 'Gulf War' just? I don't think sanctions would have worked with Saddam Hussein. A leader ensconced in a well-stocked bunker who seems to care more for his own preservation and power than the survival of hundreds of thousands of his people, will out-stubborn almost any efforts. And yet sanctions and world condemnation have encouraged South Africa to mend its racial ways. Even the most hard-hearted of regimes are not impervious to outside pressure.

All that said, it is not my belief — either as a realist or as a biblical Christian — that everlasting peace is an achievable objective in this imperfect world.

One of the problems is harmonising the Old Testament with the New Testament. War is a dominant theme in the Old Testament. Yahweh, the God of the Hebrews, is a warrior-God, 'The Lord of Hosts'. He leads his people into battle, defeats the Egyptians, the Canaanites, the Philistines, etc. David's military victories make him Israel's greatest hero. But throughout the Old Testament there is also another view: the promise of 'Shalom', peace (Numbers 6:2, Judges 6:24, Leviticus 26:6, etc.). David is not allowed to build the Temple because he is a warrior and has shed blood. The prophets from the eighth century onward stopped blessing Israel's war, and said they deserved punishment instead (Amos 5:18-20, Zechariah 8:16ff.), and turned their people's gaze towards a future Messianic era of universal peace (Isaiah 10:12-15, 9:2-7, Jeremiah 51, Ezekiel 38-39).

The idea of peace pervades the New Testament even more. Jesus is the Prince of peace (Luke 1:77-79, 2:13-14, see Isaiah 9:1-6). His is a kingdom of peace (Luke 4:5-8, 19:33ff.). He promises peace to his followers (John 14:27; 20:21), who, through his death, have peace with God (Romans 5:1, 5:10, 2 Corinthians 5:17-19, Colossians 1:21-22). Indeed, we must look at the Old Testament through the prism of the life and teaching of Jesus.

He taught that his followers must live in peace, and be actively engaged in peacemaking — even loving their enemies (Matthew 5:9, 39, 43-45). The apostles similarly urged the young churches to be communities of peace (Ephesians 4:3, 1 Thessalonians 5:13, Colossians 3:15). The question, 'Whose side is God on in this war?' must always be answered, 'God is on the side of the suffering'.

Any theological understanding of war and peace must begin with the idea of humans — mothers and fathers, sons and daughters, — being made in the image of God. What's the most important thing you can say about Saddam Hussein, Adolf Hitler, Pol Pot, Idi Amin? They are like God!

But they — and we all — are like the devil. We want our own way, and not God's. We want our own way, even at the expense of others. This is called pride. God, says James 4:6, opposes the proud. It's pride that creates an 'us and them' mentality. It's pride that wants to make our nation 'the greatest'. It's pride that makes us want to be number one. A Danish scientist-poet expresses this in the following aphoristic advice:

> The noble art of losing face
> may one day save the human race
> and turn into eternal merit
> what weaker minds would call disgrace.

Nations are proud, and go to war for all the same reasons individuals fight. And let us be realistic. Nations, like people, are selective about who they fight: they may intervene in a conflict when they shouldn't, or fail to intervene when they should (oil under the ground plays a vital part in the calculation).

What can we do to encourage peace? First, we must affirm that Christians are people of hope. Hope leads to action whereas despair leads to apathy. We must develop a vision of 'shalom community', where all are brothers and sisters, rather than allies or enemies. We begin with prayer, using the spiritual resources available to us to fight this battle on the spiritual front. Let us then unite with other Christians around the world and with them speak out prophetically against militarism. Humans have been incredibly creative in other directions: we now need new ways of thinking about conflict.

Changing our thinking will include issues like these: Is competition Christian? Is barracking for a football team a function of our fallen tribalism? A war toy is not just guns, tanks and soldier dolls. It includes all playthings which by means of their structure and advertising encourage children to play games of war and violence. This could extend to model kits, video games, cartoon shows — a very significant portion of the entertainment available for our children is based on violence. They are constantly being encouraged to see violence as both entertaining and a solution to problems...

What can nuclear nations do? Here are some options: • A nuclear freeze, stopping the manufacture of further nuclear weapons; • No 'first use' policy, using nuclear weapons only for defense, never attack; • Reduction in defense expenditure; • Agreeing to a comprehensive test ban treaty; • Partial unilateral disarmament, with just enough weapons for a second strike; • Total unilateral disarmament: the horror of nuclear war is so great that conventional defence forces only are maintained.

Governments without nuclear weapons also have several options: • Refusing to have nuclear bases on their soil; • Refusing landing or mooring rights for nuclear armed planes and ships; • Refusing to join any military alliance with nuclear powers; • Create nuclear-free zones; • Create peace research.

Wars result from teaching children to hate, to fear. Hitler used fear of the Jews to power his juggernaut. (The Fuhrer once said: 'If the Jews didn't exist, we would have to invent them'.)

Every Christian, pacifist or nonpacifist, should pray for peace; should strive for peace and in every way possible turn people's hearts from war to peace; every Christian should keenly anticipate that wonderful time when the Prince of Peace will return to this warring earth, and set up a kingdom of peace and justice and love that will never end.

To those who ask us where we have come from or who is our commander we say that we have come in accordance with the counsels of Jesus to cut down our warlike and arrogant swords of dispute into ploughshares... For we can no longer take a sword against a nation, nor do we learn any more to make war, having become (children) of peace for the sake of Jesus, who is our commander.

Origen (185-254),
quoted in *War, Peace and the Bible:* A discussion and study guide prepared for the Baptist churches in Victoria, Australia. Revised edition, 1986, p. 7.

Peace has come to mean the time when there aren't any wars or even when there aren't any major wars. Beggars can't be choosers; we'd most of us settle for that. But in Hebrew peace, *shalom*, means fullness, means having everything you need to be wholly and happily yourself.

One of the titles by which Jesus is known is Prince of Peace, and he used the word himself in what seem at first glance to be two radically contradictory utterances. On one occasion he said to the disciples, 'Do not think that I have come to bring peace, but a sword' (Matthew 10:34). And later on, the last time they ate together, he said to them, 'Peace I leave with you; my peace I give to you' (John 14:27).

The contradiction is resolved when you realise that for Jesus peace seems to have meant not the absence of struggle but the presence of love.

Frederick Buechner,
Wishful Thinking, London: Collins, 1973, p. 69.

In his epistle, James tells us that our wars and conflicts start out in our hearts, in our disordered motives (James 4:1-3). And when one Orthodox monk was asked what a monk was, he said 'A monk is someone who can weep for the whole world'.

John Garvey (ed.),
Modern Spirituality: an Anthology, London: Darton, Longman and Todd, 1985, p. xiii.

'Acquire inward peace', said St Seraphim, 'and a multitude... around you will find their salvation'.

Kallistos Ware,
'The Spiritual Father in Orthodox Christianity', in John Garvey (ed.), *Modern Spirituality: an Anthology*, London: Darton, Longman and Todd, 1985, p. 43.

More than half the world's scientists and engineers are working for the military.

David Suzuki,
Inventing the Future: Reflections on Science, Technology and Nature. Sydney: Allen and Unwin, 1990, p. 87.

The greatest happiness is to scatter your enemy and drive him before you, to see his cities reduced to ashes, to see those who love him shrouded in tears, and to gather to your bosom his wives and daughters.

Genghis Khan 1226.

Because (nuclear weapons) are indiscriminate in their effects, destroying combatants and non-combatants alike, it seems clear to me that they are ethically indefensible, and that every Christian, whatever he or she may think of the possibility of a 'just' use of conventional weapons, must be a nuclear pacifist.

John Stott,
in a sermon preached in All Souls' Church of England, Langham Place, London, 1979.

All of this means that for me and my one little life amid the principalities and powers of this day, I want to take this stance of love and humanness and attempt to hold to it against all comers. This will involve starting the battle with evil at the point where I am closest to it; namely, with the evil in my own life. I have been much impressed lately by Jesus' words in the Sermon: 'Judge not, that ye be not judged, for with the judgment that ye yield, ye shall be judged, and with the measure of a measure, it shall be measured to you' (Matthew 7:1-5). These words are utterly realistic, for whenever I conclude the problem of evil centres in you and I move toward you in attack, your reaction will always be defensive and you will proceed to counter-attack and give me back just what I am giving you. How much better it is to go to work on the beam in my own eye; that is, to begin struggling with evil as I find it manifesting itself in my life. To this kind of struggle, others with motes in their eyes may come to say: 'Help me, you who obviously realise that you have a problem too. Let's help each other with our common problem of evil'. How much wiser a strategy this is than the self-righteous attack that seems to feel the trouble is all 'over there' and none 'in here'...

If we would struggle with the beams in our own eyes, the problem of motes in others might show astonishing improvement... Such a stance of love involves trying to remain human no matter how inhuman the treatment becomes. Thus, I must attempt to keep on listening even when I am no longer listened to, to keep on being sensitive even when others are insensitive to me, to try, like he did, 'when reviled, to revile not in return'. Now to be sure, it may not work. In such a stance I realise I could get run over by the Juggernaut and nothing at all would remain to show for so fragile an approach. But even at that, it would be going down at one's best and not at one's worst by trying to remain human and not get sucked into the swirl of inhumanity. If I have got to go down, that is the way I would most prefer to go... And by God's help, this is what I most want to do. Will you join me? If there is any hope, this has to be the way!

John R Claypool,
'Living by the Sword', a sermon published by the Crescent Hill Baptist Church, 2800 Frankfort Avenue,
Louisville, Kentucky, 40206, Vol 8/No. 9, 10 May 1970.

About five years ago I was reading a book about the war and someone who was in a concentration camp, and there was a part in it that was so horrible that I would not have been able to read it if I had known what was coming, and I was absolutely shaken by the cruelty of it. The awful thing was that I put the book down and I knew for the first time how it could have happened, and I thought, 'It could have been me, committing those atrocities', and I don't think I've ever been able to pray in the same way since. I can only pray now in penitence and in adoration because God is so tremendous when you set him against what you are.

Anonymous woman in a radio interview, quoted in Margaret Hebblethwaite, *Finding God in All Things*,
London: Collins, 1990, p. 151.

Thank you, Lord, that you bring hope to this world, which is otherwise hopelessly lost. Lord, we praise you — we believe you are victorious! Thank you for the opportunity to live in these times, to serve you and witness to your kingdom in this moment of history, to find your presence in the heat of the ever-escalating arms race, to find you in the faces of the homeless and oppressed. Lord, you are with us and we thank you.

Dawn Longenecker,
'Sojourners Peace Ministry', quoted in *War, Peace and the Bible*: A discussion and study guide prepared
for the Baptist churches in Victoria, Australia. Revised edition, 1986, p. 7.

Lord, make me an instrument of your peace,
where there is hatred, let me sow love,
where there is injury, pardon,
where there is doubt, faith,
where there is despair, hope,
where there is sadness, joy.

O Divine Master,
Grant that I may not so much
seek to be consoled as to console,
to be understood as to understand,
to be loved as to love;

for it is in giving that we receive,
it is in pardoning that we are pardoned,
it is in dying that we are born
to eternal life.

St Francis of Assisi

Eternal God, our Father, may your Spirit of peace speak to us in such a way that we live out our lives with the conviction that 'all that is necessary for the forces of evil to win the world is for good people to do nothing.' Lord, give us the serenity to accept what cannot be changed; the courage to change what ought to be changed; and the wisdom to distinguish the one from the other.

Quoted in *War, Peace and the Bible*: A discussion and study guide prepared for the Baptist churches in Victoria, Australia. Revised edition, 1986, p. 7.

Jesus our inspiration, you come in the evening as our doors are shut, and bring peace. Grant us sleep tonight, and courage tomorrow to go wherever you lead. Amen.

A New Zealand Prayer Book, Auckland: Collins, 1989, p. 109.

A Litany for Peace

Leader: *We confess our continuing inability as citizens of this global village to live in peace and harmony and justice with one another, both within our own nation and within the family of nations.*
People: *Lord, lead us to repentance.*

Leader: *We confess our tendency to exempt our nation from the sins of the world and ourselves from the sins of the nation.*
People: *Lord, lead us to repentance.*

Leader: *We confess that out of our lack of clarity, pride and suspicion of our enemies, we have been blinded to your judgment of our own nation's evils.*
People: *Lord, lead us to repentance.*

Leader: *We confess that out of fear, uncertainty, and lack of faith we have allowed our nation to stockpile weapons to provide security rather than turning to the fulfilling power and promises of your son, Jesus Christ.*
People: *Lord, lead us to repentance.*

Leader: *We confess that we allow the impoverishment of hundreds of millions of the world's poor to continue, the economic and political consequence of spending billions on weapons to protect our wealth and power.*
People: *Lord, lead us to repentance.*

Leader: *We confess that we who are so few in terms of this world's population have claimed for ourselves to much of its food, wealth and natural resources.*
People: *Lord, lead us to repentance.*

Leader: *We confess that we have failed to heed your call to be stewards of the riches of this Earth which you have entrusted us to enjoy, preserve and share in a just manner with all of your people.*
People: *Lord, lead us to repentance.*

Leader: *We confess that we your church share in full measure the responsibility for this state of the world and that we have not heeded your commandments to let you be our Lord and to love our neighbours as ourselves.*
People: *Lord, lead us to repentance.*

Baptist Peace Sunday service, Melbourne, 24 November 1991.

A benediction
Go with understanding, have courage, always keep your integrity; encourage those who have no hope, support the weak, confront the strong. Love and serve the Lord. And may the grace, mercy and peace of God the Father, son and Holy Spirit go with you always. Amen.

Discuss
1. 'I have not come to bring peace, but a sword.' Read Matthew 10:34 and the following verses: what did Jesus mean?
2. Instead of 'an eye for an eye' Jesus urged 'turning the other cheek' (Matthew 5:38-48). From personal experience, how realistic have you found this advice?
3. Read 1 Peter 2:11 to 3:22. Peter urges us to 'submit to every human institution'. So was Bonhoeffer right or wrong in attempting to kill Hitler?
4. What do you think of the 'just war' theory? Could a nuclear war ever be 'just'?
5. Personal security (safety), social security (justice) and national security (arms superiority) all have to do with peace. How would you balance these priorities in the best interests of peace for your own country?

6. 'Aggression ought to be discouraged everywhere.' What about on the sporting field, or in business, or in terms of the ever-widening gap between rich and poor?

7. What can your group or church do to work for peace?

Read

Tony Cupit, *Peace I Leave With You*, Melbourne: Baptist Resource Centre, 1986. Donald Kraybill, *Facing Nuclear War*, Scottsdale, Pennsylvania: Herald Press, 1982. Ronald Sider and Richard Taylor, *Nuclear Holocaust and Christian Hope*, London: Hodder & Stoughton, 1982.

Contact

Groups like People for Nuclear Disarmament, the Uniting Church Social Justice Division, Campaign for International Cooperation and Disarmament, Pax Christi, etc. in your city.

23
Strive for greatness — be a servant

Come, bless the Lord, all you servants of the Lord, who stand by night in the house of the Lord! Praise the Lord! Praise, O servants of the Lord; praise the name of the Lord. Let the steadfast love become my comfort according to your promise to your servant.

Remember these things, O Jacob, and Israel, for you are my servant; I formed you, you are my servant; O Israel, you will not be forgotten by me.

Here is my servant, whom I uphold, my chosen, in whom my soul delights; I have put my spirit upon him; he will bring forth justice to the nations.

You are my witnesses, says the Lord, and my servant whom I have chosen, so that you may know and believe me and understand that I am he. Before me no god was formed, nor shall there be any after me.

But get up and stand on your feet; for I have appeared to you for this purpose, to appoint you to serve and testify to the things in which you have seen me and to those in which I will appear to you. Of this gospel I have become a servant according to the gift of God's grace that was given me by the working of his power. I became its servant according to God's commission that was given to me for you, to make the word of God fully known. What then is Apollos? What is Paul? Servants through whom you came to believe, as the Lord assigned to each. For we do not proclaim ourselves; we proclaim Jesus Christ as Lord and ourselves as your slaves for Jesus' sake... and made us to be a kingdom, priests serving his God and Father, to him be glory and dominion forever and ever. Amen. If you put these instructions before the brothers and sisters, you will be a good servant of Christ Jesus, nourished on the words of the faith and of the sound teaching that you have followed. Whoever serves me must follow me, and where I am, there will my servant be also. Whoever serves me, the Father will honour. Whoever wishes to become great among you must be your servant. Moreover, it is required of stewards that they be found trustworthy. Submit yourselves therefore to God. He has graciously granted you the privilege not only of believing in Christ, but of suffering for him as well. Do not lag in zeal, be ardent in spirit, serve the Lord. Render service with enthusiasm, as to the Lord and not to men and women... since you know that from the Lord you will receive the inheritance as your reward; you serve the Lord Christ... by purity, knowledge, patience, kindness, holiness of spirit, genuine love...

Whoever speaks must do so as one speaking the very words of God; whoever serves must do so with the strength that God supplies, so that God may be glorified in all things through Jesus Christ. To him belong the glory and the power forever and ever. Amen.

Preserve my life, for I am devoted to you; save your servant who trusts in you. You are my God. I am your servant; give me understanding, so that I may know your decrees.

Psalm 134:1; Psalm 113:1; Psalm 119:76; Isaiah 44:21; Isaiah 42:1; Isaiah 43:10; Acts 26:16; Ephesians 3:7; Colossians 1:25; 1 Corinthians 3:5; 2 Corinthians 4:5; Revelation 1:6; 1 Timothy 4:6; John 12:26; Mark 10:43; 1 Corinthians 4:2; James 4:7; Philippians 1:29; Romans 12:11; Ephesians 6:7; Colossians 3:24; 2 Corinthians 6:6; 1 Peter 4:11; Psalm 86:2; Psalm 119:125.

We conclude this book near where we started. Your aim in life is simply to be like Jesus. What was he like? He was a 'Servant King', as a popular Christian song puts it. You have the privilege — what an honour! — to be a servant of the king of all kings, and to serve him as you meet him in others.

Success, in Jesus' terms, is not being boss, lording it over others, but to be a servant. James and John were two of Jesus' followers who learned this the hard way. They wanted privileged thrones in Jesus' kingdom: one of them on the left side and the other on the right. The other disciples, naturally, were furious with them. Tempers flared, and there were angry exchanges. But Jesus said, 'You know that in the world those who are thought to be "successful" are those who "get to the top". They have power over others. But it's not to be like that with you. Whoever wants to be great must be your servant; whoever wants to be number one must be the slave of all. I did not come to be served, but to serve — and to give my life for others' (Matthew 20:25-28). (And those on the right and left of the Lord in the moment of his greatest triumph were two crucified thieves!). Later, these fellows revealed that they were very slow learners at this point. When they gathered to celebrate the Passover, none of them wanted to do the slave's chore, and wash the dirty feet of his friends. So Jesus gave them — and us — an object-lesson in greatness. He removed his cloak, took a towel, filled a basin with water, and started to move slowly around the group, washing their feet, and wiping them with the towel. Amazing: in Hebrew culture only slaves washed others' feet.

In that dramatic silence only the embarrassed breathing and the trickle of water could be heard. Here is God incarnate, stripping himself to wash the feet of his proud friends!

Ultimately, the cross itself was the supreme symbol of his servanthood. He served by giving his life for his friends (and that includes us!).

> When I survey the wondrous cross,
> On which the Prince of glory died,
> My richest gain I count but loss,
> and pour contempt on all my pride...

Jesus did not give his followers a blueprint about how the church should be run; there is no specific organisational model for the institution of the church in the New Testament. But there is a dynamic one: servanthood! Greatness in the kingdom of Jesus is to be a slave of others. The Chinese have a proverb: the tallest bamboo bends the lowest.

The best Christians have learned this lesson well. A theological seminary built a new office block. The president insisted his faculty take all the spacious new offices, while he took a crowded old office in a back wing. The action was both sincere and symbolic, and made a profound impression on the students. Peter Drucker, the management expert, once wrote: 'The greatest time waster for most executives is a decision that has to do with someone's status. A move into new offices for example stirs up guerilla warfare as to who gets which office'.[1]

Effective Christians are not merely those who know a lot about Christian doctrine or the Bible, but who are willing to serve others. Effective leaders are not merely those who have a following but humbly serve those they lead, helping them become the best they can be (even if that means they do 'greater works' than the leader!). In serving we become more like Jesus Christ.

Your calling is not to exalt yourself, but to exalt Christ. Theologian James Denney wrote somewhere: 'You cannot bear witness to yourself and Jesus Christ at one and the same time.

You cannot, at one and the same time, convey the impression that you yourself are clever and that Christ is mighty to save'.

The ideal Christian may not be a great orator, or a charismatic prophet, or a generous benefactor, or a giant of faith. The ideal Christian, to paraphrase 1 Corinthians 13, is patient and kind, not envious or boastful or arrogant or rude. The ideal Christian does not insist on their own way, is not irritable or resentful, does not rejoice in wrongdoing, but rejoices in the truth. He or she is long-suffering, a true believer, is hopeful and endures anything. Whatever your titles or accomplishments or outstanding gifts: they are all passing away. Only faith, hope and love will last forever. And they are the marks of a true servant.

I am like James and John, Lord, I size up other people in terms of what they can do for me; how they can further my program, feed my ego, satisfy my needs, give me strategic advantage.

I exploit people, ostensibly for your sake, but really for my own sake.

Lord, I turn to you to get the inside track and obtain special favours, your direction for my schemes, your power for my projects, your sanction for my ambitions, your blank checks for whatever I want. I am like James and John.

Kent and Barbara Hughes,
Liberating Ministry From The Success Syndrome, Wheaton, Illinois: Tyndale House Publishers, Inc.,
1988, p. 49.

Jesus taught a lot about service by washing his disciples' feet. In our highly urban culture where we wear closed shoes and socks and drive in automobiles, washing feet is not an especially effective way to express service. We read about what Jesus did; we get the basic insight that it is important to serve others; and then we try to interpret that in our culture. Maybe we read to an older person or mow somebody's lawn. For me, 'washing feet' might be to prepare coffee for my wife each morning.

Richard Foster,
'An Introduction to Spiritual Disciplines', La Vonne Neff et al. (eds), *Practical Christianity*, Wheaton,
Illinois: Tyndale House Publishers, 1988, p. 295.

Radical servanthood does not make sense unless we introduce a new level of understanding and see it as the way to encounter God himself. To be humble and persecuted cannot be desired unless we can find God in humility and persecution. When we begin to see God himself, the source of all our comfort and consolation, in the centre of servanthood, compassion becomes much more than doing good for unfortunate people. Radical servanthood, as the encounter with the compassionate God, takes us beyond the distinctions between wealth and poverty, success and failure, fortune and bad luck. Radical servanthood is not an enterprise in which we try to surround ourselves with as much misery as possible, but a joyful way of life in which our eyes are opened to the vision of the true God who chose the way of servanthood to make himself known. The poor are called blessed not because poverty is good, but because theirs is the kingdom of heaven; the mourners are called blessed not because mourning is good, but because they shall be comforted.

McNeil, Morrison and Nouwen,
Compassion — a reflection on the Christian Life, New York: Image Books, 1983, p. 31.

In an interview in the October 1983 issue of *Northwest Orient* magazine, Andre Soltner, of Lutece in New York, one of the world's premier restaurants, puts it this way: 'I am more than thirty years a chef. I know what I am doing and each day I do my absolute best. I cook for you from my heart, with love. It must be the same with service. The waiter must serve with love. Otherwise, the food is nothing. Do you see? Many times, I will leave my kitchen and go to the tables to take the orders myself. It starts right then and there. That feeling the customer must have is relaxation. If not, then his evening is ruined. Mine, too, by the way. How can he love, if he's not relaxed? People ask me all the time what secrets I have. I tell them there is nothing mysterious about Lutece. I put love in my cooking and love in the serving. That is all'.

Tom Peters and Nancy Austin,
A Passion for Excellence, London: William Collins Sons & Co Ltd, 1985, p. 289.

We must face the modern situation honestly. The biblical image of servant is not popular. In the face of much bondage, much sickness, and much sorrow, there are many professionals who are eager to offer their services for a dear price and from the protection of a status lifted far above those served... Is there still a place for the servant? I fear that if there is not, our lofty civilisation will swiftly degenerate. The social and economic proofs seem too powerful to deny... Agents of healing and deliverance are those who do not lord it over others, but identify with others in their joys and sorrows, successes and losses, recoveries and setbacks. But we have learned from our biblical heritage that such identification, and servanthood, does not grow out of heroic decisions, but out of personal deliverance from false gods and integration into the community finding true freedom in acknowledgment of the sole Sovereignty of God. The hero reaches down to save and further demeans the one in bonds. The servant of Christ experiences his or her solidarity with the one in bondage, a solidarity based on the awareness of God's love embracing both.

Earl E. Shelp & Ronald H. Sunderland (eds),
The Pastor As Servant, New York: The Pilgrim Press, 1986, pp. 17-18.

If it is true that people can grow, expand their capacities, jump higher, run harder, and compose greater music, that means that the ultimate leadership is servant leadership, for we will produce followers who will surpass us. Runners will become coaches — to train other athletes who will break their records. Executives will hire subordinates and motivate them so well that they may become their superiors. It is not easy to adjust to such a view of the development of leaders. So, when some people get to the top, they pull up the ladder with them. They cannot tolerate the ambition of the young, and see every subordinate as a potential rival. Such executives hang on by their fingernails in organisations until the last possible moment, and give their attention to fighting off rivals rather than nurturing successors. It is a foolish way to lead, inasmuch as we are always within one generation of extinction.

Reprinted from *Bringing Out The Best In People*, by Alan Loy McGinnis, copyright © 1985 Augsburg Publishing House. Used by permission of Augsburg Fortress.

• Servants lead out of relationships, not by coercion. Servants don't demand obedience or submission. They meet their followers at the point of need. Servants have a common touch, maintain living contact, and demonstrate consistent concern for their followers. • Servants lead by support, not by control. Servants give from themselves rather than take for themselves. They love and lift others rather than manipulating them. • Servants lead by developing others, not by doing all the ministry themselves. Servants, whether clergy or laity, recognise that the kingdom of God calls for the full participation of all believers. All spiritual gifts are given by God for service to Christ's body (Ephesians 4:11-13). • Servants guide people, not drive them. Volunteer organisations like churches require selfless leaders rather than selfish bosses or bullies. • Servants lead from love, not domination. Authority, in part, grows out of 'the consent of the governed'. Peter sounded this theme clearly: 'Tend the flock of God that is in your charge, not by constraint but willingly, not for shameful gain but eagerly, not as domineering over those in your charge but being examples to the flock' (1 Peter 5:2-3).

• Servants seek growth, not position. Servants aren't ambitious. They keep the growth and spiritual health of others paramount. Unlike Diotrephes, an ambitious leader in the early church who preferred to 'put himself first' (3 John 9), servants put others first.

Robert D. Dale,
Pastoral Leadership, Nashville, Tennessee: Abingdon Press, 1986, pp. 34-5.

Field-Marshal Montgomery reckoned there were seven key ingredients necessary in a successful leader in war, and all of them are applicable to spiritual warfare as well. The leader must:

1. Be able to sit back and avoid getting immersed in detail.
2. Not be petty.
3. Not be pompous.
4. Be a good picker of (assistants).
5. Trust (subordinates) and let them get on with their job without interference.

Ian Dobbie,
'The Leader' in John Eddison (ed.), *'BASH' A Study in Spiritual Power*, Basingstoke, Hants UK: Marshalls, 1982, p. 70.

It has been said of some religious leaders that they have an unusual ability to be able to strut sitting down.

Richard Lovelace,
Dynamics of Spiritual Life, Downers Grove, Illinois: Intervarsity Press, 1981, p. 248.

Will you let me be your servant,
let me be as Christ to you?
Pray that I might have the grace
to let you be my servant too.

We are pilgrims on a journey,
we are travellers on the road.
We are here to help each other
walk the mile and bear the load.

I will hold the Christ light for you
in the night time of your fear.
I will hold my hand out to you,
speak the peace you long to hear.

I will weep when you are weeping,
when you laugh I'll laugh with you.
I will share your joy and sorrow
till we've seen this journey through.

When we sing to God in heaven,
we shall find such harmony
born of all we've known together
of Christ's love and agony.

Will you let me be your servant,
let me be as Christ to you?
Pray that I might have the grace
to let you be my servant too.

Lord, make us strong enough to do what we should do calmly, simply, without wanting to do too much, without wanting to do it all ourselves. In other words, Lord, make us humble in our wish and our will to serve. Help us above all to find you in our commitments, for you are the unity of our actions; you are the single love in all our loves, in all our efforts. You are the well spring, and all things are drawn to you. So, we have come before you, Lord, to rest and gather our strength.

Michel Quoist,
'We Have too Much to Do', in Gordon Bailey (Compiler), *100 Contemporary Christian Poets*, Herts, UK: Lion Publishing, 1983. p. 136.

O thou who has so graciously called me to be thy servant, I would hold myself in readiness today for thy least word of command. Give me the spirit, I pray thee, to keep myself in continual training for the punctual fulfilment of thy most holy will.

Let me keep the edges of my mind keen: Let me keep my thinking straight and true: Let me keep my passions in control: Let me keep my will active: Let me keep my body fit and healthy: Let me remember him whose meat it was to do the will of him that sent him.

John Baillie,
A Diary of Private Prayer, London: Oxford University Press, 1963, p. 81.

Eternal God, who are the light of the minds that know you, the joy of the hearts that love you, and the strength of the wills that serve you; grant us so to know you, that we may truly love you, and so to love you that we may fully serve you, whom to serve is perfect freedom, in Jesus Christ our Lord.

St Augustine of Hippo,
cited in Tony Castle, *The Hodder Book of Christian Prayers*, London: Hodder & Stoughton, 1986, p. 18.

Kings lord it over their subjects, but with us the highest must be like the lowest, the chief like a servant. Who is greater — the one who sits at table or the servant who waits? Surely the one at table. Yet Jesus is among us like a servant. He came not to be served but to serve, and to give his life as a ransom for many. So when we have done all that we have to do, we shall simply be servants who have done our duty.

Come to Jesus, all those whose work is hard, whose load is heavy, and you will be renewed.

A New Zealand Prayer Book, Auckland: Collins, 1989, p. 117.

Lord, teach me to be generous.
Teach me to serve you as you deserve;
to give and not to count the cost,
to fight and not to heed the wounds,
to toil and not to seek for rest,
to labour and not to ask for any reward
save that of knowing that I do your holy will.

O divine Master,
grant that we may seek not so much
to be consoled as to console;
to be understood, as to understand;
to be loved, as to love.
For it is in giving that we receive;
it is in pardoning that we are pardoned;
it is in dying that we are born to eternal life.

A *New Zealand Prayer Book,* Auckland: Collins, 1989, p. 109.

A benediction
May the Lord Jesus Christ, who became one of us to serve us
and to die for us, so enrich you with his example and his love,
that you may serve and love him until your dying breath... May
his love, mercy and peace remain with you always. Amen.

Note
1. Peter Drucker, *Drucker on Management,* Management Publications Ltd, 1964, p. 15.

Rowland Croucher is a Baptist pastor with a wide experience in pastoral ministry. Currently, he is director of John Mark Ministries, encouraging clergy, church leaders and their spouses through seminars, writing and counselling.

His previous publications include the best selling *Your Church Can Come Alive!*